# SHE REPRESENTS

## Acknowledgments

To my parents, Barbara and Peter, who gave me the tools.

To my friends, who are also family—especially to Laura, Richard, and Pepe—who help me through the hard times and make the good times better.

To the team at Zest Books, who believed and listened.

I hope this book is a reflection of the powerful analysis and insistent hope that you've all given me throughout its process.

Zest Books™
An imprint of Lerner Publishing Group, Inc.
241 First Avenue North
Minneapolis, MN 55401 USA

For reading levels and more information, look up this title at www.lernerbooks.com.
Visit us at zestbooks.net.

Title font: annamiro/Shutterstock.com.

Designed by Emily Harris.
Main body text set in Tw Cen MT Std.
Typeface provided by Monotype Typography.

### Library of Congress Cataloging-in-Publication Data

Names: Donohue, Caitlin, author. | Arrington, Briana, illustrator.
Title: She represents : 44 women who are changing politics ... and the world / Caitlin Donohue ;
    illustrations by Briana Arrington.
Description: Minneapolis, MN : Zest Books, an imprint of Lerner Publishing Group, Inc., [2020]
    | Includes bibliographical references and index. | Audience: Ages 13–18 | Audience:
    Grades 10–12 | Summary: "Each of the forty-four women profiled in this illustrated YA book
    demonstrates how women are capable of political and community leadership and activism.
    Readers will be inspired to pursue their own goals of social change." —Provided by publisher.
Identifiers: LCCN 2019044553 (print) | LCCN 2019044554 (ebook) | ISBN 9781541579002
    (library binding) | ISBN 9781541579019 (paperback) | ISBN 9781728401638 (ebook)
Subjects: LCSH: Women politicians—United States—Biography—Juvenile literature. | Women
    politicians—Biography—Juvenile literature. | Women—Political activity—United States—
    Juvenile literature. | Women—Political activity—Juvenile literature. | Social change—
    Juvenile literature.
Classification: LCC HQ1236.5.U6 .D66 2020 (print) | LCC HQ1236.5.U6 (ebook) |
    DDC 320.082/0973—dc23

LC record available at https://lccn.loc.gov/2019044553
LC ebook record available at https://lccn.loc.gov/2019044554

Manufactured in the United States of America
1-47089-47889-5/5/2020

# SHE REPRESENTS

**44** Women Who Are Changing
Politics . . . and the World

CAITLIN DONOHUE

ILLUSTRATED BY BRIANA ARRINGTON

ZEST BOOKS
MINNEAPOLIS

# CONTENTS

# INTRODUCTION

I remember with awful clarity the day I learned about sexism in politics. When I was a culture section intern at the dearly departed alt weekly *San Francisco Bay Guardian*, the first newspaper that ever hired me to write something, I got stuck covering a local Democratic election night party. Up until the night in question, I had mainly been reporting on sustainable food issues, but a politics reporter was sick and the editors needed a body capable of asking questions and taking notes. Slightly out of my element, I gave it my best shot. I gamely cornered the male head of the board of supervisors and started peppering him with questions. Two queries in, we were interrupted by a local blogger, who I did not recognize but who was a notoriously foul fixture of San Francisco progressive politics. This blogger clapped the politician on the back and greeted him with a friendly obscenity. Then, "Is this your escort?" he inquired, jerking his head in my direction and effectively reducing me to my apparent sexual availability. The head of the board of supervisors muttered that I was a journalist and disappeared in a cloud of small-talk smoke, leaving me alone with the disagreeable media man. This, at a gathering of progressive leaders, in San Francisco, ostensibly one of the country's most progressive cities! I felt as though I would never want to report on politics again.

But now I am older and wiser, and I know this disagreeable blogger said what he said because for a long time, women were seen as an accompaniment or aberration in politics. It didn't matter that Cleopatra and Nefertiti ruled Egypt back in ancient times—throughout much of modern US history, if we were in a room where decisions were made, we were probably arm candy for the men who were there to call the shots.

I am happy to say that times are slowly changing. In the United States, we are electing women at record rates. In the 2018 midterm elections, 589 women ran for the House of Representatives, Senate, and the governor's office. And 125 of them won their elections, including 45 women of color. In over half the countries of the world, quotas dictate by law how many women political parties must nominate for election. In 2019 women made up 24 percent of the world's parliaments, as opposed to just 11 percent in 1995. With representation comes new norms. Every year there are fewer places where chauvinist pigs may frolic freely and make women feel bad just for being in the room.

Not only is it definitely a good thing for women that we have more opportunities for political careers, but it is a good thing for everyone. Women make up more than half the population and are often entrusted with society's hardest jobs, including taking care of their families. Just like other traditionally underprivileged groups of people, we need a voice in the way things are run—if only to keep our political system truly representative of the people it governs.

This book is a nonexhaustive who's who of the current political generation that is influencing and shaping politics—although in some moments we'll take breaks to talk about great women political leaders from history. Some are heroines, and some are villains. Depending on whom you ask, most are both. But all of their stories teach us about the segments of society they represent, both by biography and by their actions in voting and policy decisions.

Mostly, the women in the main profiles of this book are currently in office, with some key exceptions. Hillary Clinton (page 22) and Sarah Palin (page 148) haven't held elected posts in years, but I thought their influence on today's politics was too remarkable to leave them out. Former Republican congressional representative Mia Love's (page 116) exit from electoral politics (for now) may be able to teach us about the current state of her party, and Stacey Abrams's (page 10) shocking gubernatorial defeat helps demonstrate the state of US voting rights for people of color. Wendy Davis's (page 44) story shows the difficulty of fighting for reproductive rights in much of the US, and despite her 2018 resignation, United Nations representative Nikki Haley (page 80) provided leadership within the Trump administration too unique to be ignored. Brazilian city council member Marielle Franco (page 64) is no longer with us, likely assassinated by her own government's paramilitary forces. Luckily, her political legacy thrives in Brazil and beyond.

The women in this book are mainly from the United States, because that's where this book is being published. But many of them are from other countries, and I'm especially excited to share these international stories with you, dear readers. Here's the thing: the US is not exactly a role model when it comes to having women in political office. We haven't even elected a woman president, and Iceland accomplished that back in 1980! (Here's to you, Vigdís Finnbogadóttir [page 74].) And when you grow up in the United States, you often don't learn much in school about the way politics work in the rest of the world. Those omissions limit our ability to think about what is politically possible and make us really easy to dupe about our country's relationship with other nations—especially on important matters such as immigration, faraway wars in foreign lands, and international trade.

This book is coming out during the 2020 US presidential elections, when our country's voters are entrusted with making a choice that will affect the rest of the world for the next four years. We don't think often enough about how our politics, in a rich country that has dominated world politics for many decades, affect our neighbors. Especially as it becomes clearer that developed countries like the United States have contributed way more than their fair share to climate change—which soon will become the most important political issue of our time, if it's not already. This is something we really need to think about. I hope learning about the international leaders in this book will inspire you to find out more about their parts of the world. As someone who has spent a lot of her life living outside the US, lemme tell ya, understanding more about other countries can teach you a hell of a lot about your own!

I have one more thing to say about the women in this book, and it may be the most important point that I want you to take away from this introduction. This book is meant to teach you what the road to power looks like for women in modern times. *I did not write it for fangirls.* Many of the women's stories are inspirational, but politicians are not celebrities. We don't read their biographies so that we can become their #1 stans or their most loyal Instagram followers. We learn about them to understand them, because once we understand them, it is easier to forecast their future policy decisions and— get ready for this—affect their actions. Politicians work for the people who elected them, and when they make decisions we don't agree with, we need to hold them accountable. *Not all the women in this book are what I would consider heroes, and I guarantee that every last one will make missteps during her career.* If we perceive them as glittering, sassy semi-deities rather than complex professionals and human beings, we give them way too much power.

Again, that's not to say that you can't be moved to action by reading the stories of these women! It's important to remember that there are many ways to make change. Politicians can make change, but activists, teachers, parents, students, writers, and people from every other walk of life can too.

Four years after that blogger tried to make me feel small by belittling me and sex workers in one fell swoop, I was promoted to culture editor at the *Bay Guardian*. It turned out I wasn't done writing about politics after all! I interviewed a group of local, politically active people of color, queer people, and women about similarly bigoted things this blogger had done and said to them, and published it all together in an article. I learned a valuable lesson about not being a straight white guy that day: when our voices come together, it becomes unmistakable that the aberration is not us, but rather the forces that would try to minimize our power.

I hope this book does something similar by uniting the stories of these political leaders and showing the ways in which their tales—our tales—are becoming part of the voice of politics, rather than the exception to the rule. Representation does matter, as does knowing what it is we stand for. Raise your voice—we'll be listening!

# STACEY ABRAMS

**(born 1973)**

**"Practice boldness, and the world adapts."**

Years in political office: 2007-2017

Position: minority leader of the Georgia House of Representatives, 2011-2017; member of the Georgia House of Representatives, 2007-2017

Party affiliation: Democrat

Hometown: Madison, Wisconsin

Top causes: voting rights, health care, and reproductive rights

# LIFE STORY

Stacey Abrams is the second of six kids born to Robert and Carolyn Abrams, who lived in Mississippi and then Georgia so that they could study to become Methodist ministers. Following their faith was not a financially lucrative path, and the family sometimes fell back on government aid, which taught Stacey early on about the value of the social safety net.

While her mom and dad hit the books, so did Abrams. In high school, she got a job on a congressional representative's campaign—and she was so good they later hired her as a speechwriter. Abrams earned the highest grades in her high school class, becoming the school's first Black valedictorian. In honor of her academic feat, she was invited to a reception at the governor's mansion in wealthy Atlanta neighborhood Buckhead. But when her family got off the bus and tried to walk up to the governor's front door, a security guard looked them up and down and told them they did not belong at the private event.

That show of racism and classism lit a fire under Abrams. She attended Spelman College in Atlanta, a historically Black school, where she became a campus leader during intense student protests over the not-guilty verdict in the Rodney King trial, in which LA cops were charged with excessive force for savagely beating a Black man. Abrams even debated Atlanta's mayor on television, taking him to task over not supporting young people. A few months later, his office gave her a job on the city's youth services.

After attending the University of Texas and Yale University for graduate degrees, Abrams headed back to Atlanta and became an attorney. She initially worked at a private firm, but soon she was appointed deputy city attorney—reportedly, the youngest in Atlanta history. She went on to win her first election to the Georgia House of Representatives, where she worked on education and tax issues. After four years, she became the House minority leader, leading her Democratic peers in policy work. Yet again, she was the first Black person and the first woman to be appointed to the position.

# WHAT'S ON HER AGENDA

Black people have long had to fight for their right to vote in the United States. Some early voting rights activists were murdered, including Lamar Smith, the Reverend George Lee, and Herbert Lee—all from Mississippi, one of Abrams's home states. So it's no surprise that she has long been concerned about voter suppression. An organization she founded while serving in the House of Representatives, the New Georgia Project, registered two hundred thousand voters of color in two years.

When she decided to run for governor in the 2018 election, she was right to be worried about getting a fair election. Abrams's opponent Brian Kemp was Georgia's secretary of state, in charge of overseeing the gubernatorial election! He had been criticized for failing to properly secure 6 million Georgia voters' personal information and faced a lawsuit for incorrectly nullifying some 340,000 voter registrations. Former president Jimmy Carter said that if Kemp kept his seat even while running for governor, then this was a clear conflict of interest. He called for Kemp's resignation before the election, but Kemp ignored Carter's advice, citing other elected officials who had not resigned while running for higher office.

On Election Day, many were horrified at what they saw as widespread voter suppression. Over two hundred polling places were closed. Many majority-Black and low-income precincts—the exact areas with the highest concentration of Abrams supporters—found themselves without the proper number of voting machines. Thousands more voters arrived to find that their names had been wrongly flagged as inconsistent or incorrect.

Abrams wound up losing by only 54,000 votes. Given the large numbers of those who had been unable to cast their vote, she questioned the legitimacy of the election results. She had won 1.9 million votes—surpassing any other Democratic candidate in the state's history. After her call for a runoff was rejected, she gave a speech to end her campaign. In it, she made it clear that she was not in agreement with the election results. "Democracy failed Georgians," she said. In 2019 her organization Fair Fight Action sued the Georgia Board of Elections over the voter suppression tactics employed in her election. Abrams was still intent on righting the system's wrongs.

It's not every day that you see a politician launched into the national spotlight by a high-profile election loss, but Abrams's resolve led to just that. There has been much speculation about whether she would run for a US Senate seat, make another go at the Georgia governorship, or even launch a presidential campaign. This last possibility got more media attention when Abrams dismissed the notion that she would run as Joe Biden's vice president by saying, "You don't run for second place." After months of teasing supporters, Abrams officially stated she would not run for president in the 2020 elections but changed her mind on serving as VP. "I would be honored to be considered by any nominee," she said.

If anyone doubted that Abrams is a force to be reckoned with, it was dispelled when she was picked to give the Democrats' official rebuttal to US president Donald Trump's 2019 State of the Union speech. Traditionally, the speech is given after the president addresses the country on legislative priorities and gives an assessment of where the nation stands economically and socially. The rebuttal gave Abrams a chance to tell the nation what she stands for: respecting immigrants' contributions to society, prioritizing affordable health care and other economic measures that help working families, and challenging all politicians to fully respect the rights of all US residents.

## AWESOME ACHIEVEMENTS
- Abrams was the first Black woman nominated for governor in any state by a major US party.
- She was the first in her family to buy a house.
- Abrams was the first Black woman to give an official response to the president's State of the Union—and she didn't even hold an elected position at the time.
- She has written eight romance novels under the pen name Selena Montgomery, which have sold over one hundred thousand copies.

## QUOTABLES
"If you don't bother asking for permission, then anyone else's denial of your agency is irrelevant."

"Concession means to acknowledge an action is right, true, or proper. As a woman of conscience and faith, I cannot concede."

"We are a mighty nation because we embedded in our national experiment the chance to fix what is broken. To call out what has faltered. To demand fairness wherever it can be found."

"I always say that if you're not at the leadership table, then expect to be on the menu."

# JACINDA ARDERN

(born 1980)

"It takes courage and strength to be empathetic."

Years in political office: 2008–present

Position: prime minister of New Zealand, 2017–present; leader of the Labour Party, 2017–present; deputy leader of the Labour Party, 2017; member of the New Zealand Parliament, 2008–2017; president of the International Union of Socialist Youth, 2008–2010

Party affiliation: Labour

Hometown: Hamilton, New Zealand

Top causes: Māori rights, climate change, and economic equality

# LIFE STORY

Jacinda Ardern spent much of her own childhood in the rural, conservative town of Morrinsville, New Zealand. Her mother was a school cafeteria worker, and her father was a law enforcement officer who eventually became the island of Niue's high commissioner. They raised her in the Mormon faith, but repelled by the church's negative stance on homosexuality, she left it for good in her early twenties. Positive from the get-go, she started a "happy club" at school as a little girl. She says seeing the effects of economic inequality on New Zealand's Māori people inspired her early on to become a politician.

Ardern's political career started when, at the age of nineteen, she volunteered on a Labour Party Parliament member's reelection campaign. Later, she would get a job in the office of her eventual mentor, New Zealand prime minister Helen Clark, the second woman to lead the country. Ardern worked for three years in the UK in the office of Prime Minister Tony Blair on relations between small businesses and the government before returning to her home country. She was twenty-eight when she first became a member of the New Zealand Parliament, making her the youngest representative in the country. When she became prime minister at thirty-seven, she was the youngest woman in the world to be leading a nation.

This identity has made her somewhat of a magnet for people's thoughts on the relationship between womanhood and power. Take for example, the famous rugby coach who called Ardern "a pretty little thing" during a talk show appearance— while he was voicing his support for her as prime minister, no less.

Jacinda Ardern

When one of the show's cohosts commented, "Rest assured he won't leave without bruised shins," Ardern responded via Twitter, "I hope your shoes were pointy."

Ardern has a daughter named Neve with partner Clarke Gayford, who is best known as a National Geographic channel celebrity fisher (his show is called *Fish of the Day*). The politician demonstrated the importance of paid family leave when she took a six-week break from her job as prime minister after having Neve. The family does not employ a nanny, and Gayford sometimes can be spotted in the crowd, bouncing Neve on his knee, while Ardern makes speeches.

# WHAT'S ON HER AGENDA

People often use gendered language with regard to Ardern's "niceness," her civil but direct attitude that she uses with every politician, even those whose views lie far from hers on the political spectrum. Ardern certainly prioritizes the needs of families by increasing welfare benefits, paid parental leave, and quotas for the number of refugees that New Zealand can house, causes that affect the lives of women throughout the country.

A terrible crucible of Ardern's prime ministerial career took place on March 15, 2019. On that day, a shooter strode into Al Noor Mosque and Linwood Islamic Centre and killed fifty-one members of the city of Christchurch's Muslim community. He streamed the massacre on Facebook Live. The ugly and violent show of hatred terrified New Zealander Muslims and provoked sadness, anger, and helplessness in individuals far beyond their community, who watched the event and its aftermath play out via media coverage.

The world needed comfort, and a mother with a lifelong passion for social justice stepped up to provide just that. Ardern had only been prime minister for a year and a half, but she knew she needed to deliver a message of unity in the face of this violence. "We are not immune to the viruses of hate, of fear, of other," she said at the memorial service for the victims of the shooting. "We never have been. But we can be the nation that discovers the cure." She donned a head scarf to address the grieving Muslim community and the gesture was picked up by her fellow non-Muslim New Zealanders. Soon Ardern's image was being projected onto Dubai's Burj Khalifa, the world's tallest building. Above her face read the word "Peace," written in both Arabic and English.

But Ardern's response to the Christchurch shootings was not limited to encouraging speeches and symbolic gestures. After criticizing Facebook for allowing violent content on its platform, she wrote legislation to ban the assault weapons and military-style semiautomatic arms that the terrorist had used, intending to do away with the means of committing such an act. She—like the rest of the world—hoped such a massive loss of life would never happen again.

## AWESOME ACHIEVEMENTS

- The adoration shown to her from a vast portion of New Zealand's population of five million is so fervent that it's been given a name: Jacindamania.
- When Trump called her with condolences over Christchurch, he asked what the US could provide to help. She told him, "Sympathy and love for all Muslim communities."
- When Ardern gave birth while serving as the head of a country, she was only the second person to do so in recorded history. (Decades earlier, Pakistani prime minister Benazir Bhutto did it twice.)

## QUOTABLES

"Today is a new beginning. The status quo is not good enough and we will not settle for it."

"(New Zealand is) small, and our contribution to the global emissions profile is even smaller, but we are surrounded by island nations who will feel the brunt of climate change acutely. I see ourselves as having a responsibility to demonstrate that we can and we will lead the charge."

"Very little of what I have done has been deliberate. It's intuitive."

"I am not the first woman to multitask. I am not the first woman to work and have a baby—there are many women who have done this before."

# ELAINE CHAO

### née 趙小蘭 (born 1953)

## "Immigration is an issue that has helped to enrich America. It has kept America dynamic and always competitive."

**Years in political office:** 1988–1992, 2001–2009, 2017–present

**Position:** US secretary of transportation, 2017–present; US secretary of labor, 2001–2009; director of the Peace Corps, 1991–1992; US deputy secretary of transportation, 1989–1991; chair of Federal Maritime Commission, 1988–1989

**Party affiliation:** Republican

**Hometown:** Taipei, Taiwan

**Top causes:** free markets and improving US infrastructure

# LIFE STORY

Elaine Chao, the oldest of six sisters, was born to a couple who fled the Chinese Civil War (1927–1949) to Taiwan. Her dad then got a scholarship and a US student visa, but the latter didn't allow for the rest of his family's legal passage. Chao calls her father at the time "a bright young man full of promise, hopes, and dreams." Her mother encouraged him to leave the family behind when she was seven months pregnant. Her mom took care of the family until they could reunite, which ended up being three years later. The experience shaped Chao's understanding of the sacrifices immigrants make. "I understand this immigration issue on a very deep and emotional level," she reflects.

Chao was eight years old when she finally came over to the US on a thirty-seven-day cargo ship journey with her mom and two sisters. The family's first US home was a one-bedroom apartment in Queens, New York. Everything felt sharply different to Chao. She didn't like the food, and the kids at school made fun of her beginner's English. But her family persevered. "My parents were so empowering," she says. "They imbued within us the confidence that we could do whatever we wanted. Not an arrogance, just a sense that we knew our own self-worth." She got her US citizenship when she was nineteen years old.

Chao attended the women's school Mount Holyoke College and then got a business degree from Harvard University. Originally, she wanted to be a banker. But then, in 1983, she got a fellowship at President Reagan's White House. "I'm actually a Republican!" she remembers thinking in surprise while working on a speech there. One of her first political jobs was heading up Asian American outreach for George H. W. Bush's presidential campaign in 1988.

Along the way, close friends set her up with a Republican politician named Mitch McConnell, who had three kids from a previous marriage. Those mutual acquaintances knew their stuff: Chao and McConnell married and consequently became one of Washington's best-known power couples. From 2003 to 2007, he was the US Senate majority whip, and Chao has worked for four different presidents, overseeing the country's Peace Corps, Labor Department, shipping, and transportation systems. At the time of this writing, she was one of the most seasoned policy makers on Trump's cabinet, and he was the Senate majority leader.

Chao calls her influential spouse "encouraging," and dubbed him her "low maintenance husband" because he does their laundry and cooks. The subtext is that in her busy life there is little time for such domestic affairs, something that Chao has lamented. "In my generation, we were taught you could have it all," she's said. "It doesn't work like that."

Elaine Chao

# WHAT'S ON HER AGENDA

Chao has held all kinds of positions, including head of the United Way, vice president for syndications of Bank of America, and a job with conservative think tank Heritage Foundation. But when it comes to transportation, she has a particularly deep source of experience. Her family made a fortune when her father founded the Foremost Group, a New York–based shipping company that sends goods to Chinese shipyards. Chao stopped officially working with the company years ago, but her sister Angela serves as its CEO.

Some critics have suggested that this makes Chao's position as head of the governmental agency that oversees United States shipping a bit problematic, as there might be conflicts of interest. Chao and McConnell have received gifts and political donations amounting to millions of dollars from Chao's family members who work for the company, but at the time of writing this, there is no evidence that these donations broke any laws. Chao's sister Angela took offense to the notion that the family company could be working against US interests. "We are an international shipping company, and I'm an American," she told the *New York Times*. "I don't think that, if I didn't have a Chinese face, there would be any of this focus on China."

Other scandals have developed around Chao and McConnell. In 2019 it came to light that Chao had asked the US government to make arrangements so that she could bring her family members to meetings with shipping company higher-ups in China. The planned trip was quickly canceled after the press started asking questions, and she released a statement calling the scandal "a web of innuendos and baseless inferences." Other politicians have since called for investigations into Chao and McConnell's political connections and funds.

Chao is a big believer in the idea that one needs to earn their living through pure hard work, and that the government shouldn't give people handouts. "America was built on meritocracies," she once said. That's meant pretty consistent opposition to unions when she was the secretary of labor, and opposition to affirmative action, which provides opportunities for underprivileged people to attend schools they otherwise couldn't afford. She supports immigrants who follow the legal process in starting a life in the US, much as her own family did.

She's also made it clear she will not be bullied into policy decisions. When two Boeing 737 airplanes crashed in quick succession, each killing all 157 people aboard, Chao responded to calls to ground the planes by flying in one with her staff from Texas to Washington, DC.

## AWESOME ACHIEVEMENTS

- She was the first Asian American woman to serve in a US president's cabinet—and she has served in four different administrations (and counting).
- As secretary of labor, Chao served in the George W. Bush administration for the entire eight years he was in office. She was the only cabinet member to do so.
- A $40 million donation that the politician's family made to Harvard led to the construction of the first campus building named for a woman or Asian American, built in honor of Elaine's mother, Ruth Mulan Chu Chao.
- Chao is lauded for her managerial acumen—when she was transportation secretary, she oversaw more than sixty thousand employees.

## QUOTABLES

"My family are patriotic Americans who have led purpose-driven lives and contributed much to this country."

"I remember the feelings of vulnerability, of anxiety, and what it feels like to be on the outside, and I feel like that makes me more empathetic as a leader."

"I don't think any of your viewers, any new immigrant, should feel that either party is not in support of immigrants. America is a country of immigrants. We all come from somewhere else, except for the Native Americans."

"Just because there are no role models doesn't mean that you can't be the future role model that you now seek. Just pursue your life's passion—do what you really love and the way will unfold."

Elaine Chao

# HILLARY CLINTON
## née Hillary Diane Rodham (born 1947)

## "We need to understand there is no one formula for how women should lead our lives."

Years in political office: 2001–2013

Position: US secretary of state, 2009–2013; US senator from New York, 2001–2009; First Lady of the United States, 1993–2001; First Lady of Arkansas, 1983–1992

Party affiliation: Democrat

Hometown: Chicago, Illinois

Top causes: health care, education, and international women's rights

# LIFE STORY

Hillary Rodham was born in 1947 to Chicago-area homemaker Dorothy Howell and textile entrepreneur Hugh Ellsworth Rodham. She got a quick start in campaigning. The first elections she won were as safety patrol cocaptain in elementary school and junior class vice president in high school. At first, her beliefs slanted conservative, and she joined her college's Young Republicans group. Graduating with a degree in political science, she went on to Yale Law School where she met a budding—and liberal—politician, Bill Clinton from Arkansas. The two fell in love and would become the very definition of a political power couple.

In 1978 Bill was elected as the country's youngest governor in his home state. The two were married by then, but Hillary, who continued to practice law and involved herself in state-level policy work, did not match the expectations many Arkansans had for the governor's wife. When Bill lost his reelection, some said that Hillary keeping her own last name after marriage had contributed to his defeat. By the third time he ran, she had started going by Hillary Rodham Clinton—and he won. The media's scrutiny of Clinton's womanliness, which she would face throughout her career, had begun.

Bill rode his folksy charm and appeal to a broad range of voters all the way to the presidency in 1992. The couple headed to Washington with their only child, Chelsea, and cat, Socks. As she had in Arkansas, Clinton took on an unprecedented amount of policy work as First Lady, focusing on family issues such as health insurance subsidies for kids.

Rough times came. A massive scandal enveloped Bill over his affair with intern Monica Lewinsky, and his family was caught in the fray. The media endlessly discussed intimate details of the affair, and Bill came within a hair's breadth of being removed from office for lying about the situation. Clinton infamously stood by her husband throughout the ordeal, calling the scandal over her spouse's terrible behavior a "vast right-wing conspiracy." In public, Clinton was loyal to her philandering partner under media pressure and Republican-led impeachment proceedings.

# WHAT'S ON HER AGENDA

Eventually, Clinton stepped out of Bill's shadow to focus on her solo political career. She was sworn in as a US senator representing New York just seventeen days before the couple left the White House in 2001, becoming the only First Lady elected to public office. Given her fame, some were surprised when she ducked her head down to focus on committee work. She won her second Senate election by 67 percent of the

# Electoral College

The Electoral College is not a school at all but a controversial system that's been around as long as the US Constitution. It determines how the country elects its presidents. Here's how it works: When people cast their vote for president, they're actually telling their state's *electors* how to vote. The electors cast their votes for whichever candidate received the most votes throughout the whole state. So even if, say, Candidate X receives one million votes and Candidate Y receives one million and one votes, Candidate Y gets all the state's electoral votes. Only Nebraska and Maine send out electors proportionally to the percentage of votes each candidate got. There are 538 electors in the college, with big states typically having more total electors than smaller states. This means that a candidate could receive a larger number of citizens' votes (what we call the popular vote) but send fewer electors to the Electoral College and thus lose the presidency. That has happened five times in the US, most recently to Al Gore in 2000 and Hillary Clinton in 2016.

vote, but cut her term short when she felt once again called to the White House—this time, as the president of the United States (POTUS) herself.

In Clinton's first presidential campaign, in 2008, she was beaten in the primaries by rising Illinois senator Barack Obama. She supported him in the general election, and Obama appointed her secretary of state. In that position, Clinton encouraged the US to interfere with politics in the Middle East. She was heavily criticized for insufficiently supporting people's uprisings in Egypt and Libya but lauded for her work in enforcing the rights of women and children.

After beating Vermont senator Bernie Sanders in the 2016 presidential primaries, she was locked and loaded for a truly brutal showdown with real estate mogul and reality TV star Donald Trump, who inadvertently coined a feminist catchphrase when he called her a "nasty woman" during a debate. Trump saw that Clinton secretly used a private email account for official business while she was secretary of state as a clear sign of her corruption. At his campaign rallies, stadiums of his followers chanted "lock her up" to call for her incarceration. Though she ended up winning the popular vote by 2.8 million votes, Clinton lost the Electoral College to Trump. Disheartened, she announced in 2017 she would not run for public office again. She's far from perfect, but Clinton's expansion of the First Lady's potential and undaunted belief in the power of women to lead will not be soon forgotten.

## AWESOME ACHIEVEMENTS

- As First Lady, Clinton joined Attorney General Janet Reno to help open the Department of Justice's Office on Violence Against Women, which supports programs that fight domestic violence, stalking, and sexual assault. By 2019 the office had given out $8.1 billion in grants.
- Clinton's fascination with her first role at the White House led her to push for the establishment of the online National First Ladies' Library.
- She received an astronomical $8 million advance for writing her White House memoir, *Living History*, which became an international best seller.

## QUOTABLES

"Women's rights are human rights."

"If you believe you can make a difference, not just in politics, in public service, in advocacy around all these important issues, then you have to be prepared to accept that you are not going to get 100 percent approval."

"There's that kind of double bind that women find themselves in. On the one hand, yes, be smart, stand up for yourself. On the other hand, don't offend anybody, don't step on toes, or you'll become somebody that nobody likes because you're too assertive."

"Don't let anyone tell you that great things can't happen in America. Barriers can come down. Justice and equality can win."

# TATIANA CLOUTHIER

## (born 1964)

### "The right and the left no longer exist in Mexico."

**Years in political office:** 1991, 2003–2006, 2018–present

**Position:** member of the Mexican Congress, 2003–2006, 2018–present; substitute member of Congress, 1991

**Party affiliation:** National Regeneration Movement, 2018–present; independent, 2005–2018; National Action Party, 1990–2005

**Hometown:** Culiacán, Mexico

**Top causes:** reducing violent crime and empowering local government

# LIFE STORY

Tatiana Clouthier grew up one of eleven children in a wealthy family. Her father, Manuel "Maquío" Clouthier, was the president of a major national business organization. He ran as the presidential candidate for the conservative National Action Party (PAN) in 1988, but he lost. Few ever thought he stood a chance. Though his party's efforts were crucial in opening up the field to opposition parties, the Institutional Revolutionary Party (PRI) had controlled the Mexican government for sixty years.

Clouthier grew up in Culiacán, a city in northwestern Mexico, but she moved at a young age when her parents worried that she might become one of the thousands of Mexicans who were kidnapped in the '90s by drug cartels. In 1990 Clouthier became active in her deceased father's political party. Her first positions were in the city government of San Pedro Garza García, a city in the wealthy, PAN-loyal state of Nuevo León.

The PAN scored a historic victory in 2000 when the party's candidate, Vicente Fox, became the first president who wasn't from the PRI in more than seventy years. It was a validation of the Clouthiers' political work, but she—appointed as a member of the

## Mexico's Year of the Woman

When Andrés Manuel López Obrador (AMLO) won the presidency in 2018, he appointed a cabinet with full gender parity featuring eight women and eight men as ministers, including former Supreme Court judge Olga Sánchez Cordero as his secretary of the interior (a post typically considered the second most important position in the Mexican government). Claudia Sheinbaum, a scientist and Nobel Peace Prize winner for her work on climate change, was also elected mayor of Mexico City, the capital whose metropolitan area is home to one-sixth of the country's population.

In the same elections Mexican voters chose so many women candidates that the country's Senate is comprised of 49 percent women. Mexico's lower house, the Chamber of Deputies, is not far behind at 48 percent women representatives—rather astounding given that prior to the 2003 elections, they only held 17 percent of the seats. In 2019 the country's percentage of women in parliamentary chambers was still beat by those of Rwanda (61 percent), Cuba, and Bolivia (both at 53 percent).

Many of these landmarks were made possible by a federal quota system that began in 2003, which states that political parties must nominate an equal number of men and women in federal and state political races. Mexico is not the only country with a quota system—every country in Latin America besides Venezuela and Guatemala has one.

national Congress in the victory through the Mexican system of proportional political representation—was soon disillusioned. She saw Fox give preferential treatment to Chinese textile companies because of their connections to his wife's family. Even though the PRI had been defeated, their signature corruption seemed to have stuck around. "What we fought for was not what was happening," remembers Clouthier.

She left the PAN in 2005, focused on NGO activism, and eventually launched an unsuccessful run for mayor in San Pedro Garza García. She remains an advocate for putting more power in the hands of local governments so that "they don't have to pass through being nice to the governor, nice to the president to do things."

It became clear that Clouthier believes parties come second to people when she met the country's best-known left-wing politician, the former Mexico City mayor and presidential candidate Andrés Manuel López Obrador (better known by his initials AMLO), at a 2006 dinner party. Clouthier says she was impressed by his humility and restraint, a far cry from his grandstanding public persona. Clouthier had been impressed in the past with his effectiveness as mayor in reducing the robberies and kidnappings that had terrorized Mexico City residents. She decided if he could run one of the world's largest cities, he had a good shot at running Mexico.

When AMLO ran for president for a second time in 2012, Clouthier publicly supported him. When he ran for a third time in 2018, she became his campaign manager, masterminding the "Together We'll Make History" campaign that finally won AMLO the presidency. Clouthier turned down the president's offer to take a position on his cabinet. But she is the first member of Congress—again, appointed through the proportional representation system—from AMLO's MORENA Party to hold the leadership position equivalent to that of the United States' majority whip. FYI, that's the person who mobilizes votes for the political party with the most seats.

Clouthier has said that she's holding back on her political career until her two teenage daughters are older. To blow off steam, she loves exercising, playing Rummikub, and watching TV, especially CSI: Miami. She is inspired by other prominent people who have served as connections between disparate parts of their societies, such as Diana, Princess of Wales; Mother Teresa; and Mexican human rights activist and priest Father Alejandro Solalinde Guerra.

# WHAT'S ON HER AGENDA

During AMLO's 2018 run for the presidency, Clouthier took an unusually visible role for a campaign manager. But it's pretty easy to see why. AMLO is sonorous, unrelentingly serious, and perceived as a radical by middle-class Mexicans unsettled by his unflinching focus on the problems facing the country's working poor. In contrast, Clouthier has become known for her witty one-liners on social media and comes from a well-known conservative family and political tradition. Plus, she has extensive connections in her home of northern Mexico, traditionally a richer, more business-oriented, and more conservative area than the southern Mexican regions where AMLO's base has been historically concentrated. Between the two of them, a swathe of Mexico's political panorama was represented. "The worst thing that can happen for anyone winning the presidency at this moment is that the market shifts, and in that sense you need to give [business leaders and investors] security," she told US business magazine *Bloomberg* during the campaign. "I think Andrés Manuel knows that." Clouthier played a significant role in translating how AMLO's policies of supporting the voiceless could bring greater security and peace to all of Mexican society.

Her impressive performance during the campaign and continually high popularity ratings left some wondering whether she will run to fill her boss's shoes in the next presidential elections in 2024 (in Mexico, presidents serve six-year terms and are not allowed to run twice). But Clouthier has remained coy about the prospect, even suggesting that she may throw her weight behind another candidate. "All the work that would imply . . . it's not something that I long for," she told the press in 2018.

But that doesn't mean that she's sitting back and letting others run the show. In her second bout as a member of Mexico's Congress, Clouthier has proven that she's unwilling to be a rubber stamp for the president and has pushed back against some of his policy decisions. Unsurprisingly, as a woman whose life has been impacted by Mexico's skyrocketing violent crime rates, Clouthier has been particularly active on security issues. She publicly denounced AMLO's creation of a sixty-thousand-member National Guard, which many in Mexico see as an escalation of the War on Drugs against violent cartels that by 2018 had already cost an estimated 150,000 lives.

## AWESOME ACHIEVEMENTS

- Clouthier is the author of five books, including one on her politician father and another about working on AMLO's 2018 campaign.
- In 2009 she founded Evolución Mexicana (Mexican Evolution), a foundation that is dedicated to encouraging citizen participation in politics.
- Clouthier has taught college and postgraduate classes in English, Mexican history, socioeconomics, and ethics in digital media.

## QUOTABLES

"Andrés Manuel has evolved. The bankers, too, have understood that he doesn't eat children."

"The extension of the home is the municipality (local government)."

"There is a long road in front of us towards equality."

# SUSAN COLLINS
## (born 1952)

"Our success multiplies each time we lead someone else to success."

Years in political office: 1996–present

Position: US senator from Maine, 1997–present; former Massachusetts deputy state treasurer, 1993–1994

Party affiliation: Republican

Hometown: Caribou, Maine

Top causes: national security, health care, women's health, and education

# LIFE STORY

Susan Margaret Collins was born December 7, 1952, to a family of lumber company owners, judges, and political leaders. Both her parents served as mayor of the little town of Caribou, Maine, where she was raised. Her father was part of her family's four generations of state legislators, and her mother was on the boards of organizations such as the Catholic Charities of Maine.

In school, Collins shone. She represented Maine in the US Senate Youth Program and spent a month in Washington, DC, meeting the country's top politicians. There, she had a two-hour-long conversation with Maine senator Margaret Chase Smith— the first woman ever to be elected to both the House and Senate. Collins's exchange with Smith inspired her to consider a political career.

In high school, she had a job at the Caribou Public Library reading books to children. She credits those story hours for her high regard of the importance of education. Collins got the second-best grades in her graduating class at Caribou High School and received Phi Beta Kappa honors in college.

At the age of fifty-nine, Collins married Thomas Daffron, whom she had met when she was a twenty-one-year-old congressional intern. As a testament to Collins's high standing, the Senate halted their discussion of a highway bill and adjourned early so members could attend the engagement party, which was hosted by Hillary Clinton (page 22).

# WHAT'S ON HER AGENDA

Collins got going in politics right after graduating from college. She worked in the office of US representative—and subsequent senator—William Cohen for more than a decade. She later became Maine governor John McKernan Jr.'s commissioner of professional and financial regulation. Her talent gained nationwide recognition when President George H. W. Bush made her regional director for the federal Small Business Administration.

In 1994 she decided to run for an elected position and beat out seven other Republicans in the governor's race to become the first woman from a major party nominated for the position in Maine. She was eventually bested by the Democratic candidate, but maybe it was meant to be. Two years later, Collins won the election to become one of Maine's national senators. She was immediately appointed chairperson of the permanent subcommittee on investigations, a position which a woman had never held before, and used her role to expose Medicare scams that affected US residents' pocketbooks. Her debut Senate vote was to confirm Madeleine Albright as the country's first woman secretary of state—historic indeed.

Collins has held onto her Senate seat ever since, earning a reputation as an independent voter who takes her time to research issues. She's famously cast votes against the Republican party line on national health care, same-sex marriage, and abortion rights. When Georgetown University cosponsored a study of senators' voting records from 1993–2014, she was named the most bipartisan current member of the US Senate, a title that gave her a lot of strategic power in close votes within the two-party system.

That reputation of bipartisanship did get tarnished in the polarizing Trump administration, during which Collins's reputation as a swing voter put her in some hopeless political situations. In 2018 the senator weathered the biggest controversy of her career when she became one of the key votes in the confirmation of Supreme Court justice Brett Kavanaugh. Kavanaugh, nominated by Trump, had been accused by Christine Blasey Ford of attempting to rape her when they were adolescents. Aghast (and politically motivated) Democrats were adamant that he not serve in the nation's highest court, where he would likely be voting on issues important to many women, such as the survival of Roe v. Wade. After a period of intense media speculation on her vote, and pressure from both sides of the aisle, Collins delivered a forty-five-minute speech in favor of Kavanaugh on the Senate floor.

In the run-up to her 2020 reelection bid, Collins has already sought opportunities to regain the liberal base who felt betrayed by her after the Kavanaugh toss-up. In 2019, for example, she opposed Trump's nominee for a northern Texas district judge, Matthew Kacsmaryk, who had previously called pro-choice activists "sexual revolutionaries." Overall, Collins votes along with Trump's positions 69 percent of the time.

## AWESOME ACHIEVEMENTS

- Collins is an extremely hardworking politician, having never missed a single roll call vote in her entire Senate career. By December 2019 she had taken part in 7,262 consecutive votes!
- In 2007 she was awarded the Mother Teresa Award from the National Association for Home Care & Hospice for her work in promoting legislation that widens access to care for the elderly and special needs individuals.
- She worked with Senator Joe Lieberman to repeal Don't Ask, Don't Tell, the military policy that prevented members of the LGBTQ community from openly serving in the armed forces. Later, she became an outspoken opponent of Trump's crusade to ban transgender individuals from serving in the military.
- In 2014 Collins received the Corporation for Public Broadcasting's Thought Leader Award, honoring leaders who support the mission of publicly owned media.

## QUOTABLES

"Unconstrained and unfettered and unvetted, I marched over to the Senate floor, took the microphone and challenged our colleagues to come out of their partisan corners, to stop the fighting and to start legislating in a manner worthy of the people of this country."

"Our first responsibility as a leader is to create an attractive dream, to proclaim a destination, communicating it in detail to others who might be interested in joining our expedition."

"If you don't know what you want, you'll probably get what somebody else wants."

"Voting is a Senator's most important responsibility, and I feel strongly about making every effort possible to be present to make sure Mainers' voices are heard."

Susan Collins

# HISTORIC HEAVYWEIGHTS

## GOLDA MEIR

A Ukrainian immigrant living in the US, Zionist Golda Meir was drawn to take part in the creation of Israel, the Jewish state. In 1921 she and her first husband immigrated to the area of the Middle East known as Palestine, and she became a major political force there, even signing the Israeli Declaration of Independence that established the state as an independent country. Meir served on the Knesset, the Israeli parliament, and was the bearer of the country's first issued passport for her work as the Moscow ambassador. In 1969 the Israeli prime minister died in office and Meir was elected to replace him on a temporary basis. She served in the position for five years. Meir held the country together during a turbulent time but was criticized for her administration's treatment of the Palestinians.

## BELLA ABZUG

This Russian Jewish native of New York City was a civil rights lawyer before she ran for US Congress at the age of fifty. Abzug's winning campaign motto was, "This woman's place is in the House . . . the House of Representatives." She proposed a bill to end the Vietnam War (1957–1975) on her first day on the job in 1973. She sponsored the Equality Act, which would have been the country's first gay rights bill if it had passed. She also coauthored Title IX, a groundbreaking legislation that banned gender discrimination in schools. Abzug was known as Battling Bella, and she always wore a hat—because, according to her, it was the only way to get her male colleagues to treat her as a professional.

## MARGARET THATCHER

Britain's famed Iron Lady was a lifelong conservative who grew up above her family's grocery market and started her professional life as a chemist. She married rich, yet successfully portrayed herself as a penny-pinching housewife and became Britain's prime minister in 1979. Thatcher was a powerful advocate for free markets and became infamous for disassembling social welfare programs—she once cut free milk for schoolkids from the education budget. Though her legacy's effectiveness remains up for debate, she's generally regarded as one of Britain's most self-confident recent leaders.

## ANN RICHARDS

Ann Richards was a wildly charismatic, hard-drinking Texas feminist teacher. She was recruited to run for county commissioner and then won her bid for state treasurer in 1982, becoming the first woman elected to statewide office in fifty years. Her sparkling conversational skills made her a talented politician, one particularly given to memorable one-liners, as when she defended her infamous whorl of snow-white locks: "I get a lot of cracks about my hair, mostly from men who don't have any." After overcoming her alcohol addiction, she was selected to one term as governor in 1991. There, she advocated for a progressive "New Texas," racially integrating the Texas Rangers law enforcement agency and pushing for legislation that prioritized the rights of women, LGBTQ people, and people of color—whose political careers she tended to promote whenever possible.

## BARBARA JORDAN

This pastor's daughter from Houston's Fifth Ward had a deep voice some thought of as God-like. More importantly, she broke ground for Black women in US politics with her unprecedented rise to Congress. She was not a radical so much as a political master who learned the system inside and out, charming and outmaneuvering political adversaries. At the end of her first Texas state senate session in 1967, the thirty other members—all of them white men, mind you—gave her a standing ovation. She was thirty-six years old when, in 1973, she became the first southern Black woman elected to US Congress. Jordan did important work expanding the Voting Rights Act, and her reasoned denouncement of President Richard Nixon's crimes in the Watergate scandal remains one of her most famous speeches.

## BENAZIR BHUTTO

Bhutto served as Pakistan's prime minister from 1988 to 1990 and then again from 1993 to 1996. Leadership ran in the family—her father, Zulfikar Ali Bhutto, was president and then prime minister in the 1970s. The hypereducated politician (she held degrees from both Harvard and Oxford) was the first Muslim woman to lead an Islamic country, and she pushed hard for privatization and industrial development. Her administrations were plagued by corruption charges, and she was assassinated in 2007, but she was also the first modern head of state to have a child while in office. She worried about political opponents gunning to remove her from office, so she hid the pregnancy from everyone and was back on the job the day after giving birth.

Historic Heavyweights

# CARMEN YULÍN CRUZ SOTO

**(born 1963)**

"I cannot fathom the thought that the greatest nation in the world cannot figure out logistics for a small island of 100 miles (161 km) by 35 miles (56 km) long."

Years in political office: 2009-present

Position: mayor of San Juan, Puerto Rico, 2013-present;
Puerto Rico House of Representatives member, 2009-2013

Party affiliation: Popular Democrat

Hometown: San Juan, Puerto Rico

Top causes: Puerto Rican sovereignty, labor rights, and rebuilding
post-natural disaster infrastructure

# LIFE STORY

Cruz was born and raised in San Juan, the city where she would one day be mayor, and was student president of her eighth-grade class and later of her high school. She once even represented her peers at a presidential youth summit. She was an honors student and a track-and-field star, raised by a dad who was a maintenance worker and a mom who has a reputation on the island for being a staunch Puerto Rican patriot.

To further her education, Cruz went to the continental United States after high school, earning degrees from Boston University and Carnegie Mellon. She went on to work for the US Treasury Department and Scotiabank before she came home. In San Juan she entered the world of politics as an adviser of Sila María Calderon, who was then the second woman to become mayor of San Juan and who would later be the commonwealth's first female governor.

Cruz—everyone in Puerto Rico calls her Yulín—then ran for a seat in Puerto Rico's House of Representatives. She lost the first time but won after her second bid eight years later. In 2012 she set her sights on San Juan's mayorship and, with the endorsement of LGBTQ, student, immigrant, and worker organizations, she beat the three-term incumbent.

She has proven to be a fierce advocate for labor unions and for her own island. She once asked the US Congress to increase Puerto Rico's ability to self-govern and allow it to make its own trade agreements with other countries (to no avail).

*Carmen Yulín Cruz Soto*

She loves to read biographies of world leaders whose lives she finds inspirational. Her bookshelf includes titles about Supreme Court justice Ruth Bader Ginsburg (page 162) and Chicano union leader César Chávez.

# WHAT'S ON HER AGENDA

Most US mainlanders became aware of Carmen Yulín Cruz Soto in the aftermath of Hurricane María. The storm struck Puerto Rico with a fury that islanders will not soon forget, killing over four thousand people. Many of its fatalities happened after the storm, when entire communities were left without electricity and water for months. Many blamed the fact that federal aid did not arrive quickly enough to vast swaths of the island, including its capital San Juan, where Cruz had been mayor for four years.

And so on September 29, 2017, the 5-foot-tall (1.5 m) Cruz held a press conference in front of pallets filled with donated food and made a plea. "We are dying," she said, addressing her remarks to the United States' disaster relief agencies and their commander, Trump. "You are killing us with the inefficiency and bureaucracy." Later, she would liken the neglect to that which occurred after Hurricane Katrina struck New Orleans in 2005. The federal government had similarly failed to effectively respond to the disaster, resulting in heavy casualties in a poor area mostly populated by people of color.

After María, an estimated 130,000 Puerto Ricans (4 percent of the island's population) left the island for good. In response to Cruz's plea, Trump fired off a series of tweets lamenting Cruz's "poor leadership ability" in getting aid to her people.

Many US residents did not initially realize that what was happening in Puerto Rico was a national—and not an international—tragedy. Surveys show that almost half of the mainland population is unaware that the island is one of the US's territories. Colonialist Spain signed it over to the United States with the 1898 Treaty of Paris, and it has been under US control since. Puerto Ricans became full US citizens in 1917, and the island officially became a US commonwealth in 1952, but its residents still cannot vote for president. Their sole representative in Congress, called a resident commissioner, cannot participate in final votes on legislation.

In Cruz, Puerto Ricans found a dedicated leader. For three months after the storm, she led rescue missions in person and lived in a back room of Roberto Clemente Coliseum, a sports arena that had been turned into an emergency shelter.

Cruz is running for governor of Puerto Rico in the 2020 elections. She announced her campaign on March 22, the same day that Puerto Rico celebrates the abolition of slavery on the island. She wore a white pantsuit and black tee emblazoned with words in Spanish that aptly sum up her career: "¡Sin Miedo!" (Without Fear!)

In 2019 the need for new leadership on the island became even clearer when discriminatory and threatening messages written by Governor Ricardo Rosselló and his peers in private chats were made public. Thousands of Puerto Ricans protested in the streets every day for a week, and Rosselló stepped down. "It truly is about a movement led by the people and not the politicians, thank God, and a movement of unity and power," said Cruz, who Rosselló's crew had joked about shooting in the texts. "I'm proud like hell to be Puerto Rican."

## AWESOME ACHIEVEMENTS

- While mayor, Cruz supported the formation of labor unions by San Juan city workers looking to better their pay and benefits.
- She prefers to do all her own household chores to stay down to earth (even if that means her apartment gets a little messy sometimes).
- She was once the proud owner of a Harley-Davidson motorcycle.
- When she was announced as one of four national cochairs on Senator Bernie Sanders's 2020 presidential campaign, Cruz became the first Puerto Rican elected official to play such an important role in a US presidential election.

## QUOTABLES

"Politics is a rough game, and sometimes as females we are taught that you have to play nice. Sometimes you can't play nice."

"We are awake to our inequity—and our inequality."

"I often say to my friends that I felt too Puerto Rican to live in the States; then I felt too American to live in Puerto Rico. So when I settled back in Puerto Rico in 1992, I had to come to terms with all of that."

"I didn't do anything special. I did what had to be done. And I would do it again and again."

# SHARICE DAVIDS
(born 1980)

**"Many of my fellow candidates talk about being a 'voice for the voiceless.' I have built my campaign on the belief that everyone already has their own voice."**

Years in political office: 2019–present

Position: member of the US House of Representatives from Kansas, 2019–present

Party affiliation: Democrat

Hometown: Frankfurt, Germany

Top causes: gun violence, green energy, and funding public schools

# LIFE STORY

When she was a child, Ho-Chunk Nation member Sharice Davids remembers being fascinated by Bruce Lee. She fashioned her own black belt and loved to walk around the house channeling the Hong Kong American actor and martial arts legend. Her mom, who served in the military for twenty years and gave birth to Davids while stationed overseas, lacked the funds to send her to martial arts classes. But when Davids was in her late teens and able to afford the fees herself, she started getting instruction in capoeira, karate, and tae kwon do. A coach with mixed martial arts (MMA) experience convinced her to start fighting in competitions, and Davids won her first amateur MMA fight decisively in 2006. She would struggle with her role within the sport—although clearly talented, she didn't have the funds to dedicate herself to a pro career.

While still in training, Davids got her law degree from Cornell University and eventually set her sights on being a corporate transactional attorney. She worked for Denton, one of the world's largest law firms, on financing for Native tribes, equities, mergers, and other deals. Davids left the firm for projects in the world of nonprofits, at one point to create an entrepreneurship program at a high school on the Pine Ridge Indian Reservation in South Dakota.

That job, however, wasn't without its challenges—one was finding a place to live while she worked at the school. South Dakota was one of the states that doesn't protect government housing applicants from discrimination based on their sexual orientation, and Davids was an out lesbian looking for a place where she and her long-term partner could live. (The discriminatory housing policy was reversed in 2016.) The experience of that institutionalized bigotry spurred her into a political career. "I thought, 'we need more people who have experiences like I do, like my friends and family do,'" she remembers.

Always ready for a fight, in 2010 the Democrat Davids and her partner moved back to the suburban Kansas district where her mom and two brothers still lived, and Davids launched a campaign for election to Congress. Her successful run would help expose the United States' still-standing prejudices against Native Americans.

# WHAT'S ON HER AGENDA

The thirty-eight-year-old Davids's challenge was appealing to the largely white electorate in her well-to-do district that was once a shoo-in for Republican

*Sharice Davids*

candidates. It was a big deal that she was a lesbian running for Congress in Kansas, a state that just three years earlier, in 2015, had seen its governor rescind discrimination protections for LGBTQ state government employees (these protections were reinstated in January 2019). But, strategically, Davids chose not to highlight her sexual orientation or her position on the Republican president Trump in her campaign. Rather, she focused on her plans to end corporate tax giveaways and on health-care issues. She scored a major endorsement from reproductive rights group Emily's List, and emerged victorious in her primary when voters chose Davids over a progressive candidate backed by Bernie Sanders and Alexandria Ocasio-Cortez (page 140).

During the run-up to the general election, Davids attracted national media attention after receiving one of the nastiest, most inaccurate racist slurs of the electoral season. "Your radical socialist kick boxing lesbian will be sent back packing to the reservation," one Republican precinct committee member wrote in a private Facebook chat that was later made public. Leaving aside the facts that she hadn't grown up on a reservation and that Davids's moderate policies are far from socialist, the hater was wrong about Davids's political trajectory. She would go on to beat four-term Republican incumbent Kevin Yoder by 10 percent, contributing to the Democrats taking control of the House of Representatives in 2018. Davids and New Mexico's Deb Haaland (page 76) became the first Native women in Congress. "The fact that we are in 2018 and we are still seeing all these firsts is mind-boggling to me," Davids said in the run-up to her historic victory. "When I stop and think about it, it makes me very proud to be a part of this movement that is happening in our country."

Though detractors had attempted to paint her as a radical, Davids demonstrated her more moderate views when she quickly made alliances with House Speaker Nancy Pelosi (page 154) and cosponsored an immigration bill once championed by Yoder upon arriving in Washington, DC. In the early months of her congressional career, Davids said she could not commit to supporting many of the progressives' top issues, such as the Green New Deal, abolishing the Immigration and Customs Enforcement (ICE) agency, and Medicare for All. "I can't say what the next step looks like," she said, discussing health care in her first Kansas town hall after taking office. "But the things I can actually put energy into, I want them to be things that can get bipartisan support."

# AWESOME ACHIEVEMENTS

- Davids is the first openly gay person to represent Kansas in the House of Representatives and the first openly gay Native American woman in Congress.
- She won her first professional MMA fight in under a minute.
- Davids was selected as a 2016 White House fellow based on her work in economic community development for Native Americans.
- While living on the Pine Ridge Reservation, Davids founded the since-shuttered Hoka Coffee, selling roasted South and Central American beans at powwows and other community events. Her company's tagline? "Indigenous from the ground to the cup."

# QUOTABLES

"It's funny that through learning how to physically fight, you also learn how to navigate really complicated and hard conversations with people."

"We have the opportunity to reset expectations about what people think when they think of Kansas. We know there are so many of us who welcome everyone, who see everyone, and who know that everyone should have the opportunity to succeed."

"I saw first-hand the disconnect that exists when decision makers have no connection to the communities they're impacting. I saw that one new voice can change the entire conversation."

Sharice Davids

# WENDY DAVIS

née Wendy Jean Russell (born 1963)

## "Lawmakers, either get out of the vagina business, or go to medical school."

Years in political office: 1999–2008, 2009–2015

Position: Texas state senator, 2009–2015; member of the Fort Worth City Council, 1999–2008

Party affiliation: Democrat, 2006–present; Republican, before 2006

Hometown: West Warwick, Rhode Island

Top causes: reproductive rights, education funding, and marijuana decriminalization

# LIFE STORY

This future state senator was one of four kids, raised by a single mother whose education stopped after ninth grade and who worked at an ice cream store to keep the family fed. Wendy Davis jumped into the working world early, staffing an Orange Julius juice bar as a teen. She became pregnant, got married, and divorced her first husband by the time she was twenty-one, winding up living with her first kid in the trailer she and her ex had bought. "I just saw myself in a dead end," she remembers. "And I was struggling, literally struggling, to pay the bills, buy the groceries and put gas in my car."

She was waiting tables in her father's restaurant when she met her second husband, Jeff Davis, a businessperson and former Dallas City Council member who eventually adopted Davis's daughter, Amber, and fathered her second child, Dru. Able to count on his childcare and financial support, Davis got her bachelor's degree from Texas Christian University and then her law degree from Harvard. She was determined to make the most of her academic career and reportedly never missed an assignment or a day of class at Texas Christian, even while she was pregnant with Dru.

During those school years, Davis had to make some tough decisions. While at Harvard, she sent her two daughters back to live with their dad when it became clear that their life in Massachusetts while she attended full-time law school would be untenable. That kind of ambitious prioritizing of one's career goes largely unquestioned when successful men do it, but it is rarely accepted when done by women. Davis would later face political blowback for her decision to go wholeheartedly after academic success and for not switching to a less prestigious law school so that she could be nearer to her girls.

After graduation, Davis was drawn not to law but to politics. She lost her first Fort Worth City Council election ("It was the first time in my life I had tried to do something and hadn't succeeded at it," she says) but tried a second time and triumphed, eventually serving there for nine years.

By the time she reached the state senate, Davis was an established firebrand. Republicans attempted to oust her by trying to redraw the lines of her district in the hopes of making it unwinnable for a Democrat, a move that was rejected by the Supreme Court. When her name recognition in Texas soared by forty points after a pro-choice star turn (more on that later), she was encouraged to run for governor in the staunchly Republican state. But her centrist campaign avoided all mention of abortion to appeal to swing voters, and she lost by 20 percent.

*Wendy Davis*

## Filibuster

A practice dating back to ancient Rome in which a single politician or a group of them will talk a *lot* to hold up proceedings and prevent a decision being made on legislation they don't want to pass. It's a beloved tradition in the US Senate (where it can still be vetoed by the vote of sixty senators), strictly limited in the US House of Representatives, and legal in fourteen state legislatures.

Since then she has kept busy. Davis formed a nonprofit that focuses on inspiring young people to be active on issues of gender discrimination. She hangs out with her grandkids—and is also mulling over a run for US Congress. We may not have seen the last of this woman in the political fray.

# WHAT'S ON HER AGENDA

Abortion rights hit close to home for Davis, since she's had two. The first time was when she discovered that she had an ectopic pregnancy, a potentially lethal situation that happens when an embryo begins to form outside the uterus. During a later pregnancy, she and her husband were advised that their unborn daughter—whom they had already named Tate Elise—had a serious brain abnormality. "Through a great deal of pain, we ultimately made a decision that the most loving thing that we could do for her was let her go," says Davis.

In 2013 Republicans were hoping to pass Senate Bill 5 to severely limit access to abortion. In what is her most famous act as a politician, Davis stepped up to filibuster a vote on the bill on the final day of the legislative session. The rules were so strict that she had to have a catheter inserted so that she wouldn't have to leave the floor to pee! The fitness buff managed to speak for eleven hours, sharing testimonies from people who had abortions, all without leaning, sitting, or drinking. With the help of a rowdy crowd of pro-choice demonstrators who raised a vote-confusing ruckus in the chamber for the final two hours, the bill was temporarily blocked. Across the country people cheered Davis's iron resolve to stand up for reproductive rights.

Her efforts, however, seemed to be for naught. The governor called a special legislative session, and Senate Bill 5 was approved, eventually cutting the number of Texan abortion clinics from forty-two to nineteen. But then, in 2016, the Supreme Court ruled in favor of one of the clinics affected and the bill was struck down. "So gratifying," Davis said in reaction. "I truly believed this day would come."

## AWESOME ACHIEVEMENTS

- She was the first person in her family to go to college.
- The Senate Bill 5 filibuster was not Davis's first. In 2011 she provoked another special session when she spoke out against $4 billion in education budget cuts.
- The pink-and-lime Mizuno running sneakers she wore for the filibuster sold huge numbers online, snapped up by consumers looking to channel Davis's resolve.

## QUOTABLES

"When people believe that their votes are going to matter, they show up."

"Women in this country are not equal in terms of the way we're treated in the workplace and elsewhere, and it's going to take the passage of the Equal Rights Amendment (and) it's going to take some affirmative steps in terms of protecting us in the workplace and elsewhere, to ensure we become the full and equal partners in society that we ought to be."

"The day of the filibuster was such a great example of people stepping forward to do a deed. It grew on social media and it didn't stop there. It grew into people acting—thousands of people who showed up. It became a symbol for me of the way we can act to make a difference."

"People are hungry for leadership that's not afraid of political consequence."

Wendy Davis

# LEILA DE LIMA
## (born 1959)

**"No high concrete walls,
barbed wires, or caged
environment can silence me.
I remain free in spirit
and unbroken."**

**Years in political office:** 2010–present

**Position:** Philippines senator, 2016–present; secretary of justice,
2010–2015; chair of Philippine Commission on Human Rights, 2008–2010

**Party affiliation:** Liberal

**Hometown:** Iriga, Camarines Sur, Philippines

**Top causes:** human rights, electoral justice, climate change,
and abolishing the death penalty

# LIFE STORY

Leila de Lima, who would become one of her country's loudest voices for democracy, was born thirteen years after the Philippines declared its independence from the United States. De Lima comes from a family that is big on the will of the people—her beloved dad, Vicente de Lima, a lawyer, was even appointed to oversee the Philippines' national elections. But unfortunately for the island nation, when Leila de Lima was still a kid, the twenty-year dictatorial regime of Ferdinand Marcos began. By the time it ended in 1986, Marcos had stolen some $10 billion from the impoverished country and instigated repressive military violence against his fellow Filipinos.

From an early age, de Lima proved to be a bright student, eventually following in her father's footsteps and going to San Beda College of Law in Manila, the capital of the Philippines. Marcos's reign ended just as she was waiting to hear whether she had passed the bar exam, and she received the eighth-highest score in the country. De Lima started working for a Supreme Court judge and then became one of the country's few female election lawyers.

Impressed by her record, President Gloria Macapagal-Arroyo named de Lima chair of the country's commission on human rights in 2008. De Lima tore into her duties ferociously, taking on some of the country's most brazenly corrupt politicians. Perhaps no one concerned her more than Rodrigo Duterte, who spent twenty-two years as the mayor of Davao City. De Lima found that Duterte was enlisting vigilante death squads to kill drug dealers and addicts—and, by his own admission, sometimes even slaughtering them personally.

Fatefully, de Lima was elected to the Senate the same day Duterte was elected president in 2016. He had won by a landslide, powered to the top office by Filipinos who were sick of violence in the country and supported Duterte's dramatic solutions to combat crime. During his campaign, he made it clear who he would hold responsible for the country's issues: "All of you who are into drugs, you sons of bitches, I will really kill you." Soon after his election, the death squads started to kill people—primarily poor people. This violent spree reportedly cost a staggering six thousand lives in the first six months of Duterte's presidency.

# WHAT'S ON HER AGENDA

Those familiar with de Lima's tenacious nature were not surprised when the senator dug into Duterte's murderous campaigns. Her human rights committee investigation scored a real victory when Edgar Matobato testified that he participated in over fifty death squad operations at Duterte's behest. Matobato even dropped the bombshell that Duterte had ordered him to kill de Lima on one of her trips to Davao City in 2009.

In response to the confession, Duterte publicly exposed a long-running, consensual romantic relationship between de Lima and her driver-bodyguard. At one of his political rallies, Duterte even told de Lima to hang herself. Meanwhile, his allies swung into action. Days after Matobato testified, de Lima was removed from her position as head of the country's human rights committee in a motion led by senator and eight-time world champion Filipino boxer Manny Pacquiao. Charges of drug trafficking came next—the president's administration claimed that as secretary of justice, de Lima had accepted bribes from gang bosses.

Many doubted the truthfulness of these charges, and throughout the ordeal, de Lima kept her head up. "All of this—the slut-shaming, the threats—it's unprecedented," she said. "No one has ever been subjected to this by a sitting president." She delivered an impassioned speech for justice in the Philippines before being arrested in February 2017 and sent to prison, where she remains. Duterte's drug war is said to have killed over twenty thousand people.

Incredibly, de Lima continues to serve as a senator from inside her cell, even sponsoring legislation and speaking out against the president's intention to reinstate the death penalty. She's become a symbol of resistance to Duterte's presidency and its most awful crimes. Global human rights groups continue to rally for her release.

## AWESOME ACHIEVEMENTS

- President Benigno "Noynoy" Aquino III was so impressed with de Lima's service on the human rights commission that he appointed her secretary of justice in 2010.
- In 2016 *Foreign Policy* magazine named her one of its Global Thinkers, alongside German chancellor Angela Merkel (page 128), US senator Hillary Clinton (page 22), and United Nations secretary-general Ban Ki-moon.
- Not only has she written two books in prison, but she has also tried her hand at illustration. Her drawing of a songbird appears on the cover of her 2018 collection of letters from jail, *Dispatches from Crame*.
- Amnesty International, an international human rights organization, honored de Lima as a Most Distinguished Human Rights Defender. But she couldn't receive the award in person due to her ongoing incarceration.

# QUOTABLES

"My consolation is that I'm living in a prison of truth and conscience, while my tormentors are living in a prison of lies and deceptions."

"Let us fight for our rights, let us fight for justice, let us fight for democracy."

"If there is any way that a diamond can compare to a woman, it is in its strength. A woman is resilient, a woman is unbreakable."

"Slowly, eventually, inevitably, the truth will set me free."

Leila de Lima

# BETSY DEVOS
### née Elisabeth Prince (born 1958)
## "No school is as great as it can be."

**Years in political office:** 1996–2000, 2003–2005, 2017–present

**Position:** US secretary of education, 2017–present; chair of the Michigan Republican Party, 1996–2000, 2003–2005

**Party affiliation:** Republican

**Hometown:** Holland, Michigan

**Top causes:** school choice, reducing the size of the government, and vocational education

# LIFE STORY

Betsy DeVos grew up in West Michigan Dutch country in a town where, by some accounts, the company started by her father, Edgar Prince, employed a quarter of the population. Her dad invented the light-up vanity mirror used in cars' sun visors, an innovation that made his family quite wealthy, and with his money, he became one of the country's biggest donors to the Christian Right. She went to private Christian schools all the way up to her college graduation. In 1976 she volunteered on Gerald Ford's 1976 presidential reelection campaign. She married Richard (Dick) DeVos Jr., son of the family (net worth $5.6 billion) that cofounded the Amway company.

The well-monied couple first started thinking about the United States educational system in earnest when they sent their oldest son to school. They opted for a private, faith-based institution, but also decided to support a 90 percent benefactor-funded, private religious school in Grand Rapids that was attended by many students from low-income families of color and where DeVos began to volunteer. The experience taught her that many poor families didn't have the money to make the same painstaking decision that the DeVoses had made over where to send their kids to school. "It became a matter of fairness to me," she says.

The DeVoses envisioned a future in which families could get tax dollars through voucher programs to take their kids out of struggling public schools and enroll them in privately run charter schools. Critics say this would mean public schools would get less funding, putting the education of millions of low-income, developmentally disadvantaged, and rural kids who can't attend charter schools at serious risk. Inspired by the possibilities of what came to be known as "school choice" and endowed with the connections to wealthy donors and politicians that their own money brought, the DeVos family rose in Michigan's political ranks. On the promise of providing fairness in education, DeVos became her county's Republican chair, then a four-term state chairperson of the party. Her husband was the Republicans' 2006 nominee for governor.

The couple were philanthropists, donating large sums to schools that were usually private and faith-based. In 2017 the DeVos clan divulged that its five family foundations had donated a lifetime total of $1 billion to conservative and Christian politicians, committees, and organizations. "We do expect something in return," wrote DeVos in an op-ed on giving. "We expect to foster a conservative governing philosophy consisting of limited government and respect for traditional American virtues. We expect a return on our investment."

During his 2016 presidential campaign, Trump proposed giving $20 billion in private school vouchers to parents throughout the country. When he won the election, DeVos's allies, Vice President Mike Pence and Jeb Bush (son of school choice champion

President George H. W. Bush), suggested that Trump tap DeVos for his administration. He appointed her secretary of education. DeVos had finally seen a serious return on her family's support of the Republican Party.

# WHAT'S ON HER AGENDA

For all her passion for education, a soft-spoken and polite DeVos stumbled, and often, during her confirmation to the post. In Senate hearings, she expressed a lack of understanding of important concepts about her proposed job, and at one point said guns were needed in schools to "protect from potential grizzlies." (Yes, bears, which are apparently a problem at a rural school with whose administrators DeVos is friendly.) "I think I was undercoached," she would later say, in reference to the Trump administration for not giving her enough concrete information on its policies.

Her commitment to faith-based education in a secular government system made her a controversial appointee and gave her a far higher media profile than any past education secretary had held. She was confirmed by a hair— Republican senators Lisa Murkowski (page 132) and Susan Collins (page 30) voted against DeVos, leaving Pence to cast the first tiebreaking vote for a government appointee's confirmation in the country's history. Shortly after she assumed office, protesters who thought her noted support for Christian causes would lead to a deterioration in the nation's educational system physically blocked her from her first public school visit in Washington, DC. Her first budget request—which would have made large cuts elsewhere in the educational system to fund school choice programs—was denied.

During her first two years in office, DeVos mainly focused on rolling back many of the previous Obama administration's diversity protections, which she saw as an example of overreach by the former president. She withdrew memos that encouraged schools to allow trans students to use the bathroom that corresponds to their gender identity and that shifted the burden of truth onto alleged predators— rather than alleged victims—in sexual assault allegations. She has greatly limited the number of students who qualify for federal loan forgiveness programs and argued that high levels of federal spending on public education over the last decades has seen meager results. DeVos has proposed every year to cut funding to Special Olympics, a vastly unpopular prospect that was even dismissed by Trump in 2019 in a public dustup.

DeVos's beliefs represent a considerable segment of US society that, like nearly everyone else, is concerned over the state of the educational system. Since her early days of volunteering, she's shown a commitment to her ideals and a passion for making change.

# AWESOME ACHIEVEMENTS

- When the first federal budget cut to the Special Olympics was proposed, DeVos—who had made an appearance at one of the organization's events two weeks earlier—donated a quarter of her salary to the organization.
- In 2019 she broke her pelvis and hip socket in a bike accident but continued to work and make public appearances in a wheelchair.
- DeVos donates her entire government paycheck to charity. She also pays for her own security and travel expenses incurred by her trips by private plane.

# QUOTABLES

"My faith motivates me to really try to work on behalf of and advocate for those who are least able to advocate for themselves."

"As much as many in the media use my name as clickbait or try to make it all about me, it's not."

"I entered public life to promote policies that empower all families. Notice that I said families—families, not government."

# MARÍA ELENA DURAZO

## (born 1953)

**"You look around at who has the most difficult jobs, at who is doing the work we rely on every day, and it is immigrants."**

Years in political office: 2017–present

Position: member of the California State Senate, 2018–present; vice chair of the Democratic National Committee, 2017–present

Party affiliation: Democrat

Hometown: Madera, California

Top causes: immigrant rights, creating new jobs in environmentally sustainable industries, and public education

# LIFE STORY

María Elena Durazo was born in California's San Joaquin Valley to parents who had come to the US from Mexico as migrant agricultural workers. The family traveled up and down the West Coast looking for jobs. According to Durazo's sisters, sometimes they lived out of their truck, bathed in rivers, and slept underneath the stars. Durazo was one of eleven siblings, and everyone helped out in the fields, picking grapes, melons, nectarines, peaches, plums, tomatoes, and string beans. Contractors often underpaid them, and the family faced deplorable working conditions. The experience taught Durazo about exploitation, fair payment issues, and workplace safety. "No toilets, no drinking water, no shade," Durazo remembers of those years.

She was the first of her family to graduate from high school and to get a university degree. By then a single mom, Durazo began to work as a labor union organizer. In her early thirties, she led a sea change at the local chapter of a hotel workers' union in which members voted out longtime leadership who were reluctant to give translated versions of important information to its growing number of Spanish-speaking members. Once Durazo became the union's president, the organization went fully bilingual. She was determined that everyone should understand the union's strategies and contribute to the fight for their rights.

After the unexpected shakeup of leadership, the national office of the hotel workers' union sent in an organizer to help guide—and possibly control—Durazo's leadership team. That representative happened to be Miguel Contreras, another child of migrant laborers who had worked with iconic labor leader César Chávez on the United Farmworkers campaign. "You ain't gonna just walk right into this and be the boss here," Durazo remembers thinking at their initial meetings. "What ended up happening was he came in with the same ideas I had, and then I fell in love." The two were married, and with their shared passion for the labor movement, became one of California's most influential political power couples.

The '90s were a rough time for Californian Latinxs. In 1994 voters passed Proposition 187, a ballot referendum that banned undocumented immigrants from using key social services such as public schools and nonemergency health care. Those who knew how many undocumented immigrants are part of the Latinx community, not to mention the extent that those individuals' lives depend on those services, were enraged. Two years later, Contreras was elected secretary-treasurer of the Los Angeles County Federation of Labor and underlined the common political issues faced by Latinxs and other members of the working class. Contreras put a big emphasis on voter registration, and even Latinx community members whose immigration status prevented them from voting were enlisted to do outreach.

María Elena Durazo

Contreras held his position for eleven years before dying of a heart attack at fifty-two years old. In 2006 Durazo succeeded him, becoming a leader of 350 unions and six hundred thousand members. She was set on continuing the fight for the principles she'd shared with her husband, and became a powerful force in Los Angeles. Her coalition was able to pass living wage increases, ensuring new jobs and other benefits for workers—victories that critics said often emptied the city's pockets. Durazo's movement was so powerful that by 2013, two-thirds of the city council was comprised of candidates she and her allies had helped put in office.

In 2008 she left the labor federation to become the hotel workers union's general vice president for immigration, civil rights, and diversity. In 2017 she was named vice chair of the Democratic National Committee and in 2018 was elected a California state senator. She has two children, Mario and Michael Contreras.

# WHAT'S ON HER AGENDA

It's hard to overestimate the importance of Durazo's power as an organizer. In the United States, union membership has been declining since 1954, leaving workers without an organized voice in the fight for health insurance and fair working conditions. By 2013 unions represented only 11.3 percent of US workers. Durazo said that part of the reason for the labor movement's decay was that it wasn't focusing on the rights of all workers. While union membership was still concentrated in well-paying (but disappearing and moving overseas) manufacturing jobs, union organizing campaigns rarely focused on many of the country's most vulnerable individuals in low-wage positions. Durazo's labor federation focused on working with health care and service industry workers, often Latinxs and recent immigrants. She built the Los Angeles labor movement into one of the strongest in the country. As a result, rates of union membership in California rose while, in much of the rest of the US, they stagnated.

Durazo was not shy about the fact that Trump's election drove her to electoral politics. "We're at another very critical time in this state," she said. "I know what it's like to press elected officials." Her first government election was a big one; Durazo ran for the seat of California state senator Kevin de León, who was leaving the most powerful position in the state senate as president pro tempore. She easily trounced her opponent, winning 66 to his 33 percent of the votes.

As a state senator, Durazo represents over 931,000 constituents—more than most members of the US Congress represent! Her considerable name recognition and understanding of the issues of various marginalized communities have served her well in politics. She has presented bills that would provide better aid to the victims of violent crimes, as well as legislation to limit the number of charter schools, which she sees as key to continued support for public education. She has also supported bills to help California's growing number of homeless residents and protect individuals from losing money to predatory lenders.

## AWESOME ACHIEVEMENTS

- She was the first woman to head the Los Angeles County Federation of Labor.
- In 2003 Durazo became the national director of the Immigrant Workers Freedom Ride, during which caravans came from ten different cities around the US to converge for a massive demonstration in New York City. The protest updated tactics used by 1960s civil rights activists to draw attention to the struggle for immigrants' rights.
- Durazo was named vice chair of the bid for the 2024 Summer Olympics alongside basketball legend Earvin "Magic" Johnson. Los Angeles ultimately lost the bid, but was granted the 2028 Olympics.

## QUOTABLES

"We cannot fix the prosperity of the rest of the country without improving the prosperity of immigrants."

"Here in Los Angeles, and in a number of cities, officials are standing up and saying we're not going to allow our local police to cooperate with ICE (US Immigration and Customs Enforcement). Our schools are saying we're not going to allow ICE to come in."

"I am not asking you (my constituents) to send me to Sacramento. I am asking you to come with me to the State Capitol."

María Elena Durazo

# DIANNE FEINSTEIN

## née Dianne Emiel Goldman (born 1933)

### "Are you ready to make history?"

Years in political office: 1970–present

Position: US senator from California, 1992–present; mayor of San Francisco, 1978–1988; member of the San Francisco Board of Supervisors, 1970–1978

Party affiliation: Democrat

Hometown: San Francisco, California

Top causes: gun control, LGBTQ rights, and labor issues

# LIFE STORY

Dianne Feinstein was born to a Russian Orthodox surgeon dad and fashion model mom in San Francisco. Her grandparents were immigrants from Poland and Russia. Feinstein went to Stanford University and got a history degree before she entered San Francisco politics. She was elected to the town's board of supervisors in 1969 and within nine years had become its first woman president.

Tragedy struck on November 27, 1978, when a conservative supervisor walked into city hall and shot and killed San Francisco mayor George Moscone and Feinstein's fellow supervisor Harvey Milk—one of the country's first openly gay politicians elected to public office. The killer, who Feinstein counted as a friend, had recently resigned from his position on the board. That morning Feinstein was the first to discover Moscone, and it fell to her to try, in vain, to staunch his bullet wounds.

As board president, she was next in command, and on the day of the killings, she was sworn in as the first woman mayor of her hometown. The city was devastated, but with her stick-with-it, middle-of-the-road tendencies, Feinstein was able to pull San Francisco through what could have been a time of absolute fracture. She recalls showing up on the scene of every fire in town hoping to portray strength, especially to those who doubted that a woman was fit for the mayor's office. Feinstein was mayor for ten years, carrying out a vital renovation of the city's historic cable car system and hosting the 1984 National Democratic Convention.

In 1991 President George H. W. Bush nominated Clarence Thomas to associate Supreme Court justice. A law professor, Anita Hill, claimed that Thomas had sexually harassed her when she had served as his attorney-adviser. The Senate Judicial Committee interviewed Hill about her allegations. Feinstein remembers seeing two hundred people gathered around the TV at Heathrow International Airport, watching Hill's testimony and subsequent berating by an all-male panel of senators.

"It was a silent crowd, but it was a big crowd, and that said something," Feinstein remembers. The message she received was that despite her own successes in challenging gender norms, in many ways society still did not take women's concerns seriously. "It moved me to action, yes, and the action was to run [for office]," she said.

She was not the only one who heeded the call to campaign for a higher office. Politically, 1992 is remembered in the United States as the Year of the Woman because a record-breaking four were elected to the US Senate. That may not sound like a lot, but before those elections, only two women served as senators! The phrase "Year of the Woman" was used again in 2018 when fifteen women were elected to the Senate, and 102 made it to the House. Again, a judge's alleged

*Dianne Feinstein*

sexual misconduct had set the stage. Supreme Court nominee Brett Kavanaugh was confirmed a month before the country's fall elections, despite accusations of sexual assault by several women.

# WHAT'S ON HER AGENDA

DiFi is the longest-serving woman senator, and the pragmatic politician continues to crush her opposition during reelection campaigns. Her peers know her as a moderate willing to work across the aisle on issues, though those centrist tendencies have brought her under fire at times, notably from left-wing groups in her California constituency who would rather she prioritize progressive initiatives than compromise with conservatives.

The US Senate is built around rewarding seniority with power, and Feinstein, as its oldest member, illustrates the influence that long-serving senators can wield when they play their cards correctly. During her first year in the Senate, she became one of the first two women on the Senate Judiciary Committee, whose members she had watched belittle Anita Hill. Decades later, Feinstein became the committee's ranking member and, in 2009, its first woman chair.

As she's gotten older, many of her views have shifted. Though she supported capital punishment early in her career, Feinstein officially declared herself in opposition to the death penalty in 2018. At the time, she was running a tighter-than-usual reelection campaign against a Southern California progressive (she still wound up getting four times as many votes as him in the primaries). "It became crystal clear to me that the risk of unequal application [of the death penalty] is high, and its effect on deterrence is low," she explained.

Other crusades have been more consistent. The horror of the 1978 Milk and Moscone killings never left Feinstein, and she has been one of the country's staunchest advocates for gun control for decades. She wrote successful pieces of 1994 legislation limiting the sale and possession of assault weapons, and encouraged a zero-tolerance firearm policy on school campuses. In 2019 she cosponsored legislation that would further curtail high-capacity ammunition weapons. "If we're going to put a stop to mass shootings and protect our children, we need to get these weapons of war off our streets," she said.

## AWESOME ACHIEVEMENTS

- She was the first woman ever to become a US senator from California.
- Aghast at reports of waterboarding and other interrogation tactics used by the CIA on terrorist suspects after 9/11, Feinstein ordered the government agency investigated. In 2014 her staff released a shocking five-hundred-page report that exposed widespread human rights violations and earned the senator no small number of enemies in the surveillance industry, with whom she had previously had a close relationship.
- In 2012 she got more votes in a single election than any US senator in history—7.75 million!

## QUOTABLES

"What I do is I really try to bring people together, try to work out problems."

"Basically, my life is government."

"We women have been saying it for a long time; if we were in power, we would do it differently."

# MARIELLE FRANCO

## née Marielle Francisco da Silva (1979–2018)

## "How many more will have to die before this war ends?"

Years in political office: 2017–2018

Position: Rio de Janeiro city councillor, 2017–2018

Party affiliation: Socialism and Liberty Party

Hometown: Rio de Janeiro, Brazil

Top causes: human rights, stopping gender-based violence, and reproductive rights

# LIFE STORY

In Rio de Janeiro, 20 percent of the population lives in favelas. These vast, underserved hillside neighborhoods are home to much of the city's Afro-Brazilian culture. They are also among the sites of the country's bloody war between drug cartels, military police, and citizen-run paramilitary groups. Marielle Franco was born to a family of migrants from northeastern Brazil and grew up in a community of favelas named Complexo da Maré. As a child, she recalled the near-constant presence of violence and seeing the bodies of shooting victims lying in the streets.

When Franco was nineteen, she gave birth to her daughter, Luyara, and set about raising the child as a single mom. She was a brilliant student and got a scholarship to attend Rio's Pontifical Catholic University, becoming one of only two Black women in the school's sociology program.

When she was twenty years old, a friend of hers was shot by a stray bullet during a street battle between drug traffickers and police officers. Franco turned to politics out of a need for her community's concerns to be heard and started working on the Rio de Janeiro state legislature election campaign of favela youth educator Marcelo Freixo. Freixo won and was put in charge of the legislature's commission for human rights. Franco was also hired to the commission and helped families of the victims of drug war violence put pressure on authorities to properly investigate their loved ones' deaths.

By 2016 she ran for public office, earning fifth place out of fifteen hundred candidates for election to Rio de Janeiro's city council. She was one of seven women and the only Black woman elected to the fifty-one-member legislative body—pretty uneven figures when you consider that Black women make up 28 percent of Brazil's population.

As a bisexual woman, Franco was one of Brazil's only openly LGBTQ politicians. She dated architect and fellow activist Mônica Benício (who is also from Maré) on and off for fourteen years, at times interrupted by objections from both of their families. Eventually, they moved in together, along with Luyara.

On March 14, 2018, the couple were engaged to be married and considering having another child. The future was also looking bright for Franco's political future; she had been tapped as her Socialism and Liberty Party's candidate for deputy governor of Rio in the upcoming October elections.

But those plans were not to be. That night Franco was at an event at Rio's House of Black Women, where she gave a speech on political empowerment. She had just called Benício to let her know she was on her way home when two vehicles pulled up. The attackers pumped nine bullets into Franco's white Chevrolet. Four of the shots struck her in the head. Her driver was also killed, and Franco's press officer was injured by shrapnel.

Marielle Franco

It quickly became apparent that the very military police against whose corruption Franco had fought during her life were likely responsible for her death. The sophisticated tactics and professionalism of the hit indicated it had been done by police, and the bullets that killed Franco were found to have come from police ammunition stock. "You can't understand Rio unless you understand the organized crime here," one politician told the press after her death. "It's not a parallel state—it is the state."

Justice can be scarce in Brazil, where few murders are ever solved. But nearly a year after Franco's death, two former police officers were arrested in connection with the killing. Franco's supporters were unsurprised to learn that the culprits have ties to the family of Jair Bolsonaro, the far-right leader who became president of the country in 2018.

# WHAT'S ON HER AGENDA

Franco often wore bright head wraps over her hair and painted each fingernail with a different-colored varnish. No less evident were her political priorities. During her brief time as an elected politician, she challenged corruption in the expensive construction of Rio's World Cup and Olympics stadiums. She chaired the city council's commission for the defense of women, and she is perhaps best remembered politically for her fight for women's rights. She passed legislation that established after-dark, government-funded childcare programs for parents who worked the night shift and the International Day of Black Women, which is celebrated on July 25 in Rio.

Her killers almost certainly targeted her because of her emerging power. Ironically, the very day before her death, Franco wondered on Twitter whether a young man named Matheus Melo had been sent to his death by the military police, who are sometimes referred to as the "battalion of death" in the neighborhoods they run with an iron fist.

But if her killers hoped to frighten others from speaking out against human rights violations, they failed. Tens of thousands of protesters took to the streets of Maré and other neighborhoods after Franco was slain. Many saw her death as one more episode in a long history of Black genocide in Brazil, which was the last country in the world to ban slavery in 1888. Protests took place in major cities across the world, and Franco was posthumously honored on the floor of the European Parliament.

Her smiling face has become a symbol of progressive action in a country that needs it more than ever. Bolsonaro's election has brought an added threat of violence against marginalized communities but also coordinated resistance. In 2019 the country's highest court voted to ban discrimination based on sexual orientation and gender. Months after Franco's death, three more Black women were elected to the Legislative Assembly of Rio de Janeiro.

## AWESOME ACHIEVEMENTS

- Franco's master's thesis on the persecution of favela residents by police was published as a book eight months after her death.
- As a teen, she won a contest dancing baile funk, the bombastic favela genre that blends Miami bass, Brazilian rhythms, and hip-hop swagger.
- One of Rio's famed samba schools released a song for Carnaval (Brazil's massively important yearly street celebrations) honoring people's history with a line honoring Franco: "Brazil, the time has come to hear the Marias, Mahins, Marielles, Malês."

## QUOTABLES

"I am because we are."

"Phrases from the survival handbook for women in the midst of men: 'You're questioning me.' 'I just made the same joke.' 'That's the same idea I had.' 'Your macho joke is not funny.' 'Don't touch me.' 'Thank you for teaching me what I already know.'"

"Being a black woman is to resist and survive all the time."

Marielle Franco

# "FIX WHAT AIN'T RIGHT"
# LGBTQ POLITICIANS

## JÓHANNA SIGURÐARDÓTTIR

The world's first LGBTQ head of state is an Icelandic lesbian who was also the first woman to become prime minister of her country. Jóhanna Sigurðardóttir became an active union member during her early career as a flight attendant and had two kids with her husband before their divorce. She was first elected to parliament in 1978 and was prime minister from 2009 to 2013, providing calm guidance to her country during a devastating financial crisis. She is also the only person to have a spouse of the same gender while serving as head of state—longtime partner Jónína Leósdóttir, who Sigurðardóttir married the very day that their country legalized same-sex marriage.

## TAMMY BALDWIN

Baldwin is a Wisconsin pioneer who, in 1998, became the first lesbian elected to the US Congress and, in 2012, the first openly gay person to become a US senator. "All of us who are openly gay are living and writing the history of our movement," the former lawyer has said. "We are ordinary people, living our lives, and trying, as civil rights activist Dorothy Cotton said, to 'fix what ain't right' in our society." Baldwin has distinguished herself as a legislator on LGBTQ rights, cyberbullying, and veterans' issues.

## KATE BROWN

This bisexual, feminist Oregon governor proved unshakable during her 2018 reelection campaign, when Republicans spent big bucks unsuccessfully trying to get her out of the state's driving seat. Brown is a progressive leader in the Beaver State, responsible for signing some of the country's most forward-thinking pro-choice legislation and progressive gun safety laws. The former secretary of state is a bold opponent of Trump, having denounced his orders to ready National Guard troops to defend against immigrants at the US-Mexico border and his plans to ban openly trans troops from serving in the military.

## TANWARIN SUKKHAPISIT

"I spent years making films talking about the experience of transgender and LGBT people in Thailand, but it no longer felt like enough to tell the story," says trans and nonbinary movie director Tanwarin Sukkhapisit. "I wanted to change the discriminatory laws." The catalyst for their political debut was a five-year legal battle over their film about a transgender father, which the government had censored. In 2019 Sukkhapisit was one of four transgender individuals to win election to Thailand's National Assembly in the country's new progressive party, Future Forward, and plans to advocate for equal marriage rights and sex education in schools.

## AYA KAMIKAWA

Few expected a thirty-five-year-old transgender writer to stand a chance in the polls in Japan, where trans people still face serious challenges in even getting their correct gender recorded on official government records. That gave little pause to Aya Kamikawa, who has served on the local assembly of Setagaya (one of Tokyo's largest wards) since 2003. Her efforts opened the doors for others. In 2017 Tomoya Hosoda, a trans man, thanked Kamikawa when he was voted onto Tokyo's city council. "To be my real self, that's my basis for living," Kamikawa says. "I can't live in a society that doesn't admit that. That's why I decided to run in the election."

## MARY GONZÁLEZ

If you've ever been in the position where you've had to explain your sexuality, you understand what it has been like for Chicana Texas state representative Mary González. When she ran for her seat in 2012, it was widely reported that she was a lesbian. Postelection, González clarified that she loves people regardless of their gender, making her the first openly pansexual person to serve on a US legislature. She's won her reelections ever since, focusing her work on education, economic development, and agricultural issues.

# KIRSTEN GILLIBRAND

### née Kirsten Elizabeth Rutnik (born 1966)

## "You cannot silence me."

**Years in political office:** 2007–present

**Position:** US senator from New York, 2009–present; member of the US House of Representatives from New York, 2007–2009

**Party affiliation:** Democrat

**Hometown:** Albany, New York

**Top causes:** campaign funding, military sexual assault, and paid family leave

# LIFE STORY

Kirsten Gillibrand's family knows politics. Her grandmother, who was her heroine, worked for Albany, New York, Democratic kingpin Mayor Erastus Corning II. Her mother was a lawyer, a highly capable woman who "not only cooked the Thanksgiving turkey but also shot the Thanksgiving turkey," according to Gillibrand. Amid these legends, Gillibrand by her own account was "a massive kiss-ass [who] lived for positive reinforcement."

She has a bachelor's degree in Asian studies, graduating with honors from Dartmouth University, and a law degree from the University of California, Los Angeles. Gillibrand began her career as a corporate lawyer. She represented various corporations, and among her clients was a large tobacco company. She eventually left the corporate world, compelled to enter politics by Hillary Clinton's (page 22) 1995 "women's rights are human rights" speech at the United Nations. "I left the law and decided to run for Congress because I wasn't fulfilled through the work I was doing," Gillibrand remembered. "I felt like it didn't represent who I was and my values and what I wanted to accomplish in life." She found her first governmental job in the US Department of Housing and Urban Development and bought a house with her husband, Jonathan Gillibrand, in a wealthy and conservative-leaning upstate New York congressional district that seemed to be a good fit for a future Gillibrand campaign.

Many of Gillibrand's big wins have come through unusual circumstances. She beat an eight-year Republican incumbent to reach the House of Representatives—but was aided by the last-minute publication of a police report detailing allegations of domestic violence against the other candidate. (Many believed that Gillibrand's camp had leaked the documents to the press, a charge that she has never refuted.) She was appointed, rather than elected, to her Senate seat when Hillary Clinton left the post to become secretary of state. In her first Senate reelection campaign, she got 72 percent of the vote—a higher percentage than anyone running for governor or the Senate in the history of New York.

Her rise has not left her immune to charges of flip-flopping and hypocrisy. During the transition from representing her conservative congressional district to her Senate career, Gillibrand went from hyping deportations of immigrants to supporting a ten-year path to citizenship for them. She also shifted her views on gun control so dramatically that she went from an A rating from the National Rifle Association (NRA) to an F. She even called the NRA the "worst organization in the world," on the presidential campaign trail in 2019. "I had the humility to recognize this isn't good enough," explained Gillibrand when asked about her changes in opinion—but she's been unable to convince many who attribute the shifts to political convenience.

# WHAT'S ON HER AGENDA

One area in which Gillibrand has never fluctuated is her staunch support of reproductive rights and hard line against sexual assault. She was the first Democratic senator to call for the resignation of Minnesota senator Al Franken after allegations of inappropriate sexual behavior were made against him, earning her the nickname "the #MeToo senator" from the TV show *60 Minutes*. She has never backed down from that position, and Franken has become a poster boy for how the #MeToo movement has made behavior that was once normalized (such as stealing a kiss, as in Franken's case) unacceptable. In 2017 Gillibrand risked a split with her political mentor Hillary Clinton when she told the press that Bill Clinton should have resigned from the presidency over evidence of his own sexual misconduct. But some eyebrows rose when she continued to be a political ally of the Clintons, even having him campaign for her occasionally.

In 2019 Gillibrand announced her plan to run for president. Early polling placed her as a long-shot candidate, but she worked to position herself as a concerned mother and the most stridently feminist White House aspirant. She also wanted to be seen as the most anti-Trump candidate, launching her campaign outside one of the president's Manhattan hotels that she called a "shrine to division, greed, and vanity." Her haranguing of the country's conservatives continued when she appeared on Fox News and scathingly disagreed with the channel's presenters and their strong pro-life views. "I'm not sure it's frankly very polite when we've invited you to be here," said moderator Chris Wallace.

In response, the Gillibrand campaign started selling tote bags emblazoned with the words that staffers hoped would become a new feminist rally cry à la fellow 2020 presidential candidate Elizabeth Warren's "Nevertheless, she persisted" (page 180): "Frankly, not very polite."

The strategy was a tough sell in a race that started with at least six women candidates, and Gillibrand ended her campaign in August 2019. But the way she made her gender a central tenet of her politics was unprecedented. Throughout history, many women politicians have sought to minimize their femininity, rather than make it a cornerstone of their campaigns.

## AWESOME ACHIEVEMENTS

- Gillibrand is so committed to protecting women's reproductive rights that she has a 100 lifetime rating from the Planned Parenthood Action Fund.
- In 2008 she put in twelve hours of work on the House floor before giving birth to her second son, Henry, the very next day.
- A lifelong fan of fitness and known for her impressive biceps, the senator was the captain of her college squash team and went undefeated in the sport her senior year.
- Gillibrand wrote the text for a 2018 picture book called *Bold & Brave*. It tells the life stories of ten women in the United States who fought for their right to vote, including Harriet Tubman, who Gillibrand calls her political hero.

## QUOTABLES

"Women are on fire in America today. We have marched, we have organized, we have run for office, and we have won."

"It's part of your job. Let people be angry, sad—speak to you directly."

"I think the country would be so much stronger if women had greater voices."

# HISTORY'S FIRSTS
# THE AUDACITY OF SOME WOMEN!

## FIRST AND ONLY FEMALE PRIME MINISTER OF INDIA: INDIRA GANDHI

Hailing from a family of political big shots, Indira Gandhi was the daughter of the first prime minister of India, Jawaharlal Nehru. In 1966 Gandhi was appointed prime minister and, for over a decade, fended off challenges to her authority. Her government was eventually voted out, and she was locked up on corruption charges. After she emerged from prison, she led her party to power and became the prime minister again. She was assassinated in office in 1984 by her two bodyguards, who were taking revenge for Sikh casualties at the hands of the Indian army under Gandhi's administration.

## FIRST BLACK WOMAN TO RUN FOR US PRESIDENT: SHIRLEY CHISHOLM

Chisholm adopted the campaign slogan "Unbought and Unbossed" for her 1972 run at the White House. She was a pioneer, having become the second Black woman elected to the New York State Assembly and the first in the US Congress. In the House, Chisholm spoke out against the Vietnam War, helped institute the national food stamp program, and employed an all-women staff. Chisholm placed fourth in the presidential nominee race, losing to pro-segregation Alabama governor George Wallace. Chisholm opened the Democratic Party's eyes to the leadership potential of people of all races and genders. "If they don't give you a seat at the table, bring a folding chair," she liked to say.

## FIRST WOMAN TO BE DEMOCRATICALLY ELECTED PRESIDENT: VIGDÍS FINNBOGADÓTTIR

It is a distinctly Icelandic story that an experimental theater director and media personality who taught French on public television would, in 1980, become the first woman to get elected president. Finnbogadóttir was a single adoptive mother who spent her four-term administration promoting the Icelandic arts culture in which she had long worked. After stepping down as head of the country, she founded the Council of Women World Leaders, then based at Harvard University.

## FIRST WOMAN TO BE HEAD OF STATE IN AN AFRICAN COUNTRY: ELLEN JOHNSON SIRLEAF

This Liberian politician had an early reputation of being trustworthy in financial matters. She clashed with the demonstrably corrupt regime of Samuel K. Doe, was nearly put to death once, and eventually was sent to jail for criticizing the military-controlled government during a run for vice president. During her twelve years of exile, and while Liberia suffered a devastating civil war, she became a well-known World Bank economist. After the war, she returned to the country, was elected president, and spent twelve years in power from 2006 to 2018. Her administration was hounded by charges of the very corruption she once fought and had to fight against the Ebola virus that took over forty-eight hundred Liberian lives.

## FIRST FEMALE VICE-PRESIDENTIAL CANDIDATE REPRESENTING A MAJOR AMERICAN POLITICAL PARTY: GERALDINE FERRARO

In 1984 pearls-wearing Queens, New York, criminal prosecutor Ferraro was tapped by Democratic presidential candidate Walter Mondale to be his running mate. Ferraro, a congressmember and mother of three, had both conservative and progressive stances, and was a staunch supporter of a woman's right to choose. Her charisma and influential committee work made her a seemingly potent candidate, but her slate was smashed in one of the biggest Republican landslides ever. Ferraro vacated her congressional seat in 1985 and went on to become a member of the United Nations Commission on Human Rights.

## FIRST DIFFERENTLY ABLED WOMAN IN US CONGRESS: TAMMY DUCKWORTH

Fascinating fact: This Illinois member of Congress was the first person to give birth while serving in the US Senate. Another one: She is the country's first Thailand-born senator. Also, in 2004, while she was serving in the Iraq War (2003–2011), a rocket-propelled grenade was launched at the helicopter she was piloting and she lost both of her legs. There are a lot of reasons to pay respect to this Purple Heart recipient. With her legislative work in gun safety laws and veterans' rights, she's proven unafraid of a political challenge. That was most evident when she told an unsuccessful Senate challenger, "These legs are titanium. They don't buckle. Go ahead, take a shot at me."

# DEB HAALAND

(born 1960)

"How can we not be outraged by the separation of families? It's like we're reliving the past."

Years in political office: 2015–present

Position: member of the US House of Representatives from New Mexico, 2019–present; chairperson of the New Mexico Democratic Party, 2015–2017

Party affiliation: Democrat

Hometown: Winslow, Arizona

Top causes: immigration policy, universal childcare, renewable energy, and indigenous land rights

# LIFE STORY

Self-described "thirty-fifth generation New Mexican" Deb Haaland grew up as part of the Laguna Pueblo tribe, a sovereign nation that has been located outside of Albuquerque since 1300 CE. The child of military parents, Haaland moved around a lot as a kid, attending thirteen schools over the years. As an adult she became an entrepreneur and got going in the food industry, creating her own business selling salsa and even decorating cakes. Remarkably, even as a single mother, Haaland simultaneously earned her law degree and supported her family.

She first entered politics when she volunteered for Barack Obama's presidential campaign and traveled to remote areas to register Native voters. Haaland often had to seek authorization from tribal leadership before canvassing their voters. Her respect for these local constituencies did not go unnoticed, contributing to her election as head of New Mexico's Democratic Party in 2015.

In 2018 Haaland was among an unprecedented number of Native women political candidates. She was one of four Native women to run for US Congress and one of two from New Mexico (Republican Yvette Herrell, a Cherokee woman, ran in a southern district). Elsewhere in the country, three Native women ran for governor and thirty-one for seats in state legislatures. Many progressive candidates were motivated by what they saw as a lack of concern from the federal government for the well-being and sovereignty of tribes. Trump's curtailing of federal land protections and restriction of access to health care for Native communities convinced many that more Native voices were needed.

Haaland beat five opponents in her Democratic primary, going on to easily defeat her Republican challenger in New Mexico's historically progressive First Congressional

District. In doing so, she made history, becoming one of Congress's first female Native representatives alongside Kansas's Sharice Davids (page 40).

# WHAT'S ON HER AGENDA

Haaland's and Davids's arrival to Congress represented a long-overdue step toward Native communities having a say in their own governance. First Nations people were excluded from 1870's Fifteenth Amendment, which purported to give voting rights to all US citizens regardless of race. Native people did not receive their right to vote in the US until the 1924 Snyder Act, and Haaland's home of New Mexico became the last state, in 1962, to grant full enfranchisement. Inequality has wrought immense damage on Native communities, who suffer from the country's highest rates of unemployment and lowest life expectancies.

But Haaland's political agenda is far from limited to problems that affect Native people. Perhaps the sharp inequalities that affect her community have left her particularly cognizant of injustices that affect others. For example, her strident protests against the family separation policy within US-Mexico border immigrant detention camps were evident even before her election to Congress. Her own family had been wrested apart by similar forces. In the 1880s, Haaland's great-grandfather was taken from his parents during the US government's plan to force Native children to assimilate. He was sent to Pennsylvania's Carlisle Indian Industrial School, which

## What's the Difference between the House and Senate?

The House of Representatives and Senate are two chambers that comprise the US Congress, or legislature. For a bill to become a law, it can start in either chamber, but the legislation has to be passed by a majority of members in both of them. The House represents the people, with each representative having a constituency of around 711,000 people, and the Senate represents states. Every state, regardless of population size, has two senators. The two chambers' jobs are different. The House can propose new uses for the country's money (called *appropriations*), but the Senate can veto any proposed appropriation. Only the House can start the process of impeaching a president, but the Senate is charged with conducting the ensuing investigations. The Senate also votes on presidential appointees such as judges and cabinet members, and ratifies treaties with other countries. Senators stick around longer; their terms last for six years, while members of the House serve two years per term.

was founded by a US Army officer infamous for saying, "Kill the Indian, and save the man." Haaland's grandmother suffered a similar fate when she was forcibly sent to a boarding school at a young age. In these schools, Native kids were not allowed to speak their tribal languages and took classes not only on academic subjects but also non-Native US cultural norms.

In February 2019, Haaland met with refugee families at the border whose children had been taken from them by the Department of Homeland Security. Shortly before Mother's Day, she took to the floor of Congress to make clear the connection between the policy and her own family's history. "Native Americans know all too well the long lasting trauma of government-enforced family separation," she said. "Our communities still struggle with the lasting impact that cruel assimilation policy has had."

Haaland has also emerged as a leader on issues about the use of land for natural gas drilling. She led congressional delegations to remote areas to see firsthand the nature-damaging effects of natural oil and gas extraction. She was aware of those issues largely due to their geographic proximity to the sites of ancient Native communities, as in the case of Utah's Bears Ears National Monument.

## AWESOME ACHIEVEMENTS

- Haaland took four days out of her congressional campaign in 2018 for a camping trip in Bears Ears, the first site to be federally protected with the guidance of Native tribal leaders. But it wasn't exactly a break. Haaland wanted to acknowledge that Trump had bowed to uranium mining lobbyists and reduced the protected area by 85 percent, putting its legacy of invaluable cultural and environmental significance in danger.
- She was made vice chair of the House Committee on Natural Resources within weeks of taking office.

## QUOTABLES

"I choose to honor my ancestors by thinking, each day, about the sacrifices they made so that I could be here, and I will continue to work to protect what they left here for me."

"Congress has never had a voice like mine."

"I know what it's like to be on food stamps, what it's like to teach my daughter to ride the public bus, what it's like to piece together health care. I think when you've lived struggle, you can identify more with the struggles of average Americans."

"Tribes should be at the table."

# NIKKI HALEY

née Nimrata "Nikki" Randhawa (born 1972)

"With all due respect, I don't get confused."

Years in political office: 2005–2018

Position: US ambassador to the United Nations, 2017–2018; governor of
South Carolina, 2011–2017; member of the South Carolina
House of Representatives, 2005–2011

Party affiliation: Republican

Hometown: Bamberg, South Carolina

Top causes: equality in education, border security, and international relations

# LIFE STORY

Nikki Haley's mother was a sixth-grade social studies teacher. Her father taught botany at a historically Black college. Bamberg, South Carolina, was a working-class, conservative town with only one traffic light and, after the arrival of Haley's parents a couple of years before she was born, one Indian family. Finding a place to live was difficult until they met the owner of a house who was willing to sell to them—if they promised not to drink alcohol or invite guests who weren't white. Haley remembers someone calling the cops on her turban-wearing dad at a farmer's market and how her mother's sari stuck out amid a sea of moms wearing jeans. Haley and her little sister entered the town's Little Miss Bamberg beauty pageant but were disqualified when the organizers couldn't figure out what to do with them, since typically, the pageant elected one white and one Black winner.

Despite all this, the family prospered and put down roots. Their clothing business Exotica International became a multimillion-dollar enterprise. Haley—who later in her career would proudly sport a necklace featuring the palmetto and crescent moon of the South Carolina flag—went to the state's Clemson University. She got married at twenty-five, converting from the Sikh religion to her husband Michael Haley's Christian faith.

A 2003 speech by Hillary Clinton (page 22) inspired Haley to go into politics. (She says her role model is Britain's Margaret Thatcher [page 34], the conservative prime minister from 1979–1990 and a more traditional declaration for a Republican.)

When Haley was elected to the state's House of Representatives, she became the first Indian American elected to office in South Carolina. She set about tackling corruption, sponsoring a bill that would make all votes public. The prospect upset some of her Republican peers, who were used to being able to vote for special interests without their constituents' knowledge.

"It was an embarrassing moment for the Republican Party," Haley remembers of her party's reluctance to let the public know how they voted. "And I knew I had to fix it." And so, she stepped up to run for governor. Endorsed by Sarah Palin (page 148), Haley defeated an attorney general, a lieutenant governor, and a member of Congress to become the first woman and first POC to hold the position in South Carolina, as well as the country's youngest governor at the age of thirty-eight. All this, despite South Carolina state senator Jake Knotts referring to her as a "raghead" during the campaign.

Haley proved to be a popular leader, committed to improving the state's public education system and framing racial justice in approachable terms that have encouraged many of her fellow South Carolinians to take responsibility in the fight for equality.

# WHAT'S ON HER AGENDA

Many were surprised when President Donald Trump made Haley his ambassador to the UN, and not just because she was the first Indian American woman to hold the position. During Trump's presidential campaign, Haley gave the official GOP response to Obama's final State of the Union address, stating, "During anxious times, it can be tempting to follow the siren call of the angriest voices. We must resist that temptation." When questioned, Haley acknowledged that she was referring to Trump's campaign style.

But Haley became what many saw as one of the most reasonable officials on Trump's foreign policy team. She had a tough job, given Trump's complex, "America first"–driven relationship with the UN. Haley maintained a good working relationship with UN secretary-general António Guterres—a link that helped the US work closely with the intergovernmental organization despite policy differences.

Haley sometimes disagreed with Trump on international relationships as well. In July 2018, Trump met with authoritarian Russian president Vladimir Putin. Haley chose the moment to clarify to a reporter, "We don't trust Russia, we don't trust Putin. We never will." Other times, she held to the Trumpian line. She pushed hard for the US to invade Iran, even holding a press conference in front of a room of dusty missile shrapnel, which she offered as proof that Iran was aggressively accumulating weaponry.

Haley announced her resignation shortly before the 2018 midterm elections. She was a rare Trump appointee who exited on good terms with a president who had gained a reputation for delivering negative comments about his former officials. Given Haley's high popularity ratings among even Democratic voters during a sharply partisan period in US history, many think she would fare well as a future candidate for president.

## AWESOME ACHIEVEMENTS

- Haley was the first Indian American woman to become governor. To celebrate, *Time* magazine put her on its cover with the subhead, "Women Who Are Changing the World."
- In 2015, following a tragic and racially motivated shooting at a Black church in the state's capital, Governor Haley signed a bill removing the Confederate flag from the South Carolina statehouse.
- A true southerner, she loves to kill political opponents with kindness. When Haley admitted during the 2016 presidential election that she was not supportive of Trump, he tweeted that South Carolinians were embarrassed by Haley. She responded, "Bless your heart."
- Competitive in all aspects of her life, miniature golf-loving Haley told the *New York Times* that she prides herself on being "the Putt-Putt queen."

## QUOTABLES

"It was a blessing to go into the UN with body armor every day and defend America."

"We have an obligation to remind everyone that if you care about global poverty, you should support capitalism."

"Women should always feel comfortable coming forward. And we should all be willing to listen to them."

"I don't lose, so I don't have to worry about that."

# SARAH HANSON-YOUNG

## née Sarah Hanson (born 1981)

### "You are equal and you are loved."

Years in political office: 2008–present

Position: senator for South Australia, 2008–present

Party affiliation: Greens

Hometown: Melbourne, Australia

Top causes: refugee rights, fighting sexual harassment, and climate change

# LIFE STORY

Hanson-Young grew up in the small town of Orbost, four hours outside of the city of Melbourne and near Australia's southeastern coast. Living in the small community taught her the value of being active in the political system. "I was always exposed to the idea if you care about your community, if you're not happy with something, you do something to change it," she said. She met Zane Young, the eventual father of her daughter, Kora, while still a teen, and they later married and divorced. At the University of Adelaide, she was president of the students' association and active on environmental issues. After graduation she worked on the progressive Greens's political campaigns and for Amnesty International.

On a day in 2006, twenty-four-year-old Hanson-Young learned both that she had been chosen to be a Senate candidate and that she was pregnant. The second part caught her off guard, because doctors had said her polycystic ovary syndrome and the abortion she'd had at the age of nineteen had severely limited her chances of conceiving. She wasn't the only person unprepared for the baby. In her book *En Garde*, Hanson-Young writes about how other Greens politicians scolded her for hurting her political career by going through with the pregnancy and even accused her of having hidden her desire to have a kid from party officials to get the nomination. "There's nothing quite like proving those who doubt you wrong," she writes, after having her daughter, Kora, and still managing to win her election. "I was off to [Australian capital] Canberra with my little companion by my side."

Hanson-Young was twenty-five years old when she was first elected to the Senate, making her the youngest Australian ever to achieve that feat, and the first Greens representative elected in her state. Party leader Bob Brown endorsed Hanson-Young as the candidate who would speak to the needs of young voters.

Certainly, she spoke to the needs of young mothers. In 2009 Hanson-Young, who wanted to vote on a bill, brought her then two-year-old daughter, Kora, into the Senate chamber. Under Senate protocol, she was forced to remove the crying Kora, which Hanson-Young said made her feel "humiliated." But the incident may have helped kick off a slow movement for change: in 2016 the Australian parliament began to allow its members to breastfeed in the chamber.

As with many young women in power across the globe, Hanson-Young's gender and traditionally attractive appearance have made her the target of sexism and threats of violence. She once sued a magazine that superimposed a photo of her face on the body of a lingerie model. In 2018 a Sydney police officer was fined and placed on probation after calling her office and threatening to rape her younger sister. But neither of these are the most publicized case of chauvinist discourse directed Hanson-Young's way.

*Sarah Hanson-Young*

After the murder of a young woman who was walking home late at night, the Australian Senate was debating restrictions on pepper spray and tasers for self-defense. Hanson-Young said, "Men should stop raping women."

Senator David Leyonhjelm retorted that she should stop "shagging men." He went even further days later, saying Hanson-Young was "well-known for liking men." Many saw the remarks as indicative of Australia's problem with "larrikin" (foul-mouthed) politicians generally excused for their bad behavior under the pretext that they're being unconventional. Hanson-Young made no such excuses, and she sued Leyonhjelm for defamation.

When questioned why she would subject herself to such a high-profile court trial, Hanson-Young told a reporter, "I am doing this because the woman on the factory floor, or the woman who works at the bakery, or the flight attendant who has things like this held at her, comments made, harassment in the workplace, many of those women can't stand up. . . . If we can't clean it up in our nation's parliament, well, where can we do it?"

# WHAT'S ON HER AGENDA

One of the political battles for which Hanson-Young is best known is her fight for immigrant rights. In 2014 she warned the public of inhumane conditions on the island of Nauru, which the Australian government has used as a refugee detention center since 2001. A governmental review would later expose widespread abuse on Nauru, including rape and the sexual assault of minors, of its largely Asian and African refugee population. In 2015 Hanson-Young added amendments to a visa application rights bill that called for the release of all children in immigration detention. It passed the Senate but stalled in Australia's conservative-controlled House of Representatives and its unwillingness to ease the process for people coming into the country.

As evidence of inhumane treatment of refugees on Nauru mounted, Hanson-Young would comment on "[the current Australian immigration] policy that is hurting people, breaking people, and let's make no mistake about it—that is exactly what it is designed to do." In 2016 the government denied her permission to return to Nauru. The island continues to be a source of shame for many Australians, and Hanson-Young has called her country's anti-refugee campaigns "fearmongering propaganda."

Hanson-Young has also spoken out against Australia's rapid rate of animal species extinction, petitioned the prime minister for bans on plastic products, and advocated against drilling in the Great Australian Bight, a bay off the country's southern coast. She holds a sense of urgency about climate change, especially since in 2019, it was announced that Australia's greenhouse emissions had risen for the fourth year in a row—in violation of the pledges the country has made to do the opposite.

At the end of 2019, blistering droughts led to devastating bush fires across Australia that incinerated some 26 million acres (10.5 million ha) and killed one billion animals, many of them from endangered species. Hanson-Young, whose family home in Victoria's East Gippsland barely survived the flames, led a chorus of voices connecting the disaster to climate change. "What we've seen out of this bush fire crisis—this is an environment in collapse," she said, calling for the government to vastly increase the resources it was using for helping with recovery from the fires.

## AWESOME ACHIEVEMENTS

- Hanson-Young broke down in tears on the Senate floor while speaking in favor of a 2017 bill to legalize same-sex marriage. "It doesn't matter who you are, who you like, who you might have a crush on, or who you fall in love with; the nation has your back," she said. The bill passed.
- In 2018 Hanson-Young called for the establishment of a parliamentary women's caucus to provide a space for women politicians from all parties to unite against the male leaders who launch misogynist verbal attacks on their female peers.

## QUOTABLES

"With enough of us working towards it, we can build the kind of future we want, not the kind of future we are on course for."

"Our planet is in crisis, our environment is in collapse, and politicians have sat on their hands for too long and done nothing."

"Real men don't insult and threaten women, they don't slut shame them, and they don't attack them and make them feel bullied in their workplace."

*Sarah Hanson-Young*

# KAMALA HARRIS

(born in 1964)

"When activists came marching and banging on doors, I wanted to be on the other side to let them in."

Years in political office: 2004-present

Position: US senator from California, 2017-present; California attorney general, 2011-2017; San Francisco district attorney, 2004-2011

Party affiliation: Democrat

Hometown: Oakland, California

Top causes: health care, government corruption, immigration, and marijuana legalization

# LIFE STORY

Senator Kamala Harris was born to an international family in the middle of the 1960s Berkeley, California, activist culture. Her dad, Donald Harris, is a Jamaican economics professor who taught at Stanford University. Her mom is Shyamala Gopalan, a breast cancer researcher born to a prestigious family from the Brahmin caste (the top tier of traditional Indian society). Gopalan's parents—Harris's grandparents—were strident voices for Indian independence from colonialist Britain, and Harris's grandmother liked to walk the streets with a bullhorn, educating fellow women about birth control at high volume!

Harris attended political rallies with her parents from a young age. She says that this partially inspired her more conventional career in electoral politics. "When you want to improve a system, certainly there is a role to be played about marching and about banging down the door and sometimes on a bended knee," she once said. "There is also a role, which is to be at the table where the decisions are made and influence the system from that perch, and that's what I decided to do."

She attended Howard University, a historically Black college, where she was the head of the economics society and a member of the debate team. Soon she was back in the Bay Area, working at the San Francisco city attorney's office, mainly on cases that had to do with family issues like the abuse of minors and domestic violence.

Kamala Harris

Some of her activism-oriented friends were surprised when she decided to become a prosecutor, which meant she would be bringing the case against individuals charged with crimes rather than defending them.

She proved to be incredibly well suited for the job, earning a disciplined reputation that followed her all the way up to the position of attorney general of California, the state's top lawyer. Her record is not unblemished, however. When she stepped into the ring for the 2020 presidential campaign, evidence surfaced that her office had played a role in many wrongful convictions.

Along the way she met her husband, fellow lawyer and Nirvana fan Douglas Emhoff, who already had two kids in their late teens. By all accounts, Harris gets along great with her stepchildren, Cole and Ella, who call the politician Momala.

# WHAT'S ON HER AGENDA

Throughout her careers as a high-powered prosecuting lawyer and lawmaker, instead of being "soft on crime" or even "hard on crime," Harris says that she is "smart on crime." The term—not too radical or too conservative—tells you a lot about Harris's approach to politics. With her carefully chosen words, she represents herself as a rational and pragmatic politician.

Since joining the US Senate, Harris has had plenty of opportunities to use the skills she amassed during her years grilling criminal suspects as a public prosecutor. She "interviewed" (that's the official term for the process, but these dialogues sure do look like interrogation to anyone who has seen a courtroom drama) Supreme Court nominee Brett Kavanaugh during his controversial confirmation hearings. She also investigated allegations of a treasonous relationship between Trump's presidential campaign and the Russian government, questioning Attorneys General Jeff Sessions and William Barr about their offices' potential conflicts of interest.

After these televised exchanges, many voters imagined her debating Trump himself. And sure enough, at the beginning of 2019, Harris announced her campaign to run for president in 2020. Upon declaring herself a candidate, Harris changed many of the stances she had taken earlier in her career to appeal to more voters. Marijuana, as she declared when she cosponsored Senator Cory Booker's Marijuana Justice Act the previous year, should be legalized. (She had initially pooh-poohed the idea.) Harris even started talking about her belief that sex work should be decriminalized—potentially making her the first major party presidential candidate to do so. However, not everyone was buying it. Californian sex workers remembered all too well that Harris had helped to write SESTA/FOSTA, legislation that made websites that they used to find clients in a safer way illegal. The law sent many sex workers out on the street to find work, where they had little protection against abusive clients. Despite the stances she took on her campaign platform, Harris's history of working closely with law enforcement and drafting of SESTA/FOSTA may have kept her from being the top Democratic candidate. She dropped out of the race in December 2019 and endorsed fellow Democrat Joe Biden for the presidency. That being said, one thing's for certain: she isn't afraid of a challenge.

## AWESOME ACHIEVEMENTS

- While she was attending Howard University, Harris joined the country's oldest Black sorority, Alpha Kappa Alpha. Her sorority sisters regularly show up to her presidential campaign events dressed in the organization's signature pale green and pink.
- She was the first woman, Black person, and Asian American to be San Francisco's district attorney. She broke the same three barriers when she became California's attorney general!
- As district attorney, Harris built a small but comprehensive program, Back on Track, that helped keep three hundred people out of prisons.
- Apparently, she's a beast in the kitchen. Listen up, wannabe chefs: "Salt, olive oil, a lemon, garlic, pepper, some good mustard—you can do almost anything with those ingredients."

## QUOTABLES

"My whole life, I've only had one client: the people."

"I am Black and I am proud of it. I was born Black and I'll die Black and I am proud of it. And I am not gonna make any excuses for it, for anybody, because they don't understand."

"My primary interest is to pursue justice. You can call that whatever name you want, but I think that's what the American people want in a leader."

"My advice to all young women: Surround yourself with really good friends who will celebrate your successes and know that no matter what you do, you are not alone."

Kamala Harris

# MAZIE HIRONO

(born 1947)

"Give us some credit for knowing what the hell is going on around here."

**Years in political office:** 1981–2002, 2007–present

**Position:** US senator from Hawai'i, 2013–present; member of the US House of Representatives, 2007–2013; lieutenant governor of Hawai'i, 1994–2002; member of Hawai'i House of Representatives, 1981–1994

**Party affiliation:** Democrat

**Hometown:** Koori, Fukushima, Japan

**Top causes:** consumers' rights, sexual assault and harassment, immigrants' rights, and climate change

# LIFE STORY

Mazie Hirono grew up on a Japanese rice farm, where she lived with her three siblings, mother, and a father who struggled with alcoholism and a gambling addiction. Hirono's mom decided to move the family to the US—and far away from her husband—to ensure her children's future. Upon arriving in Hawai'i after a weeklong ship journey, she and the kids piled into a single boardinghouse room. Her mother later served as Hirono's political inspiration. Hirono says, "I am following the kind of example that my mother set for me when she had the courage to bring three of her children to this country so that we could have a chance at a better life in escaping an abusive marriage."

Hirono took cashier jobs at elementary school lunchrooms and delivered *Hawaii Hochi* newspapers to help her mom make ends meet. No one in the family had health insurance, and Hirono never forgot worrying about what would happen if her mother got sick and couldn't work. In school, the future senator learned English quickly. Hirono graduated with top honors from the University of Hawai'i and then headed to the mainland United States to attend Georgetown University law school. She says her political activation was partly ignited by a book: Betty Friedan's iconic *The Feminine Mystique*. The 1963 text explained second-wave feminism, which considered how family structure and the workplace contributed to the oppression of women. "Literally, the light bulb went on, and I thought, 'Why do I think that some guy is going to take care of me?'" Hirono said.

In 1994, after spending years in the Hawaiʻi House of Representatives fighting for consumers' rights, Hirono decided to run for lieutenant governor. The leading gubernatorial candidate, Ben Cayetano, took her out for breakfast and tried to talk her out of it, saying she had limited name recognition and would be of little help to his own campaign. "I said, well, Ben, that's all fine and good but it's all bullshit and I'm running," she remembers. Hirono received sixteen thousand more votes than Cayetano in the primaries and served in the No. 2 spot for eight years. In 2002 Hirono's failed candidacy for governor yielded her career's only electoral defeat. Four years later, she regrouped and successfully ran for the US House of Representatives. Eventually, she was elected to the US Senate, becoming the only immigrant senator at the time.

Hirono got married at the age of forty-two to Leighton Oshima, a man she had dated thirteen years earlier after the two met at a Young Democrats meeting. She is an avid opera fan and misses traditional Hawaiian foods such as poke and squid lūʻau while she's in Washington, DC.

# WHAT'S ON HER AGENDA

Hirono was diagnosed with kidney cancer in 2017, the same year she ran for Senate reelection. Ten days after a painful operation to remove parts of her ribs, she was back on the Senate floor to deliver an improvised, impassioned speech against the repeal of the Affordable Care Act (a.k.a. Obamacare), which brought government-subsidized health care to many in the United States. Hirono spoke about her own battle with cancer. She recounted how many of her Republican colleagues—who were largely dead set on getting rid of the legislation—had written her get-well-soon notes, sharing tales from their own family's serious health challenges. "You showed me your care," Hirono said, raising her voice to deliver the next lines, "You showed me your compassion. Where is that tonight?" The repeal failed, and many gave Hirono credit for tipping the scale.

Hirono was one of the Senate Judiciary Committee's four women members when sexual assault allegations against Hollywood producer Harvey Weinstein catapulted the #MeToo movement into the mainstream. Since those bombshells dropped, she has asked every governmental nominee questions about their history with sexual misconduct and does not waver on the issue, even when allegations arise against her fellow Democrats. When sexual harassment allegations surfaced against her friend and Minnesota senator Al Franken in 2017, she firmly called on him to step down from his office. (He did.)

Hirono was also vocal in the Brett Kavanaugh investigations, despite his eventual confirmation to the nation's highest court. "I just want to say to the men in this country: just shut up and step up," said a frustrated Hirono. "Do the right thing for a change."

Trump derided her for the comment, calling her "the crazy female senator."

Now in her seventies, Hirono has become known for her direct, fiery manner of speech, particularly when it comes to her criticisms of Trump. "To call the President a liar, that is not good," she said. "But it happens to be the truth." She says injustices perpetuated by his administration have forced her to step out of the stoic role stereotypically assigned to Asian women *kūpuna* (a Hawaiian word for "elders"). "It's been a journey because not all of us just kind of pop out and start popping off," she said. "You don't see too many Asian people out there, Asian women."

Hirono has also spoken out on immigration and criticized Trump's proposed ban on immigrants from six Muslim countries. "Our country is made up of groups of immigrants who came here hoping for a better life," she said. "They created America."

## AWESOME ACHIEVEMENTS

- She is Hawai'i's first woman senator and first Asian American senator. She's also the United States' first Buddhist senator and its first woman Asian American senator.
- Hirono adopted her rotund feline shorthair, Hemic, at an Oahu animal shelter. Sixteen years later, the comely Hemic took home top honors in the House Cat division of the Humane Society's congressional pet photo contest.
- Hirono was a cosponsor of the Senate resolution supporting the Green New Deal.

## QUOTABLES

"People are getting screwed in this country every single second, minute, hour of the day. And, by our efforts, if we can decrease that number, we will be making a difference."

"You work with others, you compromise . . . (while) maintaining your core, and know how far to go and being able to walk away from anything."

"I think it's important for people to recognize that it's not just white guys who are serving in Congress."

"Immigrants . . . have a sense of the opportunities that this country provides. We do not take those for granted."

Years in political office: 2009–present

Position: prime minister of Iceland, 2017–present; chairperson of the Left-Green Movement, 2013–present; minister of education, science and culture, 2009–2013

Party affiliation: Left-Green Movement

Hometown: Reykjavík, Iceland

Top causes: climate change, women's rights, and refugee rights

# LIFE STORY

Katrín Jakobsdóttir grew up among individuals who made their mark not only in policy but also in the world of arts and culture. Her family tree features grandfather Sigurður S. Thoroddsen, a member of parliament; poet Dagur Sigurðarson, her uncle; and her older twin brothers, who teach at the University of Iceland.

Early on, she made her career in academia, getting a master's degree in Icelandic literature. She developed a reputation as one of the intellectual authorities on Nordic crime fiction and also worked as a language consultant at a public broadcasting news agency. She was inspired to enter politics by the controversial construction of the Kárahnjúkar Hydropower Plant in the east Icelandic wilderness, which at the time was one of Europe's largest unspoiled natural areas. Iceland's Left-Green movement, committed to the environment, took a stance against the building of the dam, and Jakobsdóttir joined them. Despite her family's political history, she had never been registered to an official party until that moment. Jakobsdóttir would go on to become a leader in the party, first as its minister of education, science, and culture in 2009 and then its chairperson in 2013. Four years later, she was appointed prime minister of her country.

The prime minister has three sons, which in many places of the world would complicate a woman's political career. Luckily, in Iceland, an equal distribution of parenting responsibilities is encouraged between parents. The law says that employers have to give moms and dads nine months off work with pay—three months for one partner, three for the other, and three that they can decide how to allot between the two of them.

# WHAT'S ON HER AGENDA

Her country calls her simply Katrín. In Iceland, all people are known by their first names, which tells you something about the intimacy that is possible in a country of 340,000 people—about the same population as Honolulu, Hawai'i! But aside from tradition, Jakobsdóttir does seem to be more beloved in her country than your average global policy maker. The pragmatic ex-literature professor arrived in the nick of time for her country, which was on pretty shaky ground after its government collapsed twice, in 2016 and 2017. Jakobsdóttir was the fourth prime minister to take office in two years.

Iceland's woes began in 2008, when the Nordic country was a canary in the coal mine regarding the global financial crisis that brought down entire stock markets. (A woman guided the nation through that dark time as well: trade unionist Jóhanna Sigurðardóttir [page 68], who became the world's first openly LGBTQ leader of a country when she was elected prime minister.) The country is still struggling to get its feet on solid ground and saw its last head of government step down after a family scandal.

But Iceland seems to have Jakobsdóttir's back. One month after her election, a Gallup poll showed that 75 percent of Icelanders supported the new government. She may have won some of that faith because of her willingness to compromise. That flexibility became apparent when she formed a coalition in the parliament between her feminist and socialist Left-Green Movement, the conservative Independence Party, and the center-right Progressive Party. Some of the leftists weren't too happy with that alliance, but Jakobsdóttir thinks that such a show of consensus building is key to maintaining voters' confidence in a country where things have been going a little haywire. "Doing it this way, having very different parties—in both their political perspective and their cultures—working together . . . Yes, it's a gamble," she said. "But I really think it's an opportunity for us to rethink, reinvent ourselves."

Even with the coalition between different parties, under her watch, the country doesn't appear to be abandoning its historically progressive values. Early in the Jakobsdóttir administration, the government not only mandated equal pay for men and women but required companies to submit regular proof that it paid people the same regardless of gender. Months later, the prime minister joined women across Iceland in a walkout protest against the enduring wage gap. Jakobsdóttir thanks the #MeToo movement for empowering Icelandic women to speak out against the gender-based harassment they face: "One of the things the #MeToo revolution has taught us all is that oppression of women thrives in silence."

Environmental issues are another of Jakobsdóttir's primary concerns, which shouldn't be surprising since Iceland was an early witness to climate change. Fishing is one of the country's top industries—but its fish stocks have plummeted as ocean temperatures have risen. Under her watch, the country has promised that it will reduce its greenhouse gas emissions by 40 percent come 2030.

## AWESOME ACHIEVEMENTS

- When she was elected in 2017, she became the youngest woman serving as head of government in a European country.
- She was elected to Iceland's parliament when she was just thirty-one years old.
- Jakobsdóttir and husband Gunnar Sigvaldason translated a book together on environmentally sustainable methods of raising kids.
- In 1996 she starred in a music video for her friends' rock band. In it, a young Jakobsdóttir makes a milkshake in a chic 1950s outfit and gets chased around Reykjavík by the members of the group. It's called "Listen Baby" by Bang Gang, if you want to check it out.

## QUOTABLES

"Crime fiction is about not really trusting anyone. And that's generally how politics works."

"I don't see the struggle for women's rights as a box-ticking exercise, this is a battle for fundamental human rights and it demands a shift in our cultures; we need to change how we treat and perceive each other."

"I think this is something you can learn from a small country: Sometimes, we can do this."

"It's really weird that I'm the second woman (to be prime minister), I should be number fifteen or so. So in fact to rectify this injustice, there should really be fifteen women prime ministers in a row after me."

# PRAMILA JAYAPAL

## (born 1965)

"A message to women of color out there: stand strong. Refuse to be patronized or minimized."

Years in political office: 2015–present

Position: Washington member of the US House of Representatives, 2017–present; Washington state senator, 2015–2016

Party affiliation: Democrat

Hometown: Chennai, Tamil Nadu, India

Top causes: immigration, health care, civil rights, LGBTQ rights, and college tuition support

# LIFE STORY

Jayapal was born in the megacity of Chennai, India. Her Malayali Indian family lived in Indonesia and Singapore, but young Jayapal decided at the age of sixteen to attend a pair of top-tier educational institutions in the United States— first, Georgetown University in Washington, DC, and then Chicago's Northwestern University for her master's degree in business administration.

Between academic programs, she worked as a Wall Street financial analyst. She realized from that experience that her life needed to take an entirely different direction. "I felt empty," she remembers, "and looking at people around me, how they were empty." After graduation, she tried a variety of jobs, including working for a nonprofit in Thailand and in sales and marketing for a midwestern company that made cardiac defibrillators. A position at an international public health NGO (nongovernmental organization, or nonprofit) meant she got to travel to developing countries to oversee loans for women's health programs. One of her assignments sent her on a two-year stint in India.

But things got complicated when the baby she and her husband at the time were expecting came early. Her child, Janak, was in the emergency room for six weeks, preventing Jayapal from returning to the United States to take care of the necessary paperwork for renewing her green card in time. Though Janak was an automatic US citizen because of their father, these events put Jayapal's future in the country

Pramila Jayapal

at risk. She had to make a special appeal to immigration authorities to let her back in the United States, and even then the delay set her back three years in getting her permanent citizenship. Seeing firsthand how immigration bureaucracy has the potential to break up families like her own convinced Jayapal that she had a bigger role to play in national policy.

In the wake of the attacks of September 11, 2001, in which Islamic militants hijacked planes and crashed into buildings in New York City and near Washington, DC, Jayapal grew concerned about the dangers and discrimination immigrants were facing after the tragedy. She started an organization called Hate Free Zone (later known as OneAmerica) that grew from a single-room office in Seattle to a $2.1 million organization with seventeen full-time employees. Hate Free Zone successfully sued the administration of President George W. Bush to stop the deportation of more than twenty-seven hundred Somali refugees. Jayapal became a nationally recognized voice for immigrants, and in 2014 she joined a hunger strike protesting the high numbers of deportations by the Obama administration.

# WHAT'S ON HER AGENDA

As someone so determined to make a difference in the world, Jayapal felt called to government. Jayapal's first position was on the Washington State Senate, but within a few years she was representing Washington in the US House of Representatives. There, she showed her strong opinions right out of the gates, joining more than sixty Democrats who refused to attend Trump's inauguration.

Jayapal has since developed a reputation as one of the House's most progressive thinkers and also as someone with enough political savvy to get left-of-center ideas considered by her more centrist Democratic peers. After just two years in the House, she had risen to coleader of the Congressional Progressive Caucus, which represents almost half of her party's members and places her in a prime position to bend House Speaker Nancy Pelosi's (page 154) ear when it comes to legislative priorities.

During a floor discussion of a 2019 anti-LGBTQ discrimination bill, Jayapal even made a last-minute decision to share the story of her nonbinary child, Janak, to sway her colleagues to support the bill. She's also spoken out about having an abortion after doctors told her the child would likely face a birth process as risky as Janak's was.

Even though she's a relative newcomer herself, Jayapal has taken a crucial role as mentor to the wave of young women of color who were elected to Congress in 2018. Some of her key advice has been to make the connection between broad policy issues and the ways they affect United States residents. She's even been known to invite fellow Democrats to her house for dinner, as the world learned when she,

House representative Alexandria Ocasio-Cortez (page 140) of New York, and a box of tomato soup showed up on AOC's Instagram feed.

As of 2019, Jayapal was one of the 13 percent of US congressional members who are immigrants or children of immigrants. In 2018, after the family-separation policy of US immigration enforcement agencies was exposed, she became the first congressperson to meet with people in immigration detention centers being held separate from their children.

## AWESOME ACHIEVEMENTS

- In 2008 she oversaw one of the biggest voter registration drives in Washington State history through OneAmerica, signing up twenty-three thousand voters in Seattle and Puget Sound.
- Jayapal helped establish Seattle's $15 minimum hourly wage by serving on an advisory committee convened by the city's mayor.
- During her term, she was the only woman of color in the Washington State Senate.
- She's the first woman with Indian heritage in the US Congress.

## QUOTABLES

"I think there's a lot of people who, because I'm a woman, because I'm a person of color, and because I look younger than people think I am, they take me for granted. And that's helpful sometimes, because you don't always need to be loud from day one."

"My beautiful, now twenty-two-year-old child told me last year that they were gender non-conforming, and over the last year, I have come to understand from a deeply personal mother's perspective . . . their newfound freedom . . . to rid themselves of some conformist stereotype of who they are, to be able to express who they are at their real core."

"It's really important not to let the outside world define you, and to be strong in standing up for what you believe in, but also be strategic."

"A fair and forward-looking immigration system must be at the heart of America's moral imagination."

Pramila Jayapal

# ANDREA JENKINS

**(born 1961)**

"We don't just want a seat at the table—
we want to set the table."

Years in political office: 2018-present

Position: vice president of the Minneapolis City Council, 2018-present

Party affiliation: Democrat

Hometown: Chicago, Illinois

Top causes: affordable housing, higher minimum wage, and racial equity

# LIFE STORY

Jenkins grew up in the underprivileged neighborhoods of Chicago's West Side. At six years old, still outwardly presenting as a boy, she was riding the bus with her mom when they saw two drag queens. She felt an inexplicable sense of connection with them, but when she saw that other people on the bus were making fun of the queens, Jenkins resolved to keep her thoughts a secret. "I remember I used to pray, 'God, why me?'" she says. "'You gave me this perfectly male body that some people even envy, but it doesn't match up with my internal concept of who I am.'"

Jenkins's mother eventually moved the family to a South Side neighborhood where there was less violence. Jenkins caught the attention of her middle school teachers, who helped her enroll in a college prep school. She was a Cub Scout and played football in high school. At eighteen years old, she worked on her first political campaign for Harold Washington, Chicago's first Black mayor. Jenkins would eventually become the president of her University of Minnesota fraternity but was forced out of the brotherhood when another member found her in an intimate situation with a man. She went on to marry a woman, with whom Jenkins would have daughter Nia before the couple divorced.

Jenkins started out her professional career as a writer and eventually went back to school to get not only her bachelor's degree but a master's degree in community economic development and a master of fine arts in creative writing. In the late 1970s, when she was in her thirties, she started work as a vocational counselor for Hennepin County (of Minnesota) government. During that time, she encountered the University of Minnesota's human sexuality program, through which she found educational resources that empowered her to start her own gender transition. "It was there I learned there are many, many, many other people who feel like this, and there's a

Andrea Jenkins

process to help you sort of come to a recognition of congruency with your mind and body," she says. Work colleagues remember how Jenkins's newfound self-confidence put those around her at ease, even if they didn't entirely understand the importance of her transition at the time.

By 2001 the openly trans Jenkins was receiving offers to work on political campaigns, and after she helped Minneapolis's Eighth Ward city council candidate Robert Lilligren get elected, he hired Jenkins to his staff. Later, she worked as an aide to another Eighth Ward council member, Elizabeth Glidden, for eight years. In 2017 she campaigned to become Glidden's successor and won handily with 73 percent of the votes and many key endorsements from the state's Democratic-Farmer-Labor Party. In so doing, Jenkins became the first transgender woman elected to a major US city council—and the first openly transgender Black woman to be elected to public office in the United States. (The first openly transgender woman of color elected was Kim Coco Iwamoto, who had successfully run for Hawai'i's Board of Education in 2006.) Phillipe Cunningham, a trans man, won his race to represent the Fourth Ward in the same election. It was a groundbreaking moment for trans representation in the Minneapolis City Council.

Regardless of her many accomplishments in the political world, Jenkins is adamant that her elected office does not define her—and indeed, introduces herself as a poet to new acquaintances. "I always lead with 'poet,' because it's my deep passion to be an artist, an educator, and a humanitarian," she says. She has a long-term partner and is the grandmother of two.

# WHAT'S ON HER AGENDA

Perhaps it is no surprise that Jenkins has taken the lead on trans issues through her work with the City of Minneapolis. While she was Glidden's aide, Jenkins was instrumental in creating a transgender issues work group, which developed successful legislation regarding gender-neutral bathrooms and training for law enforcement agents on trans issues. The work was crucial—transgender people in Minnesota, and the country as a whole, face threats of violence and severe discrimination. Jenkins herself has been the target of bigoted comments. The morning after she won her election to the Minneapolis City Council, Minnesota member of the House of Representatives Mary Franson tweeted, "A guy who thinks he's a girl is still a guy with a mental health condition." Unfortunately, there was no mistaking who the comment was intended to describe.

But as a legislator, Jenkin's focus has primarily been on issues of racial and economic inequality. In 2017, through her position as an aide, Jenkins helped the city's workers win an increase in the minimum wage to fifteen dollars an hour. As a member of the city council, she has used her background in community economic development to take a leading role in revitalizing Minneapolis's 38th Street. Jenkins worked on this strategically to prioritize the needs of the majority-POC community that had lived in the area for years and focused on building the strength of existing neighborhood organizations. A writer and performance artist herself, she has also been a strong voice for artists of color and has worked on the issues of youth violence that affected her own childhood in Chicago.

Jenkins has also sought to raise the volume of trans voices beyond politics. She worked for the University of Minnesota—site of one of the country's first academic health centers that provided trans people with gender confirmation surgery as far back as the 1960s—leading its Tretter Transgender Oral History Project. Jenkins conducted two hundred interviews with trans people from ages eighteen to eighty on their life histories, which, among other things, were used to help write policy to improve the lives of the trans community.

## AWESOME ACHIEVEMENTS

- She is the author of various books, including a 2015 collection of poetry focused on the trans experience, *The T Is Not Silent*.
- Jenkins achieved her first city council electoral win despite being diagnosed with multiple sclerosis, an autoimmune disease, during the campaign.
- Just after winning that first election, Jenkins's peers elected her vice president of the city council—a great honor for a public office newbie.

## QUOTABLES

"Transgender people have been here forever, and Black transgender people have been here forever."

"We need people laying on the street in the middle of the freeway saying 'Black Lives Matter' but we also need people in city hall, in state legislature, in the White House and in Congress saying those same things."

"I'm not sure if I would have the same sort of concepts and ideas around human justice if I weren't transgender."

"There are moments in history that prove that this grand experiment—that we call the United States—is working."

Andrea Jenkins

# AMY KLOBUCHAR

## (born 1960)

## "There is a difference between being bold and being rash."

Years in political office: 1999–present

Position: US senator from Minnesota, 2007–present;
county attorney of Hennepin County, Minnesota, 1999–2007

Party affiliation: Democrat

Hometown: Plymouth, Minnesota

Top causes: mental health issues, climate change,
and lowering prescription drug prices

# LIFE STORY

Amy Klobuchar grew up in the suburbs of Minneapolis-St. Paul. She is the Swiss Slovenian granddaughter of an iron miner. Her mother was a schoolteacher, and her father was a renowned columnist at the *Minneapolis Star Tribune* newspaper. Her dad was also an alcoholic. "When you're only seventeen years old, and you're going up with your dad to visit your grandma for Christmas, and you see him drinking out of the trunk, and you have to say, 'No, I'm taking the keys away'—yeah, that doesn't happen to most kids that age," she remembers. After numerous DUI charges, her dad had to write an apology to his readers at the newspaper but eventually overcame his addiction and repaired his relationship with Klobuchar.

Despite these challenges at home, the future senator triumphed in academics. She was her high school's valedictorian and graduated magna cum laude from Yale University before getting her law degree at the University of Chicago. While still at Yale, she interned for the then vice president Walter Mondale, and after graduation, she worked at a large Minneapolis law firm.

At the age of thirty-eight, she was elected county attorney in Hennepin County, Minnesota's most populous county that includes the city of Minneapolis, becoming the first woman to hold the post. She served from 1999 to 2007, during which Minneapolis was known as Murderapolis for its high rates of violent crime. In this role, Klobuchar pushed to require police to videotape all interrogations so as to help prevent the abuse of suspects, pursued white-collar criminals, and raised penalties for multiple drunk-driving offenders. Klobuchar prosecuted juveniles in many instances and came under fire for not bringing charges against two dozen cases in which police killed civilians—largely Black and Native American individuals—under her watch. Critics pointed out that two-thirds of the Hennepin County residents sent to state prison during her terms were African American and worried that she was putting her concerns for law enforcement officials above those for communities of color. But her tough-on-crime reputation, established during this time, helped her cause when she ran to fill a retiring US senator's seat in 2006. Klobuchar won and has held onto the position ever since.

Klobuchar met her husband, John Bessler, a University of Baltimore law professor, in a pool hall. Many consider him an expert on the issues surrounding the death penalty. Klobuchar is proud that he became active in the Senate spouses' club upon their arrival to Washington—one of the only husbands to do so. Their daughter, Abigail, was born with a health condition that made her unable to swallow and spent the first few years of her life in and out of the hospital. Like her mom, Abigail Bessler wound up graduating from Yale. She works for a member of the New York City Council.

Years later as a US senator, Klobuchar's family history would play a role in national politics. While questioning Supreme Court nominee Brett Kavanaugh, Klobuchar asked if he'd ever blacked out while intoxicated. Kavanaugh turned the question back on her. "I have no drinking problem," she evenly replied. Kavanaugh would later apologize to her. But the moment went viral and was even parodied on *Saturday Night Live*. To some, Klobuchar looked like a woman who could maintain her composure under pressure. Many think the moment inspired her future political moves.

# WHAT'S ON HER AGENDA

In the Senate, Klobuchar focuses on practical bipartisan issues like bolstering protections for consumers and curbing prescription drug costs. She demonstrated her ability to efficiently pass legislation when a Minneapolis bridge collapsed in 2007, killing 13 people and injuring 145. She helped to quickly push through a federal funding package, and the bridge's reconstruction was completed on a relatively short timeline. And during the 2016 Senate session, she either sponsored or cosponsored twenty-seven bills that were eventually signed into law—more than any of her peers.

Among Klobuchar's other legislative victories were a ban on lead in children's toys and stricter laws on swimming pool safety. In recent years, she has demanded that social media networks be subject to the same transparency laws that govern television channels and radio stations. She also took on voting rights protection, introducing several bills in the area. One of these proposals would let people register to vote on Election Day, another would institute voter education programs in high schools, and still another would require states to register individuals automatically as voters when they turn eighteen.

In 2019 Klobuchar announced her candidacy for the White House in front of the same Mississippi River bridge whose reconstruction she had helped assure. The bridge served as a metaphor for Klobuchar's powers of diplomacy. "We are all tired of the shutdowns and the showdowns, the gridlock and the grandstanding," she said, referencing Trump's government shutdown of early 2019. "Our nation must be governed not from chaos but from opportunity. Not by wallowing over what's wrong, but by marching inexorably toward what's right."

Running against some more progressive candidates in the Democratic primaries, Klobuchar staked her campaign on her reputation as a friendly midwesterner and on her belief that the US needs a unifying, centrist candidate that could woo swing voters. "I am your neighbor," she said at a February campaign event in Des Moines. "I think you all know we had some difficulty in some of the states in the heartland in 2016. But I'm someone who's been able to win in difficult counties."

Supporters' excitement over Klobuchar's announcement was dampened when multiple anonymous former staffers came forward with claims that she was a cruel boss prone to delivering needlessly harsh admonitions, once even hurling a binder at an employee. Some of her supporters chalked the accusations up to sexism. But the stories troubled many, particularly given Klobuchar's reputation for being a levelheaded legislator. The anecdotes may have explained why her office had the highest staff turnover rate in the Senate from 2001 to 2016, even as she decisively won several elections.

Klobuchar's office did not deny any of the specific claims, and she quickly apologized for her aggressive demeanor. "I know I can be tough," she said. "I know I can push people too hard, and I also know I can do better—and I will." However, after failing to secure much support in the early 2020 Democratic primaries, she dropped out of the race and endorsed former vice president Joe Biden.

## AWESOME ACHIEVEMENTS

- Klobuchar made the announcement that she was running for president in the middle of a snowstorm, making many of her hardy midwesterner constituents proud!
- She's not afraid to talk about her most embarrassing moments, including when she got ditched by her date at her high school's prom and the time she got dumped on Halloween while she was wearing a Christmas tree costume.
- With a passion that stemmed from Abigail's harrowing birth, and before ever taking public office, Klobuchar successfully pushed for Minnesota to pass laws guaranteeing moms and their newborns a forty-eight-hour postpartum stay in the hospital.
- Klobuchar was the first woman to be elected to the US Senate in Minnesota.

## QUOTABLES

"We need someone in the White House (who's) a hero for their time."

"If the past is an indication, when women are given a job to do in Congress, they get it done."

"Courage is whether or not you're willing to stand next to someone you don't always agree with for the betterment of this country."

Amy Klobuchar

# BARBARA LEE

née Barbara Jean Tutt (born 1946)

## "We are not dealing with a conventional war. We cannot respond in a conventional manner."

Years in political office: 1990-present

Position: member of US House of Representatives from California, 1998-present; member of the California State Senate, 1996-1998; member of the California State Assembly, 1990-1996

Party affiliation: Democrat

Hometown: El Paso, Texas

Top causes: checks on military power, HIV/AIDS research, racial equity in education, and subsidized childcare

# LIFE STORY

When Barbara Tutt's mother, Mildred Adaire Tutt, experienced health problems while giving birth to her daughter, racist hospital staff declined to treat them. Adaire was left to suffer in the hallway on a gurney. White family members intervened, but they came too late for a safe C-section. Doctors had to remove Lee from her mother's body using forceps, leaving the girl with a scar above her eye. "I literally came into this world fighting to survive," Lee says.

Her mother was one of the first students of color at the University of Texas in El Paso. Her father was a lieutenant colonel who served in the Korean War. The family moved around a lot, but racism seemed to follow them. Lee remembers being refused service at segregated restaurants and movie theaters.

From a young age, Lee understood hardship. She was prevented from joining her high school cheerleading team because of her race, and as an adult, she had to go on welfare to support her two kids. She eventually enrolled in Oakland, California's all-women Mills College. She participated in the local Black Panthers movement, and was even elected Black student union president at Mills. Her life changed when her government professor assigned students to volunteer for a political campaign. "I told my professor that I was definitely going to flunk because the politicians who were running locally at the time weren't speaking to issues that were important to me," Lee remembers. But then Shirley Chisholm (page 74), the first Black woman to run for president and to serve in the US Congress, came to Mills to give a speech on wage equality and subsidized childcare. Lee was inspired and wound up becoming one of the key Northern California organizers for Chisholm's campaign. Chisholm didn't win the Democratic nomination, but she did inspire generations of future women politicians. Lee got an A in her government class.

The experience was enough to set Lee on a lifelong career in politics. After she got a master's degree in social work, she worked for Ron Dellums, the mayor of Oakland, California, and a member of the US Congress. Lee was elected to the California state legislature and then won Dellums's seat when he retired from Congress. She was the hundredth Black person elected to the US Congress and its twentieth Black woman. Though she has been a consistent progressive voice, Lee lost to the younger New York representative Hakeem Jeffries in a 2018 run for caucus chairperson of the House Democrats. Eager to have an experienced woman of color in the ranks of their party's leadership, Speaker of the House Nancy Pelosi (page 154) created a position on the influential Steering and Policy Committee just for Lee the week after her defeat.

Lee keeps her personal life firmly under wraps but reportedly has a serious green thumb.

# WHAT'S ON HER AGENDA

The 9/11 attacks happened three years after Lee was elected to the US Congress. On September 11, 2001, terrorists flew hijacked airplanes into the New York City World Trade Center, and the US Pentagon, near Washington, DC, killing thousands. In response, the Bush administration asked the House for an unusually wide-ranging Authorization for Use of Military Force (AUMF) "to use all necessary and appropriate force against those nations, organizations, or persons" responsible for the terrorist attacks, with no limit on geographic reach or an end date.

Lee decided that she could not support what she saw as a dangerous overextension of executive power. It wasn't that she is opposed to military intervention of any kind, and complicating matters, her chief of staff had even lost a cousin on one of the hijacked 9/11 planes. But when the Bush administration rushed the AUMF vote a mere three days after the attacks, Lee voted against the government's proposal. She was the only politician among 435 representatives and one hundred senators to do so. Speaking about her dissent on the House floor, Lee summarized a pastor whose words had impacted her deeply at a 9/11 memorial service: "As we act, let us not become the evil that we deplore." Many mistakenly said the vote would cost her reelection.

By 2018 the War on Terror authorized by the AUMF had cost half a million Iraqi, Afghani, and Palestinian lives, over seven thousand US troops, and $6 trillion. Lee—who did win many more elections—calls it the "perpetual war." Some of her peers have begun to agree that the AUMF must end and that the US must find a way to aid the Middle East in its reconstruction. "We bombed the heck out of these countries," says Lee. "We have a moral responsibility to figure out how to help."

## AWESOME ACHIEVEMENTS

- Lee displays a photograph of herself as a high school cheerleader in her office. It's not about glory days but rather in remembrance of the time the NAACP had to step in to get her on the squad. The team had never had a Black member before she joined.
- Lee is one of the biggest champions in the US legislature for women and girls with HIV/AIDS. She was the mastermind behind the President's Emergency Plan for AIDS Relief and the Protection Against Transmission of HIV for Women and Youth Act, among other bills she penned on the issue.
- Lee has held the titles of chair of the Congressional Black Caucus and cochair of the Congressional Progressive Caucus.

## QUOTABLES

"In my opinion, the use of force should be the last option; the military option should be the last option."

"When I'm in the room and nobody else that looks like me is in the room, it makes a big difference."

"Understand: racism and institutional racism, sexism, bias, hatred, bigotry are all part of the fabric of this country."

# MIA LOVE

née Ludmya Bourdeau (born 1975)

"I am unleashed, I am untethered and I am unshackled, and I can say exactly what's on my mind."

Years in political office: 2004-2019

Position: Utah representative of the House of Representatives, 2015-2019; mayor of Saratoga Springs, Utah, 2010-2014; Saratoga Springs City Council member, 2004-2010

Party affiliation: Republican

Hometown: Brooklyn, New York

Top causes: pro-life issues, immigration reform, and faith-based initiatives

# LIFE STORY

Mia Love often opens her stump speeches with the story of her parents. In 1974 Jean Maxine and Marie Bourdeau left their home in Haiti, which at the time was reeling from the corrupt, violent regimes of the authoritarian Duvalier political dynasty (1957–1986). Love says her parents immigrated with very few resources—"$10 in their pocket," as she stated at the 2012 Republican National Convention. Her mother, Marie, arrived in New York City a few months before Love was born.

When Love was five years old, her family moved to a working-class neighborhood in Norwalk, Connecticut, and both her parents held jobs to keep them afloat. Her mom was a retirement home nurse, and her dad held various positions, including factory worker, school janitor, and bus driver.

From a young age, Love wanted to be an actress—from all accounts, she also has an amazing singing voice! She eventually got her bachelor's degree from the University of Hartford, but all the while her sights were set on Broadway. Her life took an unexpected turn when her older sister Cynthia decided to convert to Mormonism. Love didn't know much about the faith—she had been raised Catholic— but was inspired when she heard a Mormon sermon directed toward men that told them to love their wives "the way Jesus Christ would love the church." Though there are relatively few Black members of the Mormons' Church of Jesus Christ of Latter-day Saints (Black people were prohibited from becoming full members of the faith until 1978), Love decided to convert.

In college she met her future husband, Jason, while he was working as a Mormon missionary in Connecticut. He remembers being impressed by her talent for singing show tunes. But the relationship didn't go any further than friendship until after Love graduated, got a job as a flight attendant, and decided to move to Salt Lake City, the geographic center of the Mormon faith. There, she connected with Jason again, and soon the two were engaged.

After her marriage, Love's pursuit of an acting career was over. Her big break had come when Broadway producers called her about the lead role in a musical the same week as her wedding—and Love turned them down over the scheduling conflict!

Her first steps toward activism came out of necessity, when a fly infestation that had taken over the family's neighborhood became intolerable. Love came to her distraught community's rescue by convincing the neighborhood's developer to get rid of the pests, affirming her talent for advocacy.

# WHAT'S ON HER AGENDA

Faith was what motivated Love to run for elected office. She was concerned that the Supreme Court was considering the removal of the words "under God" from the Pledge of Allegiance, so much so that she launched a campaign for a Saratoga Springs City Council seat. She became the first Black woman elected to public office in the county. Townspeople were so impressed with her work on the council that they eventually elected her mayor, and she managed to reduce the town's debt dramatically.

Love's political star was on the rise. She first ran for the US House of Representatives in 2012 and, after losing, rebounded to win a second campaign in 2014. That year she was one of five Black women elected to the House—and, of them, she was the only Republican.

Though Love takes much pride in her conservative values, she has found herself at odds with her fellow Republican, President Trump, on multiple occasions. She spoke out against his move to limit protections for Haitian refugees, who came to the US after a cataclysmic earthquake hit the island nation in 2010. Then, in 2018, Trump called Haiti and other developing nations "shithole countries." Love, the country's first Haitian American member of the House of Representatives, called on him to apologize for his description of the country her parents were from. He did not.

Their chilly relationship lasted through Love's failed reelection campaign. She lost by less than a percentage point to her Democrat challenger—but before the final votes had even been counted, Trump derided Love for not seeking his help in appealing to voters, saying, "Mia Love gave me no love. And she lost. Too bad."

In her concession speech, Love spoke directly to her party, saying that Trump's words and her loss "shine a spotlight on the problems Washington politicians have with minorities and Black Americans. It's transactional. It's not personal." She concluded that Republicans need to make more effort to attract voters of color, the majority of whom vote for Democrats.

Her remarks inspired a *Washington Post* study that found that nominating Black Republican candidates for office does lead more Black Americans to identify as members of the party. We'll have to wait and see what happens with Love's own political career—at the very least, her experience could open doors to other people of color who are considering making their mark on US politics.

## AWESOME ACHIEVEMENTS

- Love was the first Black mayor in Utah.
- She is the first Black Republican woman, Haitian American woman, and Mormon woman to be elected to Congress.
- Though once critical of the influential Congressional Black Caucus, Love became a respected member of the group after her election to the House due to her bipartisan take on some policy issues.

## QUOTABLES

"I'm no victim. I'm perfectly comfortable in my skin. My parents always told me, in order for people to see you as an equal, you need to act as an equal and be an equal, not make excuses for what you look like. I'm proud of having the skin color I have. It's a feature I'm not ashamed of."

"I'm kind of a nightmare for the Democratic Party. They don't want me there. But I'm coming."

"We must do a better job of connecting with individuals and families that may not traditionally vote Republican. We must listen to their experiences, visit them in their comfort zones and take their priorities to heart."

# SANNA MARIN

## (born 1985)

## "We have work to do."

Years in political office: 2013–present

Position: prime minister of Finland, 2019–present; minister of transport and communications, 2019; member of Parliament, 2015–2019; head of Tampere's city council, 2013–2017

Party affiliation: Social Democratic Party

Hometown: Helsinki, Finland

Top causes: fighting climate change, access to childcare, and LGBTQ rights

# LIFE STORY

Sanna Marin learned about equality—and what happens in its absence—from an early age. After her mother and father split, the future prime minister's mother began a relationship with another woman. Marin grew up living with the two in the southern Finnish town of Tampere and refers to her home as a "rainbow family." She remembers feeling that she couldn't openly discuss her home life with others because of a homophobic stigma. The experience left Marin convinced of the importance of fighting for equal rights for all.

The family struggled financially at times, and Marin delivered magazines and worked as a cashier when she was a teen. Later, when she was appointed leader of Finland's government, a far-right politician from Estonia mocked her for her industriousness, dismissively calling her a "sales girl." His remarks did not seem to trouble Marin.

"Here, a poor family's child can educate themselves and achieve their goals in life," she tweeted in response.

Marin got a university degree in administrative sciences and then ran in her first election for Tampere's city council when she was just twenty-two. By the age of twenty-seven, she had been named head of the council. In 2015 she became a member of the Parliament of Finland representing the Social Democratic Party, and in 2019 Marin was named the country's minister of transport and communications.

## Parliamentary System

Many countries, including Japan, Britain, and South Africa, are run by parliamentary systems, which combine the functions of the United States' executive (presidential) and legislative (the House and Senate) branches. Parliaments tend to have two congresses and are subject to different rules in different countries. The parliamentary system puts the emphasis on political parties over individual politicians. The party that emerges with the most seats after an election gets to appoint the leader of the government, known as the prime minister or sometimes chancellor, who typically is the leader of the party. It's a lot easier to get rid of a parliamentary leader than a president. They can be subject to relatively easy-to-call "votes of confidence" by members of Parliament, regardless of when their term is set to end. If enough lawmakers vote against them during one of these roll calls, they're out.

Sanna Marin

It wasn't long before she started to serve in the country's highest leadership position. In 2019 Prime Minister Antti Rinne was forced to step down. One of the political parties in Rinne's coalition announced it had lost confidence in his ability to lead after he poorly handled a labor dispute with postal service workers. Because Marin was one of Rinne's favored political protégés, the Social Democratic Party called on her to succeed him.

Her selection as prime minister at the age of thirty-four made Marin one of five woman leaders among EU countries. She's far from the only young woman running things in Finland. In 2019 voters elected a record number of women in the country's parliamentary elections. At the time of Marin's appointment, all five of the country's major political parties were headed by women, and all but one of them were younger than thirty-five! In fact, Finland has a long history of granting women equal representation in politics. It was one of the first countries in the world to give women full voting rights and let them run for Parliament, landmarks that happened all the way back in 1906.

When Marin became prime minister, her daughter, Emma, was only two years old. The politician's husband and parents stepped up to take over Emma's childcare while mom was running the country.

# WHAT'S ON HER AGENDA

Though some of her critics say she is too uncompromising on her leftist views to be a truly effective leader, Marin's support for the social welfare state keeps with Finland's traditionally progressive politics. But that's not to say that her term will be without its challenges. Many labor conflicts in the country threaten to disrupt Finland's day-to-day operations. The rise of the far-right anti-immigrant populist Finns Party could also prevent her from advancing her progressive political goals.

One issue that Marin tackled early as prime minister was climate change. Within the first few weeks of her term, Marin headed to a two-day summit where EU political leaders were set to discuss how the EU could become carbon neutral, or how the countries would eliminate as much carbon dioxide as they emit, by the year 2050. There, she expressed her concern on global environmental issues. "We have to do more, we have to do it faster," urged Finland's new leader.

## AWESOME ACHIEVEMENTS

- She is the youngest person ever to lead Finland and its third woman prime minister.
- Marin received kudos from women leaders the world over when she was appointed head of government, including Hillary Clinton (page 22), who hailed the country's new female-led administration.
- As transport and communication minister, Marin was vocal about her goal to reduce the Finnish workweek to four days a week, six hours a day. "Some may think it sounds utopian and unfeasible. . . . But people thought the same about five-day work weeks and eight-hour workdays," she told the press.

## QUOTABLES

"We have promised change. Now we need action."

"I have lived in a welfare state and am grateful for how society gave me support in the tough times of my life."

"(I) never thought about my age or gender. I think of the reasons I got into politics, and those things for which we have won the trust of the electorate."

"I want to build a society where every child can become anything and every person can live and grow in dignity."

*Sanna Marin*

# MARTHA MCSALLY

(born 1966)

"I felt the need to let some people know
I, too, was a survivor."

Years in political office: 2015-present

Position: US senator from Arizona, 2019-present; member of the US House of Representatives, 2015-2019

Party affiliation: Republican

Hometown: Warwick, Rhode Island

Top causes: border security, deficit reduction, tax reform, and ending sexual assault in the military

# LIFE STORY

Martha McSally says one of her life's biggest motivations has been to make her dad proud. Her father, Bernard McSally, a lawyer and politician, died after a heart attack when she was twelve. Her mom became a reading specialist to support her and her four siblings. But her father's death deeply impacted McSally, a defiant kid who often clashed with the nuns at her all-girls Catholic high school. Nonetheless, she became her class valedictorian and, after graduating, went on to attend the US Air Force Academy on a scholarship.

From the jump, McSally was uninterested in gender-based restrictions. She dreamed of becoming a fighter pilot. Air force rules against women holding that position and height requirements—she's 5 foot 3 (1.6 m)—be damned. She pestered her Air Force Academy teachers about letting her fly, but to no avail. McSally filled up her postgraduation years by getting a master's degree in public policy from Harvard University's John F. Kennedy School of Government and winning Ironman triathlons. Then, in 1993, word came down that seven women would be able to become air force pilots. Destiny had arrived, and McSally began training on a single-seat A-10 Warthog jet, in her gleeful words, "an ugly down-and-dirty tank killer."

Initially deployed to Kuwait, she became the US military's first woman fighter pilot to fly in combat. McSally patrolled the sky above Iraq, enforcing the no-fly zone in effect between the First Gulf (1990–1991) and Iraq (2003–2011) Wars. During a

Martha McSally

stint in Saudi Arabia, McSally—by then the highest-ranking woman fighter pilot in the air force—came into conflict with military leadership. She sued Secretary of Defense Donald Rumsfeld over the policy that women personnel had to adhere to some parts of Islamic cultural norms when they went off base, such as wearing "host nation attire" (in this case, a full-body garment called an abaya) and always having a male driver for car trips. "I can fly a single-seat aircraft in enemy territory, but I can't drive a vehicle," McSally told a *60 Minutes* host during a stretch of media appearances she did at the time. She believed the abaya rule was a violation of her own Christian faith.

In response to the lawsuit, US Central Command downgraded the guidelines from requirements to "strongly encouraged" practices.

In 2010 McSally retired from the air force after twenty-two years. She came back to the United States and announced her intention to run for the US House of Representatives. As a moderate Republican, she largely ran on the strength of her biography, leaning heavily on her military experience. McSally lost her primary election but was victorious when she tried again in 2014. She served in Congress for two terms.

In 2018 McSally ran for the US Senate and lost in a close election to the Democratic candidate, her fellow member of Congress, Kyrsten Sinema. McSally delivered her concession speech sitting on a couch next to her golden retriever, Boomer. But in a strange turn of events, McSally would still become a senator a little over a month later when the Arizona governor appointed her after the resignation of Jon Kyl, who took over the role after the death of military veteran and much-respected John McCain. The move made her one of eight Republican women in the Senate. Since Trump was elected to the White House, McSally has largely championed him and has voted in line with his position on 95 percent of all bills since she's been in office—a departure from her hero McCain, who was frequently a Trump critic.

## WHAT'S ON HER AGENDA

In Congress, McSally proved to be an extremely effective politician. During her freshman year, she managed to pass five bills, the second-highest number of any incoming member of Congress during that session. Legislatively, she focused on immigration security and veterans' issues, even passing HR 2835, a unanimously approved measure that encouraged vets to become border officers.

McSally showed her toughness during her military career, and she again showed courage when she took on the issue of sexual assault. In 2018, during her first Senate campaign, she told the press that she had been sexually abused by her high school track-and-field coach. "I was looking for ways not to be powerless," she says of her decision to go public with the accusations. (The coach has denied any misconduct.) Then, in March 2019, she went public with allegations that must have been even harder for the proud veteran. McSally testified to the Senate Armed Services Subcommittee that she had been raped by a superior officer. Her account put a well-known face on a dire problem. A report from the Pentagon found that reports of sexual assault and harassment in the military had gone up by 38 percent between 2016 and 2018.

"I was horrified at how my attempt to share generally my experiences was handled," she said. "Like many victims, I felt like the system was raping me all over again." In the hearing, she demanded that the military work on "those distortions in the culture" that permitted sexual assault to happen and often punished its victims. Though some of her peers have proposed more radical reforms, such as shifting the responsibility of responding to allegations away from commanding officers (who critics say are sometimes too biased to hold offenders accountable), McSally prefers to pursue further study on the issue before supporting such drastic changes.

## AWESOME ACHIEVEMENTS

- McSally was the first woman to command a fighter squadron in the US military.
- She served six tours of duty in Afghanistan and retired as a colonel.
- In 2017 McSally joined with nine other Republicans in sending a letter to House Speaker Paul Ryan asking for protections for immigrants who had come to the country as children participating in the DACA program.

## QUOTABLES

"When I see something is broken, I fix it. When something is wrong, I stand up to make it right."

"I was too busy shooting 30mm out of my A-10 at the Taliban and al-Qaeda to even learn to cook!"

"You want to talk about a war on women? Walk in my shoes down the streets of Kabul. Walk in my shoes down the streets of Riyadh, where women have to be covered up. Where they're stoned, where they're honor killed if they've been raped, where they can't drive, and they can't travel without the permission of a male relative. That's a war on women."

Martha McSally

# ANGELA MERKEL

née Angela Kasner (born 1954)

## "We will manage it."

**Years in political office:** 1991–present

**Position:** chancellor of Germany, 2005–present; leader of the Christian Democratic Union of Germany, 2000–2018; general secretary of the Christian Democratic Union, 1998–2000; minister for the Environment, Nature Conservation, and Nuclear Safety, 1994–1998; minister for Women and Youth, 1991–1994; member of Bundestag, a.k.a. German federal parliament, 1991–present

**Party affiliation:** Christian Democratic Union, 1990–present; Democratic Awakening, 1989–1990

**Hometown:** Hamburg, West Germany

**Top causes:** strengthening the European Union, balancing the needs of refugees and lifelong Germans, and infrastructure development

# LIFE STORY

Angela Kasner, who would become the most powerful European leader of her era, grew up in rural, Communist-run East Germany. Her father, a highly educated Lutheran pastor, ran a center for mentally disabled individuals. Growing up under a regime in which 274,000 citizens were paid to spy on their neighbors taught her to keep her opinions to herself, a skill she later employed as a famously tight-lipped politician.

Merkel got a PhD in quantum chemistry and started her career as a chemist, marrying at the age of twenty-three and divorcing five years later. But her life changed dramatically with the fall of the Berlin Wall in 1989. The wall had been erected in 1961. Germany was divided between the western Allies and the Soviet Union. Built by the Soviet-controlled East Germany, the wall divided Berlin's residents and prevented them from accessing the other half of their own city. Its fall was the greatest symbol of the end of the Cold War (1945–1991), and also signaled the beginning of a Germany that was unified for the first time in twenty-eight years.

During this time, the then-thirty-five-year-old Merkel entered politics. She presented herself at the office of a new conservative political party, Democratic Awakening. When East and West Germany fully integrated, she joined the center-right, culturally conservative Christian Democrats. The fresh-faced East German woman from the country was quiet and prone to tears early in her career. Nearly everyone underestimated her—to their political peril. By 1990 she had been elected to the Bundestag and appointed the minister of women and youth by the country's head of government and Christian Democrats leader, Chancellor Helmut Kohl. Kohl became her mentor and liked to call Merkel his "girl," a condescension that may have eventually led to his professional demise. In 1999 Kohl entered into a scandal over campaign finances. The cunning Merkel announced in the press that it was time for him to resign, and he found he had no choice but to do so. In 2005 Merkel was appointed the country's first woman chancellor, made possible by a new alliance she forged between her party and the Social Democrats.

She married again in 1998. She and her husband, a physical and theoretical chemistry professor, live as quiet a life as possible in an average apartment in central Berlin.

# WHAT'S ON HER AGENDA

In 2010 the massive debt of Greece, a European Union country, triggered devaluation of the euro, the official currency of most countries in the EU. As Germany's chancellor, Merkel was head of the EU's largest nation, and she set about developing a strategy to lead the EU away from total collapse. The process moved slowly. Many Germans find her painstaking consideration of issues—which they call *merkeln* ("Merkeling")—both exasperating and comforting. But Merkel's decisions tend to be effective. To face the euro crisis, Merkel pushed for austerity measures, or severe governmental budget cuts, across the EU. These left deep wounds in public services for the financially stressed countries of Spain, where she was booed by crowds of hundreds, and Greece, where her visits were still igniting virulent protests in 2019. But Germans came to trust and rely on Merkel, who guided the country in her unchanging signature outfit of a colored blazer and black pants. They called her Mutti, German for "mom."

That trust was tested during the 2015 refugee crisis caused by such factors as the Syrian Civil War and economic depression in Africa. Merkel made the controversial decision to open Germany's doors to about one million refugees from the Middle East and Africa, saving a vast number of lives. But this also tested Germany's *Willkommenskultur*, or "welcome culture," because of the demands that were placed on the country's social services from the influx of refugees. Dissatisfaction among native-born Germans triggered the disintegration of the political consensus Merkel had carefully built over the last three election cycles and cued the rise of the far-right nationalist party Alternative for Germany, whose anti-immigrant policies echoed ultraconservative governments that had swept into power in Poland and Denmark. But Merkel never backtracked on her decision. "We can manage it," she said, invoking her motto of the moment. "I lived behind a fence too long for me to now wish for those times to return," she supposedly told the Hungarian prime minister, harkening back to her childhood within the walls of East Germany.

Merkel is nothing if not complex. Though she is lauded outside Germany for her progressive stance during the refugee crisis, on other issues she's proven more conservative. She has voted against same-sex marriage and endorsed a ban on burqas (full-body Islamic garments) in Germany "wherever legally possible." Despite a record of supporting environmental issues, her government has been accused of helping Germany's giant car companies to cheat their way out of pollutant emissions testing.

Voters disgruntled from the fallout of the refugee crisis have shaken the once near-absolute hold the Merkelator had on her country, though she has continued to play an important role in Europe's reaction to the United Kingdom leaving the EU because of its Brexit decision. She has remained unshaken by Trump's recurrent disdain for diplomacy with European allies, as when he publicly ridiculed French president Emmanuel Macron's approval ratings and when he refused to shake her hand during a press event at the White House. In 2018 she stepped down as the leader of her party and announced that she will not seek reelection when her current term ends in 2021—though there are rumblings that she may be deposed, or removed, before then.

## AWESOME ACHIEVEMENTS

- In 2015 *Time* magazine named her Person of the Year, calling her "Chancellor of the Free World" for the humanity she showed to refugee communities.
- An international environmental conference in Berlin that she organized early in her career resulted in the first major resolution to cut down on greenhouse gas emissions.
- In addition to being the first woman to lead Germany as its chancellor, Merkel is its first leader who grew up in East Germany.

## QUOTABLES

"In many regions war and terror prevail. States disintegrate. For many years we have read about this. We have heard about it. We have seen it on TV. But we had not yet sufficiently understood that what happens in Aleppo and Mosul can affect Essen or Stuttgart. We have to face that now."

"Never try to change your negotiating partner's mind, but find and exploit the wiggle room within their thinking."

"Fear has never been a good adviser, neither in our personal lives nor in our society."

"If the euro fails, Europe fails."

"It goes without saying that we will help them and take in people who seek refuge with us."

# LISA MURKOWSKI

(born 1957)

## "I'm working for my state first."

Years in political office: 1999-present

Position: US senator from Alaska, 2002-present; Alaska House of
Representatives member, 1999-2002

Party affiliation: Republican

Hometown: Ketchikan, Alaska

Top causes: climate change, health care, and natural gas projects

# LIFE STORY

Senator Lisa Murkowski says she gets her iron backbone from the expansive northern territory she represents. "I come from a pretty independent state," she once told an interviewer. "Alaskans are pretty opinionated, and we're not afraid to share our opinions." Murkowski is a second-generation Alaska resident and has roots in the fishery town of Ketchikan, where her dad, former Alaskan governor Frank Murkowski, grew up.

Interested in politics from a young age, she went to Georgetown University in Washington, DC, to get her bachelor's degree in economics. She then attended law school; moved to Anchorage, Alaska; and became a lawyer. She married small-business owner Verne Martell, who promised to take care of the kids while she kicked off her political career in 1998.

That year Murkowski was elected to Alaska's House of Representatives, and was reelected twice before her life took an unexpected turn. Her dad became governor of Alaska in 2002. He hadn't finished his term as senator, and as governor, he could appoint his own replacement. He talked publicly about the possibility of choosing a novice Republican politician named Sarah Palin (page 148), but in the end, he opted for his own daughter. Palin nursed a grudge over this blatant nepotism and wound up taking his job in the next round of elections for governor, cementing a political rivalry between the families. Still, Murkowski proved to be a good fit for the position, and she has been reelected for fifteen years and counting.

The long-lasting senator has built a strong reputation for self-reliance. Though Murkowski identifies as a staunch conservative, she's never been afraid to buck the party line. She was one of only three Republicans to vote for the DREAM Act.

---

## DREAM Act

The Development, Relief, and Education for Alien Minors (DREAM) Act is legislation first proposed in Congress in 2001 that continues to be fought over to this day. If passed, it would create a permanent path to citizenship for the roughly 3.6 million people who immigrated to the United States as children without documentation but who have since built a life in the country. In 2012 Obama got tired of waiting and established a temporary two-year program called Deferred Action for Childhood Arrivals (DACA), which permitted nearly eight hundred thousand DREAMers to live without fear of immediate deportation. Trump canceled the program and is phasing out its protections, but efforts continue to establish a permanent version. In June 2019 the House of Representatives passed the American Dream and Promise Act, which would do just that, though the bill was not approved by the Republican-controlled Senate.

*Lisa Murkowski*

In 2010 she, along with seven other Republicans, voted to repeal the 1994 Don't Ask, Don't Tell policy that forced LGBTQ military members into the closet.

More recently, she's spoken out against Republican president Trump. During the presidential election, she withdrew her support when videos emerged that showed him using misogynistic language. Once he was in office, she voted against the government shutdown Trump proposed in an attempt to get more money to spend on a US-Mexico border wall.

# WHAT'S ON HER AGENDA

Murkowski stood out as independent during the Senate vote to confirm Trump's candidate for the Supreme Court, Brett Kavanaugh. Murkowski, because of her bipartisan voting record, was seen as one of the deciding votes in the matter. After telling a reporter of her own "#MeToo moment," referring to the movement that encouraged people across the country to speak out against sexual harassment, Murkowski voted against Kavanaugh's confirmation. Murkowski's rebellion earned her harsh words from Trump, who said her *no* vote would cost her Senate reelection in 2022.

The senator is a firm believer in the need to take action against climate change and has witnessed the effects of it up close. Her home state of Alaska is an enormous piece of land dominated by Arctic tundra. The state is on the front line of climate change, experiencing sea ice erosion and shifting migratory paths of caribou and other animals that some Alaskans depend on for food. Murkowski has advocated for her voters' concerns about the changing landscape of their state. For instance, she urged Trump not to pull out of the Paris Agreement and acts as the chair of the Senate's Committee on Energy and Natural Resources.

She is also an advocate for Alaska's oil industry, which, since 1977 when the trans-Alaska oil pipeline started pumping, provides a whopping average of over 80 percent of the state's budget. To maintain, or even boost, this income for her state, Murkowski wants to begin oil mining in the Arctic National Wildlife Refuge, a 19-million-acre (76,890 sq. km) park that has been federally protected since 1960. Murkowski has used her position in the Senate to make that drilling happen.

Some find these two stances contradictory, while others consider her pragmatic for considering both environmental and economic concerns. Murkowski remains adamant that diesel is an important source of heat and energy for many isolated Alaskan homes and that the project will create much-needed jobs, boosting the quality of life and livelihoods of her constituency. To her critics, she says that it's impossible to understand the needs of her state from afar. "In Alaska it's beyond rural, it's frontier," she says. "It's beyond what most people can relate to . . . you have to experience it."

# AWESOME ACHIEVEMENTS

- She is the first person born in Alaska to be elected to the US Senate.
- In 2010 she lost the Republican primary for her reelection to Senate, but she headed to the general election as an independent candidate and won. It was the first time a Senate candidate had been elected by a write-in vote since 1954.
- She once caught a 63-pound (29 kg) king salmon (which is Alaska's state fish).

# QUOTABLES

"I believe that our climate is changing and we're seeing the impacts."

"I shouldn't view whether what is right and what is wrong based on the political affiliation of the individual that we are considering."

"There is a balance that goes on in Alaska that I'm proud to talk about, because we've made sure that the balance is there for the people first who live there, who need not only the jobs and resources, but the economy that comes with it."

Lisa Murkowski

# ELEANOR HOLMES NORTON

### née Eleanor Holmes (born 1937)

## "I will not yield, sir!"

**Years in political office:** 1977–present

**Position:** delegate to the US House of Representatives from Washington, DC, 1991–present; chair of the Equal Employment Opportunity Commission, 1977–1981

**Party affiliation:** Democrat

**Hometown:** Washington, DC

**Top causes:** Washington, DC, voting rights; college tuition support; and nuclear disarmament

# LIFE STORY

This third-generation Washington, DC, resident is the eldest of three sisters. Her middle-class family was led by a schoolteacher mom and government worker father. Norton became aware of the civil rights movement at the age of twelve, when her community members picketed a department store that would take Black shoppers' money for purchases but not let them use its restroom. As a child, she attended racially segregated schools. She remembers her teachers crying from joy when the Supreme Court outlawed segregation in 1954's *Brown v. Board of Education* decision.

She went on to attend Ohio's Antioch College, where she became the leader of the local chapter of the National Association for the Advancement of Colored People (NAACP). While studying to become a civil rights lawyer at Yale Law School, she spent her free time coordinating actions for the Student Non-Violent Coordinating Committee (SNCC). At one point, she even met face-to-face with influential civil rights leader Medgar Evers. In 1963 she provided administrative support for the two-hundred-thousand-person March on Washington that many say laid the groundwork for the passage of the Civil Rights Act a year later.

In 1970, five years after she was appointed the assistant legal director of the American Civil Liberties Union (ACLU), Norton took issue with the extremely limited number of roles for women in the journalism industry. Representing sixty women employees of *Newsweek*, she successfully sued the company for gender discrimination, asserting that the publication only hired men as reporters and forcing the publication to give women better employment access.

Norton took free speech quite seriously, so much so that on more than one occasion she fought on behalf of clients who held beliefs light-years away from her own. She represented pro-segregation presidential candidate George Wallace, who had been barred from using New York City's Shea Stadium for a campaign rally by the mayor. "I loved the idea of looking a racist in the face," she explained. "Remember, this was a time when racism was much more alive and well than it is today—and saying, 'I am your lawyer, sir. What are you going to do about that?'"

When President Jimmy Carter appointed Norton head of the Equal Employment Opportunity Commission in 1977, she and her husband, Edward Norton, headed back to DC. There, Norton worked to establish some of the country's first federal guidelines around sexual harassment in the workplace. She stayed in the position for four years. In 1982 she became a professor at Georgetown University Law Center.

Norton managed to win her first election to the US House of Representatives in 1990 even after a controversy emerged over her and her husband's failure to file tax returns from 1982 to 1989. She won again in 2010 despite the publication of

Eleanor Holmes Norton

a voice message of her asking a lobbyist for a campaign donation—essentially, a request for a bribe to have her work on their issue. She continues to handily defeat her opponents for the position—in 2018 she batted off Kim Ford, a former member of the Obama administration, by winning 76.7 percent of the vote. Norton says, even as she approaches three decades in office, that she sees no reason to retire. Divorced from her husband, she lives with her adult daughter, Katherine, who has Down syndrome.

# WHAT'S ON HER AGENDA

The residents of Washington, DC, despite living in the US capital, are the only mainland US citizens with no vote on the floor of the House or the Senate. (Five noncontinental US territories also don't have floor votes: American Samoa, Guam, the Northern Mariana Islands, Puerto Rico, and the US Virgin Islands.) That DC isn't a state also provides political cover for the continued geographic lapse in democracy in the nation's capital. But the omission is also largely based on racial injustice. In the 1950s, Washington, DC, would become the country's first major city with a majority Black population. Well before that, white politicians saw the growing Black community as a political threat to their control over the city. In 1874 Congress abolished the District's city council and mayor in favor of appointed commissioners, effectively taking self-rule away from DC.

It wasn't until 1961 that the DC residents regained the right to vote for president. Washington, DC, must seek congressional approval for its own city budgets and continues without some voting rights—despite the fact that the District is home to more people than either Vermont or Wyoming. That means Norton cannot vote, even on legislation she helped author, except in committee before a bill is ready to go to its final floor decision. But she can speak, and she will be heard. "I will not yield, sir!" she once roared at a fellow representative who attempted to cut her off while she was speaking on the history of her city. "The District of Columbia has spent 206 years yielding to people that would deny them the vote. I yield you no ground."

Voting rights have been one of Norton's key issues. On occasion, she has managed to bring the issue to a vote, as in 2007 with the District of Columbia House Voting Rights Act. The bill would have added two seats in the US House: one for DC and one for a conservative-leaning part of Utah—a package deal meant to entice the Republicans into supporting the proposal. But though the bill passed the House, Senate Republicans filibustered the bill, and it was defeated.

Political allies on the issue have been hard to come by. On the campaign trail, Barack Obama said he supported DC voting rights but didn't mention it in the White House. Some have criticized Norton's lack of solid gains toward getting DC political self-determination, calling her complacent. But Norton hasn't been entirely unsuccessful. She has, on occasion, been extended senatorial courtesy in recommending DC's federal judges, the US attorney, and federal law enforcement officeholders, a right granted to her by Presidents Clinton and Obama. She also managed to broker the passage of legislation that grants up to $10,000 for qualified Washington, DC, residents who attend college.

## AWESOME ACHIEVEMENTS

- Norton cofounded the National Black Feminist Organization in 1973.
- She was the first woman to lead the Equal Employment Opportunity Commission—no wonder she was responsible for groundbreaking work against gender-based harassment.
- Norton was one of only three Black women in Congress when she first took office in 1991.

## QUOTABLES

"It was important to foster the notion of solidarity that no single woman should ever have to (sue their employer on the basis of gender-based discrimination). But if all of us do it, then we have something real here."

"It's time that the District of Columbia told the Congress to go straight to hell."

"I am deep DC."

# ALEXANDRIA OCASIO-CORTEZ
**(born 1989)**

"We've got people, they've got money."

Years in political office: 2018-present

Position: New York member of US House of Representatives, 2018-present

Party affiliation: Democrat

Hometown: New York City

Top causes: universal health care, education costs, environmental issues, and immigration justice

# LIFE STORY

In the mid-1990s, Puerto Rican house cleaner Blanca Ocasio-Cortez and architectural firm owner Sergio Ocasio were convinced that their two kids would thrive if they had access to top-notch education. The couple moved north, away from their home and family in the Bronx, to a wealthy town in Westchester County, New York, where their kids were among the only people of color at school. From an early age, their daughter, Alexandria Ocasio-Cortez, was a "dorky kid." The woman who would later be known by her initials, AOC, loved science and, early on, dreamed of becoming an obstetrician-gynecologist.

Her dad passed away from lung cancer during her college years, and Ocasio-Cortez says his last words to her were, "Hey, make me proud." Determined to do just that, she moved back to New York City, where she worked at an education nonprofit by day and bartended at night to cover her student loans and health insurance. When Senator Bernie Sanders first ran for president in 2015–2016, she saw herself and her community reflected in his discourse. She too was frustrated that she and her peers had to work more than one job to make a living, that they didn't have affordable health insurance—that the economic cards were stacked against her generation.

Feeling confused and saddened by the presidential victory of Donald Trump in November, Ocasio-Cortez took off with a group of friends to the Standing Rock Indian Reservation in North and South Dakota, where the Native residents were facing off against developers who wanted to build an oil pipeline through the

*Alexandria Ocasio-Cortez*

reservation. The community's resistance was "transformational" for AOC, and when she received a phone call from Brand New Congress, an organization supporting unconventional challengers within the Democratic Party, her ears perked up. With their support, she decided to run for the House of Representatives against the Queens borough's Democratic boss and two-decade incumbent, Joe Crowley.

To keep Crowley from taking the race seriously, Ocasio-Cortez's team ran her campaign under the radar. In underestimating the massive outreach that AOC was carrying out in Queens and the Bronx, Crowley fatefully misjudged his opponent. When they finally faced off, he was ill-prepared and overconfident that his track record was impervious to critique.

Ocasio-Cortez defeated Crowley by earning 57 percent of the vote. She went on to easily beat her Republican opponent in the general election. She wore red lipstick and gold hoop earrings to her congressional swearing-in ceremony as a tribute to Supreme Court justice Sonia Sotomayor (page 162), who had been cautioned against sporting her trademark red nails for her own 2009 confirmation hearings. AOC says that "women like me aren't supposed to run for office—or win," a reminder that women of color are still fighting for acceptance and respect on the political stage.

# WHAT'S ON HER AGENDA

Alexandria Ocasio-Cortez was born in 1989, two years after Speaker of the House Nancy Pelosi (page 154) won her first election to the House of Representatives. The way that fellow politicians and much of the media perceive AOC is definitely influenced by her youth. She has been blasted for being too showy, too social media–oriented, and too unwilling to compromise. But even if she is young, Ocasio-Cortez has been eager to address her legislative concerns.

Among her top priorities when she joined Congress was the Green New Deal, a proposal designed to create jobs and cut back on planet-harming industrial emissions. The name is based on President Franklin Delano Roosevelt's New Deal, a jobs plan to end sky-high unemployment rates during the Great Depression (1929–1942). The Green New Deal proposes projects that would build green energy networks and other sustainable technology.

Another goal that has set her apart from many other Democrats has been her unchanging stance on abolishing the Immigration and Customs Enforcement (ICE) agency. Ocasio-Cortez was elected during a moment when images of caged children in ICE's detention centers were surfacing, proof of the agency's policy on separating refugee families arriving in the country.

This woman from the Bronx often seems unfazed when faced with political challenges that might cause more seasoned politicians to flinch, such as fighting ageism and questioning entrenched governmental agencies. But sometimes the political beliefs that got AOC elected—ending ICE, winning health care for all, and battling climate change—present their own challenges. The same policies that endeared her to her own constituency and gave her political power have made her threatening in the eyes of conservatives, as well as Democratic peers who believe she is too radical.

## AWESOME ACHIEVEMENTS

- This here is the youngest woman ever elected to Congress.
- An MIT lab named an asteroid after her when she came in second place at a science competition as a high school senior. (Night sky enthusiasts, look for 23238 Ocasio-Cortez.)
- In her twenties, AOC founded a children's book publishing company to give kids more stories that take place in communities like the Bronx.
- The politician inspired a comic book called *Alexandria Ocasio-Cortez and the Freshman Force*, which features parodic takes on her congressional adventures in Washington, DC, including one story where her political environment is reimagined as a wrestling ring.

## QUOTABLES

"Just like catcalling, I don't owe a response to unsolicited requests from men with bad intentions. And also like catcalling, for some reason they feel entitled to one."

"No American should be too poor to live."

"I don't think that we can compromise on transitioning to 100 percent renewable energy. We cannot compromise on saving our planet. We can't compromise on saving kids. . . . We have to do these things. If we want to do them in different ways, that's fine. But we can't not do them."

"For so long, people have thought of climate-change legislation as saving polar bears, but they don't think of the pipes in Flint. They don't think of the air in the Bronx. They don't think of coal miners getting cancer in West Virginia."

"The fundamental question, in the beginning, is, 'Why you?' The reason 'why' was 'cause, nobody else would. So literally anybody could, right? Because the alternative is no one."

# ILHAN OMAR
(born 1982)

"Here in Minnesota, we don't only welcome immigrants—we send them to Washington."

Years in political office: 2017-present

Position: member of US House of Representatives from Minnesota, 2019-present; member of Minnesota House of Representatives, 2017-2019

Party affiliation: Democrat

Hometown: Mogadishu, Somalia

Top causes: gun safety laws, renters' rights, and raising the minimum wage

# LIFE STORY

Ilhan Omar's Yemeni mother died when the future US congressperson was two years old, leaving Omar's father a single parent in charge of seven kids. When she was just eight years old, her family fled a civil war tearing apart their home country of Somalia to a refugee camp in Kenya. They lived in the makeshift community for four years before they were granted asylum in the United States. Eventually, they settled in Minneapolis, Minnesota, the city with more Somali residents than any other in the country. At the time, Minnesota had some of the worst rates of racial inequity in employment, education, and the criminal justice system in the US.

Omar's dad drove taxis and worked at the post office to support the family. When Omar was seventeen, she became a US citizen, and a patriotic one at that. In later years, she was known to quote the Declaration of Independence to remind others of the greatness that the Founding Fathers' egalitarian words promised. At nineteen she married Ahmed Hirsi in a faith-based ceremony, and the couple had two kids before they split. Omar married another man, got divorced, and then legally married Hirsi and had a third child with him before filing for divorce from him in 2019.

Amid the rampant Islamophobia that followed the 9/11 attacks, Omar began to wear a hijab as a statement that she would never be ashamed of her Muslim faith. She graduated from a state university and then worked in Minnesota public school nutrition programs, on political campaigns, and as a city council policy aide. Omar scored a seat in the Minnesota state legislature in 2016, beating an incumbent who had spent forty-four years in office.

Also in 2016, Donald Trump made a stop on his first presidential campaign at the Minneapolis–St. Paul International Airport. The election was two days away, and at the podium he said members of the local Somali population were "spreading their extremist views all over our country." Trump won the presidency, and the next year, members of an anti-Muslim militia group bombed a Bloomington, Minnesota, mosque. Many felt his racially biased speech had emboldened the perpetrators, and the *Washington Post* found that across the country, counties that hosted a 2016 Trump rally saw a 226 percent rise in hate crimes.

Two years after that speech, Omar was elected to the US Congress, becoming, alongside Michigan's Rashida Tlaib (page 172), one of the first two Muslim women to do so. Omar took over the seat formerly held by Keith Ellison, the first Muslim ever elected to the House of Representatives. Six candidates had run for Minnesota's most firmly Democratic district, but Omar beat the closest competitor by 18 percent.

Omar's heroes are women of color who dare to make themselves known. She uses Beyoncé gifs to congratulate colleagues, as she did when Ayanna Pressley became the first Black woman elected to represent Massachusetts in the House of Representatives. A pencil drawing of Shirley Chisholm (page 74) hangs in the waiting room of Omar's Capitol Hill office.

# WHAT'S ON HER AGENDA

Though relatively new to office, Omar has taken on a high profile in Congress. In her first few months as a representative, she sponsored a bill that would bar schools from shaming kids whose families are late on their school lunch payment, and another resolution denouncing Sharia law in Brunei that would punish by death offenses like blasphemy, theft, and gay sex. She helped author a piece of legislation to provide childcare to the federal employees affected by Trump's thirty-five-day government shutdown in early 2019.

Like Ellison before her—and Palestinian Tlaib, to a lesser degree—Omar has found herself at the center of the debate over Israel's actions in the Middle East. She believes that the considerable monetary aid the United States gives to Israel is used to violate the human rights of Palestinians. That view is contested by those who hold that military force is the only way Israel can survive as a Jewish homeland, and some point out that critics of Israel often overlook the actions of other US allies with worse human-rights violations.

Omar has publicly supported the Boycott, Divestment, and Sanctions movement. This movement aims to protest Israeli West Bank settlements, which have displaced many non-Israeli individuals, by withdrawing support for the country's products and businesses.

In response to criticism of that support, she once tweeted, "It's all about the Benjamins baby," implying that US politicians were influenced by money from pro-Israel lobby groups. But critics pointed out that her remarks echoed a long history of anti-Semitic stereotypes.

Omar has apologized for some of her remarks on the matter, as in the case of that since-deleted tweet. She acknowledged that she had unintentionally played into harmful stereotypes of Jewish greed by responding, "Anti-Semitism is real, and I am grateful for Jewish allies and colleagues who are educating me on the painful history of anti-Semitic tropes."

But she insists that people must acknowledge a difference between bigotry directed toward Jewish people and criticism of the State of Israel, its US lobbyists, and the aid packages the US sends its way. "I am told everyday that I am anti-American if I am not pro-Israel," she once tweeted. "I find that to be problematic and I am not alone." Progressives including Elizabeth Warren (page 180) and Alexandria Ocasio-Cortez (page 140) have agreed with Omar on these views, but her remarks have alienated more conservative Democrats such as Nancy Pelosi (page 154), as well as Republicans like Representative Lee Zeldin and House Minority Leader Kevin McCarthy.

In 2019 Trump told the four first-year members of Congress known as the Squad—Omar, Ocasio-Cortez, Pressley, and Tlaib, all of them women of color—to "go back" to the countries they came from. In response, Omar quoted Maya Angelou's famous poem "And Still I Rise," whose lines speak of triumphing over those who would diminish the author's strength.

At her 2019 swearing-in ceremony on the Quran, Omar wore an orange-and-red-striped hijab. Wearing the garment was made possible by a very recent revision (for which Omar had pushed) of a 181-year House floor ban on headwear. Later, a pastor complained that "the floor of Congress is now going to look like an Islamic republic."

Omar responded swiftly: "Well sir, the floor of Congress is going to look like America. . . . And you're gonna have to just deal."

## AWESOME ACHIEVEMENTS

- Omar was appointed to the House Committee on Education and Labor, as well as the House Foreign Affairs Committee, in her first year in office.
- She once caught thirteen Mississippi River fish to win the Minnesota governor's fishing season opening day contest, besting her political peers. She kept the achievement on her Twitter bio for years.
- She is the first Somali member of the US Congress, as well as its first representative born in an African country.

## QUOTABLES

"I always find conflicts to be the best sources for organizing."

"I know what it means to be American, and no one will ever tell me otherwise."

"We should never look at anyone and say, 'You can lead tomorrow.' Everyone needs to understand the urgency of leading today."

# SARAH PALIN
## née Sarah Louise Heath (born 1964)

## "The difference between a hockey mom and a pitbull? Lipstick."

Years in political office: 1992–2004, 2006–2009

Position: governor of Alaska, 2006–2009; chair of the Alaska Oil and Gas Conservation Commission, 2003–2004; mayor of Wasilla, Alaska, 1996–2002; member of the Wasilla City Council, 1992–1996

Party affiliation: Republican

Hometown: Sandpoint, Idaho

Top causes: antiabortion causes, natural gas drilling, and gun rights

# LIFE STORY

This future governor's family moved to Alaska when she was three months old and eventually settled in Wasilla, a small town 45 miles (72 km) north of Anchorage. Sarah was the cocaptain and point guard of her state championship–winning high school basketball team. After getting a bachelor's degree in communications, she married champion snowmobiler and oil production operator Todd Palin, who has Yupik Eskimo heritage and with whom she would have five kids. One of her first jobs postgraduation was as a sports reporter, working for both a print publication and as a TV anchor on a local NBC affiliate.

Wasilla's population was growing rapidly, and many of the newcomers were evangelical Christians. Hockey and PTA mom Palin, a born-again Protestant herself, helped to form Watch on Wasilla, a group of the town's prominent citizens who worked to get the community its own police force and succeeded in 1993. She joined the city council, and four years later, concerned with high taxes, ran for mayor.

That race set the tone for her later career. In a supposedly nonpartisan election that traditionally focused on local issues like road quality and the police force, Palin showcased how she differed from her more liberal three-term incumbent opponent, John C. Stein, on hot-button topics such as abortion and gun rights. The town proved eager for its first born-again mayor, and with the financial support of the state's Republican Party, Palin triumphed. Once in office, she forced out city employees who had supported Stein and talked with the town librarian about banning books due to inappropriate language.

After Palin reached the end of her mayoral term limit, she worked for Alaska's powerful oil and gas commission, and then decided to run for governor. Her Christian sensibilities faded into the background, her religion no longer her major talking point. On a state level, the issue of the day was government corruption, and Palin shifted gears to tackle the fat cats. Her opponent in the Republican primary was incumbent Frank Murkowski, who had passed over Palin in favor of his own daughter Lisa Murkowski (page 132) as his replacement in the Senate when he was elected governor. Palin defeated him by 30 percent and went on to win the race.

As governor she showed she was willing to rethink the system, breaking with the precedent set by previous officeholders by declining to automatically give lucrative drilling contracts to the oil industry's top corporations—Exxon, BP, and ConocoPhillips. Palin also took on policy makers that she saw as having questionable ethics, even within her own party. But her rise was complicated when allegations were raised that she had fired a public safety commissioner because he refused to dismiss a state trooper who was going through a messy divorce with Palin's sister. (Officials didn't buy Palin's explanation that she had only given him the axe to subsequently offer him a job heading another agency, to which she thought he would be better suited.)

*Sarah Palin*

Despite the "Troopergate" scandal, the charismatic hockey mom undeniably became a rising star in the Republican Party. In 2008 Palin was at the Alaska State Fair when Republican presidential candidate and political moderate John McCain called to ask her to be his vice-presidential nominee. She had only been in the governor's office for a year and a half. But in the remarkably self-assured Palin, McCain saw a fellow maverick. He liked that she was unafraid of reform and that she even went after the establishment Republicans in her state. Despite her popularity, Palin's comparative lack of experience became clear during interviews on the campaign trail. Most famously, she answered questions regarding her experience in foreign relations by telling a reporter that it was possible to see Russia from certain parts of her home state.

The McCain-Palin slate lost to the Barack Obama–Joe Biden ticket. Palin would not be quick to fade from the spotlight, though her story became more complex. In 2009 she stepped down from the governor's office, saying that she was unable to do her job properly while legally defending herself against fifteen alleged ethics violations. "It hurts to make this choice but I am doing what's best for Alaska," she said.

She remained an influential voice in Republican politics for many years. Palin started her own political action committee, SarahPAC; became a best-selling author; and joined Fox News as a correspondent. She was an important voice in the rise of the antigovernment, conservative Tea Party movement, and she courted speculation in 2016 that she would run for president herself, though she eventually handed over her support to Donald Trump.

# WHAT'S ON HER AGENDA

When McCain, who prided himself on being able to work on bipartisan issues, chose Palin as his running mate, he put her particular, folksy brand of conservatism on the national stage. Many US residents who saw themselves as having been forgotten

## PACs and Super PACs

It's no secret that money runs the game when it comes to US politics. The way that funds from wealthy special interests make their way to politicians can occur through political action committees (PACs), which can be formed by industry groups, labor unions, or any other kind of affiliated group. Super PACs are groups that don't contribute in dollars to political funds, but are legally allowed to help out in other ways, such as by buying ads or sending informational material in the mail.

by Obama-era Washington power players liked what they saw and identified with the phrases she coined. "Lamestream media" (a play on "mainstream media") and "Normal Joe Sixpack Americans" were among the terms that she popularized in her speeches, which resonated with many people's sense that the US elites were not acting in the best interests of rural, mainly white citizens.

Though McCain pushed back when some of his supporters made racist and xenophobic remarks about Obama, Palin was accused of tolerating and even encouraging them. "I am just so fearful that this is not a man who sees America the way that you and I see America," she once told a crowd of supporters. Critics believed that by aligning herself with citizens who saw Obama, who has an international, mixed-race heritage, as "un-American," Palin encouraged fear and dislike of a candidate who looked and thought differently. Her supporters called Obama an Islamic extremist, a communist, a threat to the country—and worse.

Though she failed to make it to the White House, in many ways Palin's ideals and public speaking style are echoed by Donald Trump's populist, elite disparaging stump speeches. Indeed, she even showed up to support him during the 2016 presidential campaign, at times wearing a spangly silver bolero jacket. She's been out of office for many years, but her rhetoric and ideas remain immensely influential in today's political scene.

## AWESOME ACHIEVEMENTS

- She was the first Alaskan and second woman to be nominated by a major US party for the presidential slate.
- During her first term in the governor's office, Palin announced that she had given birth to her fifth child. She was back at work three days later.
- Her classmates elected her Miss Wasilla, and she took second place at the 1984 Miss Alaska contest.
- Her business acumen in dealing with Alaska's oil contracts got results—in 2008 Palin's administration was able to send $1,200 to every qualifying Alaskan from the state's surplus petroleum revenues.

## QUOTABLES

"We say keep your change; we'll keep our God, our guns, our Constitution!"

"This government isn't too big to fail; it's too big to succeed."

"Mr. President, the only thing that stops a bad guy with a nuke is a good guy with a nuke."

"Only dead fish go with the flow."

# NOTEWORTHY FIRST LADIES

## ABIGAIL ADAMS (SERVED 1789–1801)

The second First Lady was the first to take an interest in politics and was a staunch supporter of US independence from Great Britain. Her extensive correspondence with her husband, John Adams, has been well preserved, allowing us to read Abigail Adams's early reminders for him to prioritize women's rights. She said in one 1776 letter she wrote while he prepared to write an early draft of the Declaration of Independence, "If particular care and attention is not paid to the ladies, we are determined to foment a rebellion."

## EDITH WILSON (SERVED 1915–1921)

This glamorous divorcee had President Woodrow Wilson courting controversy when he married her in 1915 shortly after the death of his first wife, Ellen Wilson. Edith Wilson famously brought in sheep to graze on the White House lawn during World War I, opposed women's suffrage (though it became legal during Woodrow Wilson's administration), and may have even run the country for five months—when he suffered a stroke during his second term, she took charge of his correspondence. Critics grumbled that the US was under a "petticoat government."

## ELEANOR ROOSEVELT (SERVED 1933–1945)

Franklin Delano Roosevelt's illustrious wife changed the game for First Ladies by becoming a politician in her own right. Two days after his 1933 inauguration, she held her first women-only White House press conference, a recurring event that not only made it necessary for newspapers to employ women reporters to get scoops but inserted Eleanor Roosevelt's agenda into the headlines regularly. She was particularly influential in children's issues, housing, and rights for women and Black people.

## BETTY FORD (SERVED 1974–1977)

Previously a modern dancer, Betty married Gerald Ford one month before his first election to the House of Representatives. In 1974, their first year as the presidential couple, the radically candid Betty shared news of her mastectomy, a key step in promoting breast cancer awareness. She championed pro-choice politics (he was pro-life) and the Equal Rights Amendment, and became an important voice for mental health after leaving the White House. Her legacy lives on in a Southern California rehab center she founded after overcoming her painkiller dependency.

## ROSALYNN CARTER (SERVED 1977–1981)

Having worked hard on the political career of her husband, Jimmy Carter, in the Georgia state senate and governor's mansion, the practical Rosalynn Carter continued her efforts in the White House. She made sure her chief of staff was paid as much as Jimmy Carter's, and became known for her pragmatism, planning low-cost state meals and wearing the same gown for various important occasions. Her main political issue was mental health, about which she testified in front of a US Senate committee in 1979, making her the first First Lady to appear before Congress since Eleanor Roosevelt.

## NANCY REAGAN (SERVED 1981–1989)

Like her husband, Ronald Reagan, Nancy Reagan was a former Hollywood actor, bringing a shiny gloss to the White House quite contrary to Rosalynn Carter's strict budgeting. When counseled to dial down the glitz, Nancy Reagan released a dramatic anti-addiction campaign, coining the phrase "Just Say No." As with many First Ladies before her, naysayers said she had too much influence over policy. She replied, "For eight years I was sleeping with the president, and if that doesn't give you special access, I don't know what does."

## BARBARA BUSH (SERVED 1989–1993)

President George H. W. Bush's wife presented herself to voters as a "traditional" First Lady, which to her meant keeping her political beliefs largely to herself. She was very active in encouraging reading skills, perhaps motivated by her son Neil Bush's dyslexia. She carried out her First Lady duties and established the Barbara Bush Foundation for Family Literacy while undergoing radiation treatment for Graves' disease, an autoimmune disease of the thyroid. She wrote two children's books narrated by the family's cocker spaniels, Millie and C. Fred.

## MICHELLE OBAMA (SERVED 2009–2017)

Princeton and Harvard graduate Michelle Robinson met Barack Obama when he was hired at the law firm where she was a junior associate. As he climbed the political ladder, she served as the Chicago mayor's assistant, founded a leadership training program, and worked in community outreach for the University of Chicago. In the White House, the country's first Black First Lady promoted healthy living, memorably planting a veggie garden on the lawn of the presidential home. Her 2018 book, *Becoming*, helped drum up speculation that she would run for office. She says she prefers "a normal life."

## MELANIA TRUMP (SERVED 2017–PRESENT)

Few First Ladies have succeeded in maintaining their private life as well as Donald Trump's third wife, the Slovenian former model Melania Trump. She's rejected the First Lady's characteristically chummy relationship with the press and didn't relocate to the White House until months after her husband's inauguration so that their son, Barron, could finish his school year in New York City. In office she has spoken out against online bullying and the country's opioid addiction crisis. She's reportedly mastered five languages and is the only First Lady of the last two hundred years not to have been born a US citizen.

Noteworthy First Ladies

# NANCY PELOSI

### née Nancy Patricia D'Alesandro (born 1940)

## "No one gives you power. You have to take it from them."

Years in political office: 1976–present

Position: Speaker of the US House of Representatives, 2007–2011, 2019–present; House minority leader, 2011–2019; House minority whip, 2002–2003; member of the US House of Representatives, 1987–present; chair of the California Democratic Party, 1981–1983; Democratic National Committee member, 1976–1996

Party affiliation: Democrat

Hometown: Baltimore, Maryland

Top causes: health-care access, Wall Street reform, and HIV/AIDS funding

# LIFE STORY

Pelosi was born to Annunciata D'Alesandro and Thomas D'Alesandro Jr., otherwise known as Big Tommy, the mayor of Baltimore. The family home in Little Italy was the heart of the Baltimore Democratic political machine. Young Nancy attended to the home's eight phone lines, an early lesson in the complex network of communication that makes politics work. (Many years later, her aides would find themselves fielding urgent calls from the workaholic politician well into the night.) Her brother was groomed for and eventually won his father's mayoral post, but Pelosi's family had other hopes for their girl. Her mother reportedly wanted her to become a nun!

Pelosi briefly considered law school, but her first career was taking care of her family, a much more common choice for women at the time. Pelosi had raised five kids with her husband, Paul Pelosi, by the time she became a volunteer organizer for the Democratic Party in his hometown of San Francisco. Her political ally US representative Phil Burton passed away—and then his wife, Sala Burton, won his seat in a special election. Before her death from cancer several years later, she backed Pelosi for her seat, which Pelosi won in a special election. That year, 1987,

## Speaker of the House

The Speaker is a member of the US House of Representatives who is elected head of the political party that holds the majority of seats, thus becoming the presiding officer of the chamber. Speakers of the House stay in office until their party loses the majority, or their fellow party members vote for a replacement. Among their tasks are opening House sessions, recognizing members who wish to speak, and keeping order. That last part can be challenging! To deal with the pressure, Speakers of the House traditionally wield a gavel that they pound on the table when things get rowdy, although the tool has become slightly less crucial since Congress installed microphone systems. Speakers also have the responsibility of assigning their party's members to various committees, choosing which bills go to which committee, and selecting which legislation is ready to be voted on by House members. The Speaker of the House generally gets the blame, the credit, or both for the party's success during the term. For their peers to see them as effective, they have to make sure a lot of legislation gets passed. Another important part of the job is that the Speaker of the House is third in line, after the vice president, as the president's replacement if the commander in chief dies in office or is otherwise unable to serve.

Pelosi's youngest child entered her senior year of high school. Pelosi has won her reelections ever since.

Being a woman in politics was difficult when Pelosi entered the House. At the time, she only had twenty-three female peers. "I always say to people, think of going to a dinner with 450 people—and two tables are women in that whole room," Pelosi once told a reporter. Though she remembers being regarded as somewhat of a curiosity at the time, she proved capable of influencing consensus among party members and working sexist expectations to her advantage. That insight has made her one of the most influential women in politics in US history, first as minority whip, then minority leader, and then Speaker of the House—twice!

Pelosi has a serious sweet tooth and is an unrepentant proponent of eating ice cream for breakfast. She is now a grandmother of nine.

# WHAT'S ON HER AGENDA

Pelosi's paradox is that despite—or perhaps, because—of all her skill and power in Washington, DC, she is despised as few other politicians. She has progressive views on controversial issues such as labor, abortion, and LGBTQ rights, and as head of the Democrats in Congress, she is often portrayed derisively as a "latte liberal"—a term referring to specialty coffee preferences that targets Pelosi's perceived disconnect from the working class—or worse by Republican attack ads during close elections throughout the country.

Such insults fail to bother Pelosi; she's incredibly thick-skinned and impossible to knock down for long. She was demoted from Speaker back to minority leader when the Republicans took the majority of House seats in 2010. As a well-respected, longtime politician, she maintained much support until the Democrats won the majority of the House eight years later. Though there were some protests from members of Congress who wanted new party leadership, Pelosi was appointed Speaker of the House again in 2019.

In early 2019, Trump shut down the federal government, halting social services, closing down many public facilities including state parks, and leaving thousands of government employees out of work. Trump resorted to the shutdown to secure funding to build a complete wall along the US-Mexico border. If Congress agreed to fund the wall, then the government would reopen. During this tense period, Pelosi held the Democrats firm in their unanimous rejection of Trump's proposal. Negotiations continued to go nowhere, with both Trump and Pelosi refusing to back down. Pelosi finally secured victory when she refused to let Trump give his State of the Union address in the House chambers due to "security concerns"—his Secret Service guards had been reduced during the shutdown. The president gave in, and after thirty-five excruciating days, the government reopened. Pelosi had once again demonstrated the woes that befall those who underestimate her as an adversary.

As Speaker, Pelosi prioritizes increasing party strength. She's also taken charge on guiding the country on important topics such as health care, as when her Congress passed Obama's Affordable Care Act in 2010, and the Lilly Ledbetter Fair Pay legislation.

Pelosi is also a longtime champion for people with HIV/AIDS. Back in 1987, San Francisco was in the darkest years of the AIDS epidemic and President Ronald Reagan seemed intent on ignoring the disease. That year Pelosi gave the epidemic's victims much-needed visibility—and her peers a pointed invitation—in her first speech at Congress. "Now we must take leadership, of course, in the crisis of AIDS," she said. "And I look forward to working with you on that."

## AWESOME ACHIEVEMENTS

- When she became the US House Democrat minority leader in 2003, she was the first woman to lead one of the two major parties in Congress.
- She was instrumental in getting the AIDS Memorial Quilt displayed for the first time on the National Mall. The quilt debuted at 1987's National March on Washington for Lesbian and Gay Rights and honors those lost to AIDS and its related symptoms.
- The gavel that Pelosi used as Speaker of the House the first time around has a new home in Washington, DC's Smithsonian Museum. She donated the gavel in 2018.
- She is the first woman to become the Speaker of the House.

## QUOTABLES

"Jobs mean freedom for workers to support their families."

"If I weren't effective, I wouldn't be a target."

"We don't twist arms, we build consensus in our caucus."

"Everything in (Washington, DC) is perishable; you just don't know the date."

Nancy Pelosi

# DANICA ROEM

(born 1984)

"Discrimination is a disqualifier."

Years in political office: 2018-present

Position: member of Virginia House of Delegates, 2018-present

Party affiliation: Democrat

Hometown: Manassas, Virginia

Top causes: improving water and transportation infrastructure, LGBTQ education policy, and strengthening freedom of information laws

# LIFE STORY

Danica Roem's early life was marked by tragedy: when she was three years old, her father committed suicide two days after Christmas. She was raised by her mom and grandfather, who encouraged the still-closeted Roem to become a baseball player on boys' teams, despite dubious athletic skill. Roem developed coping tactics to deal with the merciless teasing to which she was subjected at school, doing her hair in girly styles and eventually learning to play the guitar.

After graduating from a Catholic college, she launched her career in journalism. As a reporter for the *Gainesville Times* and *Prince William Times* on education and politics, she had a unique opportunity to talk to Virginians about everyday issues in their lives. In 2012 she began to medically transition, starting hormone replacement therapy, and changed her name to reflect her true gender. The evolution was remarkably unremarked upon. "No one cared," she remembers. "It was great. I could just keep doing my job."

Roem's boyfriend has a kid whom she considers her stepchild. She keeps their identities secret to avoid harassment. But her stepchild attends public school, and that led her into activism. Roem publicly denounced Virginia House of Delegates member Bob Marshall and his opposition to a plan that would add gender identity and sexual orientation to the local school board's discrimination guidelines.

Danica Roem

Her eloquence and boldness caught the eye of the House Democratic Caucus, which was scouting new talent to run against Republican incumbents. Caucus campaign chair and Virginia delegate Rip Sullivan called her to ask if she had ever considered running for office. "I was a reporter, so no," Roem recalls answering. "But I didn't take much convincing."

After all, her would-be opponent was Marshall, a man who had once called himself "Virginia's chief homophobe" and who had sponsored a failed "bathroom bill" that would have been banned trans people from using the restroom that corresponds to their gender identity. He had been in his seat for twenty-six years, and it might prove to be tough to oust such a long-sitting politician.

Despite Marshall's low blows during the 2017 campaign, Roem kept her head firmly on her shoulders, staying classy (if subtly sassy) through the end. She beat him decisively by eight percentage points. Afterward, a reporter asked Roem for her thoughts on her vanquished opponent. Roem replied, "I don't attack my constituents. Bob is my constituent now."

# WHAT'S ON HER AGENDA

When Roem decided to take on Marshall, she knew she had to present an alternative to voters who wanted practical representatives addressing more pressing issues than which bathrooms trans people used. Luckily, she had a keen understanding of Virginians' concerns after years of reporting on them. She identified top issues that had clear solutions, and during the campaign, she spoke to her fellow Virginians about their aging water pipes and the untenable traffic that was choking Route 28 in the northern part of the state. "Terrible traffic doesn't care if you're trans or if you're not trans," she said. "It doesn't care what the color of your skin is, it doesn't care about anything. It's traffic."

Marshall failed to consider Roem a true threat to his seat. Throughout the race, he misgendered Roem and refused to debate her publicly. Meanwhile, Roem outfundraised him and proudly let it be known she is a trans woman, wearing a rainbow-striped head scarf when speaking with voters. Her straightforward campaign priorities reminded Virginia that the cis and trans communities had similar concerns and needs. After all, everyone hates traffic! "The campaign that I ran was focused on building up our infrastructure instead of tearing down each other," Roem says.

Now that she's in office, she's had to navigate the potential pitfalls of being a local candidate who is adored by the national media—a situation that can lead to confusion over legislative priorities. But true to her campaign promises, Roem has pushed forward on the Route 28 improvements. She's intent on showing the country that things work better when ideas—and not hate—lead the way.

## AWESOME ACHIEVEMENTS

- Roem has been the singer of a thrash metal band called Cab Ride Home since 2006. She gives credit to the Virginia metal community for supporting her through her gender transition process.
- She's the first openly transgender state representative to be elected in the United States.
- As a reporter, Roem has won seven Virginia Press Association awards.
- The only corporate donation she accepted in her election to the House of Delegates was from GWARbar, a heavy metal joint in Richmond, Virginia, where a chef named BalSac the Jaws o' Death oversees the food menu.

## QUOTABLES

"To every person who's ever been singled out, who's ever been stigmatized, who's ever been the misfit, who's ever been the kid in the corner, who's ever needed someone to stand up for them when they didn't have a voice of their own. This one is for you."

"You can't spend a whole campaign talking about bullshit; you have to talk about core quality-of-life issues that you will directly deal with in your job in elected government."

"I always think of myself as a reporter before I think of myself as a politician. I will be critical of specific issues that come up in reporting, but you never, ever hear me condemn 'the media,' you never, ever hear me condemn reporters."

"Just because I sing in a heavy metal band while spinning my head in circles and getting paid to do it, why can't I run for government?"

Danica Roem

# WOMEN JUDGES AND JUSTICES

## FLORENCE ELLINWOOD ALLEN

Allen came of age before women had the right to vote in the US (which they earned with the Nineteenth Amendment in 1919) but would go on to study law and break serious gender boundaries with every step of her judiciary career. She became the first woman on a state supreme court when she was appointed to Ohio's in 1922. In 1934 President Franklin D. Roosevelt named her to the US Court of Appeals, making her the first federal woman judge in the US and launching twenty-five years of service. Less remarked upon is the fact that Allen was a music journalist before her judiciary career.

## SANDRA DAY O'CONNOR

In 1981 O'Connor was nominated by President Ronald Reagan to be the first woman US Supreme Court justice. The Senate confirmed her unanimously. Besides a career in law and as a justice, she was the country's first woman majority leader as a Republican in the Arizona Senate. She did not always express the opinions one might expect for a Republican-appointed judge, and sometimes supported abortion rights—as when she voted against a requirement that women tell their husbands before aborting—and campaign finance laws. She retired in 2006 to take care of her Alzheimer's-afflicted husband.

## RUTH BADER GINSBURG

The Notorious RBG, as she was dubbed after publishing a fiery dissent to the Supreme Court's 2013 curtailing of the Voting Rights Act, has become the subject of many a headline. She faced early difficulties in getting any job in the legal system other than secretary. But by the time President Bill Clinton nominated her in 1993 to be the second woman on the country's highest court, she was a noted feminist and civil rights lawyer. This Jewish, Brooklyn-born jurist has proven a sharp advocate for women's rights in her dedication to reproductive health services and anti-gender discrimination laws. She is a four-time cancer survivor, should anyone still doubt her toughness.

## SONIA SOTOMAYOR

Born in the Bronx to Puerto Rican parents, Sotomayor was the US Supreme Court's first Latinx justice. She says the TV show *Perry Mason* inspired her legal career, which started with top honors at Princeton University and then a law degree from Yale. She was appointed to her first judgeship by President George H. W. Bush (a Republican), then to the US Court of Appeals by President Clinton (a Democrat), and eventually as the third female US Supreme Court justice by President Obama (a Democrat). Sotomayor's norm-busting practice of wearing high heels as a court justice is showcased on the cover of her bilingual, autobiographical 2018 children's book, *Turning Pages*.

## ELENA KAGAN

In her high school yearbook's photo of the members of student government, Kagan is wearing a judge's robe and gavel, standing next to a quote from a US Supreme Court justice. She's shown a lifelong dedication to the law. Before being confirmed to the nation's highest court in 2010, she was a law professor, eventually becoming the dean of Harvard Law School. Kagan was skilled at maintaining order among conflicting factions in the legal community. She was also the country's first woman solicitor general. Kagan is very knowledgeable about technology and pop culture.

## DEBORAH A. BATTS

Deborah A. Batts is the first openly gay Black person to serve as a federal judge in the United States. Philadelphia-born Batts went to Radcliffe College and Harvard University, and then worked at a New York City corporate law firm before becoming Fordham University's first Black faculty member. In 1994 President Clinton nominated her as a US district judge for New York's Southern District. Among her big cases are the litigation between the Exxon Mobil Corporation and the government of Venezuela, and the injunction Batts issued to stop an unauthorized *Catcher in the Rye* sequel from going to press.

## JACQUELINE HONG-NGOC NGUYEN

She came to the US in 1975 as a child, fleeing the fall of the South Vietnam government with her parents and five siblings. They lived in a refugee camp on a military base before moving to Los Angeles, California. After graduating from law school, she worked for California's Central District US attorney and then became the country's first federal judge to come from Vietnam. In 2011 she was nominated by President Obama to the US Court of Appeals, making her the first Asian American woman to serve as a federal appellate justice. While she is generally neutral on many political issues, she is a strong advocate for increasing racial diversity in the US legal community.

# JEANNE SHAHEEN
### née Cynthia Jeanne Bowers (born 1947)

**"I think women are often better about worrying less about who takes credit for things and more about how do we get something done."**

Years in political office: 1992–present

Position: senior US senator from New Hampshire, 2009–present; former governor of New Hampshire, 1997–2003; former New Hampshire state senator, 1992–1996

Party affiliation: Democrat

Hometown: Saint Charles, Missouri

Top causes: health-care reform, reproductive rights, equal pay for women, and education

# LIFE STORY

Shaheen was born on January 28, 1947, to a suburban church secretary mother and a father who managed a shoe factory. She attended Shippensburg University in Pennsylvania and got married one year before receiving her master's degree in political science from the University of Mississippi. Shaheen remembers that watching TV coverage of the student protests against the Vietnam War inspired her to consider her own politics. She started teaching at a Mississippi high school, and then she opened a jewelry business with her husband, Bill Shaheen, with whom she has three kids and seven grandkids.

She became active in elections through work for other candidates. The first politician Shaheen put her weight behind was Jimmy Carter, working on his successful presidential campaign in 1976. She was also Gary Hart's New Hampshire campaign manager in 1984.

In her electoral politics debut, Shaheen served four years on the senate of the Granite State (that's New Hampshire's nickname) before she became state governor. She did important work on energy efficiency programs to make New Hampshire families and businesses more environmentally friendly. She served two terms before running for the US Senate. Here's where her career hit a rare snag: she was defeated by her Republican opponent John Sununu. Later, Republican consultants confessed to jamming the phone lines at Shaheen's campaign office, possibly costing her the election. Funny business or not, the loss stuck and it stung.

Left without an elected position, she worked on John Kerry's 2004 presidential campaign and as the director of the Institute of Politics at Harvard University's Kennedy School of Government. But she wasn't ready to give up on her dream of working in the Senate. "I remember wondering how I would respond to my grandchildren if I decided not to try and run for the Senate for a second time," she says. Convinced that her country needed her, she challenged Sununu again for the Senate seat—and won.

# WHAT'S ON HER AGENDA

Want peace? Get women involved, says Shaheen. The sole representative of her gender on the US Senate's Committee on Foreign Relations, Shaheen has pushed for women to be at the forefront in global peacemaking processes, such as those between the United States and the Taliban in Afghanistan. In 2017 she spearheaded the passage of the Women, Peace, and Security Act, which requires that the United States seek women's voices in international efforts toward conflict resolution.

*Jeanne Shaheen*

## Roe v. Wade

A monumental case decided by the Supreme Court in 1973 declaring that laws limiting access to abortion violate personal privacy. It's the basis for access to legal abortion in the United States, but pro-life activists have been trying to strike down or limit *Roe v. Wade* ever since it passed and have focused their protests on Planned Parenthood, a national health organization whose clinics provide low-cost reproductive care. Note: At the time of the *Roe* verdict, abortion was largely seen as strictly a women's issue, but we now recognize that some trans men and nonbinary folk need abortions too and that reproductive justice goes beyond abortion rights.

Her other career highlights include working to eliminate tax cuts to industries that are harming our country's environmental future, and bolstering relations between the US and the important international alliance NATO (North Atlantic Treaty Organization). She is also one of the advocates in the long-standing fight to get civil rights leader Harriet Tubman on the twenty-dollar bill. She managed to get a commitment from the Obama-era Treasury Department, but the Trump administration has yet to make the shift.

As a long-standing politician, Shaheen is able to reevaluate her positions over time. Though she was against marriage equality as governor of New Hampshire, she reconsidered her position and sponsored legislation in 2009 that would have made same-sex unions legal across the country. (Such unions weren't actually legalized until 2015, with the Supreme Court's *Obergefell v. Hodges* verdict.) She also voted in favor of throwing out the homophobic Don't Ask, Don't Tell military policy.

One of Shaheen's top priorities is defending reproductive rights. In 2019 a wave of state-level legislation was passed that severely restricted access to abortions. She delivered remarks on the Senate floor admonishing the legislators who had passed the laws, calling the bills "draconian" and describing them as part of a national plan to dial back rights that had been won with the Supreme Court's *Roe v. Wade* decision.

## AWESOME ACHIEVEMENTS

- Shaheen was the first woman elected governor of New Hampshire.
- Out of the twenty-one senators who sit on the committee on foreign relations, Shaheen is the only woman. (The lack of parity is not awesome, but it's nice that she's up there representing.)

- One of Obama's first acts as president was to sign into law the Lilly Ledbetter Fair Pay Act, which Shaheen cosponsored. It gave women more tools in the fight against bosses who pay them less than men.
- She can trace her lineage back to Pocahontas, the Powhatan woman best known for her work as a go-between for the colonists and her tribe.

## QUOTABLES

"Moments of sympathy are just not enough. This Senate, this Congress, needs to pass common sense gun safety legislation supported by nine out of ten Americans."

"If we continued at the same rate that we had been electing women to Congress, it will take us one hundred years to reach parity. So I'm not willing to wait that long."

"I think it's important to remind people that if half the population doesn't have the same access to opportunities, everybody is worse for that."

"Democracy only works as well as those who participate, and if young people are turned off, then it's not going to be good for the next generation."

Jeanne Shaheen

# ELISE STEFANIK

## (born 1984)

**"It has become crystal clear to me that I am a unique voice among my colleagues that I serve with."**

Years in political office: 2015–present

Position: member of the US House of Representatives from New York, 2015–present

Party affiliation: Republican

Hometown: Albany, New York

Top causes: veteran health care, rural health care, and supporting Republican women running for office

# LIFE STORY

Elise Stefanik's family owns Premium Plywood Products, a successful company where she worked in sales, marketing, and delivery up until her first run for the US Congress in 2014. Her dad was a former forklift operator, and the family took a big chance when it created its own business. "They really put everything we had in terms of finances and they took the ultimate risk," Stefanik remembers of her parents.

From fourth to twelfth grade, Stefanik attended the Albany Academy for Girls, a college preparatory institution where she had a reputation for being sweet and supportive of her classmates. In sixth grade she was elected secretary of the student council. In one of her most memorable policy victories, she convinced the school to allow kids to purchase from vending machines during lunch. She was also a theater kid, starring as Gretel in *The Sound of Music* and as Peter Pan in various productions. Stefanik balanced her time in the spotlight with playing on the lacrosse team.

Her involvement in electoral politics wasn't restricted to school government for long. In eighth grade she started taking a bus to volunteer at the campaign office of Rick Lazio, a Republican running for the US Senate who would eventually be defeated by Hillary Clinton (page 22). Stefanik made homemade signs for Lazio's candidacy. She went on to study at Harvard University, becoming involved with Harvard's Institute of Politics. One memorable experience included hosting the campus visit of Ted Sorensen, who had been President John F. Kennedy's speechwriter and adviser.

After graduating, she got a job as a domestic policy council staff assistant for President George W. Bush and later worked for the president's second deputy chief of staff. She fondly remembers her parents' first trip to Washington, DC, during this period, when Stefanik had the honor of introducing them to Bush in the Oval Office. Later, she hit the campaign trail, helping Congressperson Paul Ryan of Wisconsin prepare for debates during his unsuccessful candidacy for vice president in 2012.

After she served on one last Republican campaign—as policy director for Minnesota governor Tim Pawlenty's brief 2011 presidential bid—and worked for a pair of conservative think tanks, Stefanik decided it was time to focus on her own candidacy. She moved to upstate New York's Essex County, two hours from where she'd grown up. There, she could not only challenge Bill Owens, the two-term incumbent Democratic member of the House of Representatives, but also go back to work for her family's business.

In a surprising move, Owens dropped out of the race, leaving the field open to Stefanik and a roster of Republican and Democratic challengers. The young politician hit the road, determined to cover her enormous district. Essex County stretches from just north of Albany to the Canadian border, making it the second-largest district on the East Coast. Stefanik reportedly ran up 100,000 miles (160,934 km) on her F-150 truck during the campaign, driving vast distances to meet with even the smallest groups of voters.

Initially, she had little help from her party on her campaign—the National Republican Congressional Committee declined to support her in the primary election. But Stefanik's experience in the party earned her some key endorsements from Ryan and his 2012 running mate, Mitt Romney. After winning the primary, she beat her opponent in the general election by twenty-two points and started her term in the US Congress in 2015.

# WHAT'S ON HER AGENDA

When Stefanik became the first woman to serve as chair of recruitment for the National Republican Congressional Committee, she made it clear that her priority was getting more Republican women into office. Republican leaders criticized her decision to offer early backing to female candidates in political primaries, but she remained adamant in her initiative. Still, only one of the one hundred women who ran as a Republican for the House of Representatives in the midterm elections was elected in 2018. The rout left only thirteen Republican women in the House, the lowest number since 1994.

The defeat may have left Stefanik even more motivated to create future change. "Take a look around," she told a room of mainly white men at a Republican forum a few days after the 2018 election. "This is not reflective of the American public."

Stefanik is proud of her reputation for working across the aisle and likes to remind reporters that she holds "one of the top 10 percent most bipartisan records in this House and one of the most independent records." She has dissented publicly on some of her party's policies, breaking with most of her fellow Republicans when it comes to matters such as LGBTQ and refugee rights. In Congress she has led the legislative charge on bipartisan issues, such as health care in rural areas and support for the country's war veterans.

In the run-up to her own 2020 election campaign, Stefanik emerged as one of her party's top defenders of Trump. During the intense House Intelligence Committee impeachment hearings over allegations that Trump had inappropriately used foreign policy decisions to forward his personal political agenda, Stefanik was prominently positioned. "We're not here to talk about tweets," she said, chastising a witness who focused on the president's social media presence. "We're here to talk about impeachable offenses."

At one point, Stefanik attempted to question a witness on fellow Republican House member Devin Nunes's allotted time, thereby violating the chamber's procedure. The committee's Democratic chairperson interrupted her, informing her she was violating the rules. "You are gagging the young lady from New York," responded Nunes, a line that echoed across media coverage of the hearings. The remark launched Stefanik into her largest press moment yet and gave her a new reputation as one of Trump's most supportive team players.

## AWESOME ACHIEVEMENTS
- In 2015 she was then the youngest person, at the age of thirty, ever elected to the US Congress.
- Stefanik was the sole Republican woman on the House Intelligence Committee during the high-profile Trump impeachment hearings.
- During her high school years, Stefanik developed an astronomy course for fourth graders that her school integrated into the official curriculum.
- She was the first member of her immediate family to go to college.

## QUOTABLES
"I think overall it's good to have as many female role models as possible, regardless of what your political ideology is."

"There's a number of Democratic organizations that invest very early in women candidates. Republicans just haven't developed as built out of an ecosystem, and we're trying to change that. I'm trying to change that."

"Women bring a unique perspective. I think having more at the table makes us more effective policymakers."

# RASHIDA TLAIB
## née Rashida Harbi (born 1976)

## "I will always speak truth to power. #unapologeticallyMe"

Years in political office: 2009–2014, 2019–present

Position: member of the US House of Representatives, 2019–present; member of the Michigan House of Representatives, 2009–2014

Party affiliation: Democrat

Hometown: Detroit, Michigan

Top causes: international human rights, single-payer health care, and environmental racism

# LIFE STORY

Rashida Tlaib does not hesitate to share where she came from: the home of two immigrants from Palestine's West Bank. She was born and raised in Detroit, Michigan, as the eldest of fourteen siblings, and her father worked at a car manufacturing plant. The family struggled financially and, at times, relied on government assistance to make sure everyone got fed. They spoke Arabic at home, and young Tlaib learned English when she started school. She thrived in the academic world, eventually putting herself through law school. Afterward, Tlaib started working for a nonprofit that helps Arab immigrants.

The future member of Congress learned early on about Islamophobia (fear of or discrimination against Muslim people) in the United States. She often rushed to defend her mother when people reacted with trepidation to the woman's hijab. After New York City's Twin Towers were targeted in a terrorist attack on September 11, 2001, acts of fear and ignorance toward Arabs increased. Tlaib remembers her little sister coming home upset on 9/11 because, as her class watched the skyscrapers burn and tumble after being hit by airplanes apparently hijacked by Islamic extremists, a classmate asked the teacher if they'd have to kill Tlaib's sister as revenge for the attack. Worse still was when someone called a national security hotline and claimed that members of Tlaib's family had been acting suspiciously and could potentially have something to do with the 9/11 attacks. The FBI surrounded their house and interrogated her parents. Of course, no evidence was found to link them to any crimes. The persecution convinced Tlaib that the US needed a change. "I decided to do policy work at that moment," she says.

In 2004 she got an internship with Michigan state representative Steve Tobocman, who eventually took her on as a member of his staff. When he reached the end of his term limit, she ran for his seat and won. In 2018, after a five-year break from politics in which she focused on activism and worked at a nonprofit law center, she ran to replace civil rights hero John Conyers in the US House of Representatives. She did not declare victory in her primary election until every vote was counted (she won by a single percentage point and had no Republican opponent in the general election). In front of the crowd who had accompanied her until the early morning, Tlaib wrapped herself in the Palestinian flag. "I won!" she said, before reconsidering the sentiment. "We won."

Tlaib married Fayez Tlaib when she was twenty-one. The two were in love, but Tlaib says the decision to marry also had to do with getting her strict parents off her back. Though they are now divorced, the two maintain a close relationship and coparent their two sons, Adam and Yousef.

Rashida Tlaib

# WHAT'S ON HER AGENDA

As a state representative, Tlaib helped lead a fight against a toxic by-product of petroleum production called petcoke. The substance was being stored in a facility near the Detroit River, where wind was picking up the small-grained, heavy metal–infused dust and depositing it on Detroiters' cars and houses—a serious health risk. "What is really, really disturbing to me is how some companies treat the city of Detroit as a dumping ground," Tlaib told a reporter.

Her blunt speaking style makes her stand out in the diplomacy-centric world of national politics, for better or for worse. Hours after being sworn into Congress, Tlaib ignited a firestorm when she used an obscenity to refer to Trump. At a party organized by progressive public policy group MoveOn, she told a crowd: "And when your son looks at you and says, 'Mama, look, you won. Bullies don't win,' and I said, 'Baby, they don't'—because we're gonna go in there and we're going to impeach the motherfucker." Conservative pundits took major offense over her remark, and even some senior Democrats chastised Tlaib for what they saw as disrespectful language.

The politician has also been criticized for her belief that the Israeli government mistreats Palestinians. Many Palestinians have been displaced from their homes as more Jewish settlers, who started coming to the area in the wake of the Holocaust, move to Israel. (Tlaib's grandmother and other relatives still live in the contested West Bank area.)

In the face of these criticisms, Tlaib has made an effort to express respect and reverence for Jewish people. In 2019 she talked about the "calming feeling" she gets when thinking about how her Palestinian ancestors welcomed the Jews after the tragedy of the Holocaust (admittedly, not a historically accurate view of the region's history). But her views on how the Israeli government treats Palestinians remains contentious. Some conservative politicians, including Trump, skewed her words to make it seem as if she had said that she felt calmed by the Holocaust, a mischaracterization which Tlaib reports led to her receiving death threats.

## AWESOME ACHIEVEMENTS

- Tlaib is the first Arab American woman to serve in either house of the US Congress, and she and fellow member of Congress Ilhan Omar (page 144) share the title of first Muslim women to serve in the House of Representatives.
- In 2016 she showed up with a group of activists to heckle Trump about his treatment of women and other issues at a speech he was giving to the Detroit Economic Club.

- Palestinians across the country were thrilled when she wore her mother's traditional dress (called a *thobe*) to be sworn into Congress. The outfit inspired a hashtag #TweetYourThobe, highlighting the garments' *tatreetz* style of embroidery, which is important in Palestinian culture.

## QUOTABLES

"I want people across the country to know that you don't need to sell out. You don't have to change who you are to run for office—and that is what this country is about."

"Yeah, we look differently. But we also serve and fight differently."

"A lot of my strength comes from being Palestinian."

# CAMILA VALLEJO DOWLING

## (born 1988)

## "We do not want to improve the actual system; we want a profound change."

Years in political office: 2014–present

Position: member of the National Congress of Chile's Chamber of Deputies, 2014–present; president of the University of Chile students' association, 2010–2011

Party affiliation: Communist

Hometown: La Florida, Chile

Top causes: education reform, labor rights, and wealth redistribution

# LIFE STORY

Awareness of class politics came early to Camila Vallejo Dowling, who grew up in an eastern suburb of Santiago, the Chilean capital. Her great-grandfather was a member of the National Congress of Chile, and Vallejo's parents were Communist Party members. Her mother was a homemaker, and her father owned an air-conditioning and heating business. "They never tried to influence me politically," Vallejo says. "But they educated me on the values of solidarity and social justice." Nevertheless, as a teenager, she began to follow in her parents' footsteps by joining a communist youth group.

Once enrolled at the University of Chile, Vallejo realized the injustices of the education system in her country. At the time, public university degrees cost the equivalent of $3,400 USD a year, making the degrees extremely expensive relative to the average annual income of $8,500. These policies placed education out of reach for many Chileans. "I became conscious that what was happening in the public university was the most important thing in the country," Vallejo says.

Education's impossibly high price tag was a holdover from the regime of General Augusto Pinochet, who rose to power with financial support from a US government rattled by the popularity of South American socialism. Pinochet spearheaded a bloody 1973 coup that resulted in the death of democratically elected President Salvador Allende, as well as an untold number of citizens who stood up to the general's new military regime. At least ten thousand dissenters disappeared during the Pinochet administration, though many say the actual number is closer to thirty thousand. Until 1990, when he accepted the results of a referendum in which Chilean voters denied him more time in office, Pinochet instituted policies that made Chile one of the least economically equitable countries in the world.

Talented at expressing complicated political ideas in straightforward language, and inspired by Chilean communist feminist heroes such as Mireya Baltra and Gladys Marín, Vallejo became a leader in campus politics. In 2010 she was elected president—though reluctantly—of the University of Chile's powerful student association, FECH. She would later admit to feeling pressured by her peers to accept the role. The conventionally attractive Vallejo was only the second woman to lead the then 104-year-old organization, and detractors said she'd been chosen based on her looks. "Machismo was very present in all leftist movements, and changing that was not something among the demands of the student movement," she remembers. "But it was in my discourse and that of my women comrades."

She would go on to rise to near-folklore status by leading the Chilean Winter, the largest civil uprising the country had seen since resistance to Pinochet. It was driven by students' demand for education reform, and they had support from all parts of

Camila Vallejo Dowling

society. At the height of the protests—which saw hundreds of thousands of citizens take to the streets in raucous, impassioned revolt—the movement's approval ratings stood at 80 percent, shaming President Sebastián Piñera, whose rating dipped as low as 26 percent.

Vallejo did not win reelection as the president of FECH. Her fellow students saw her as too willing to work within the system and collaborate with institutions that weren't as radical as their own. She proved them right when she successfully ran for the National Congress of Chile's Chamber of Deputies in 2013, representing her hometown, La Florida, for the Communist Party.

The politician has a daughter, Adela Sarmiento, with Julio Sarmiento, a Communist Youth leader. Vallejo's favorite painter is Gustav Klimt, and she loves to dance salsa and cumbia. She says she dreams of leaving politics someday to work in geography, in which she majored at the university.

# WHAT'S ON HER AGENDA

Under Vallejo's watch, the Chilean Winter movement was in turn joyful and hard line. Kiss-ins at La Moneda, the presidential palace, alternated with violent clashes with the Chilean police. When Piñera said there was no way the government could lower education costs, students brought $70,000 USD–worth of used tear gas bomb canisters to the plaza in front of La Moneda—bombs police had used to injure their peers during protests. They formed a peace sign with them and the nose ring–wearing, twenty-three-year-old Vallejo posed in the middle of the arrangement. Such high-profile moves earned her vehement critics. A minor government official in the ministry of culture was once fired for saying of Vallejo, "Kill the bitch, problem solved."

The challenges based on her gender also proved to be constant. "When I saw what came out in the press it was shocking," she said. "Everyone was talking about how I was a woman, and that I was a woman, and that I was a woman . . . they didn't ask me about my political goals or what it was that I represented, what I wanted to do."

Global media fell in love with Vallejo, with readers of the UK *Guardian* voting her Person of the Year in 2011. But much of the media coverage focused on her looks as much as her organizing prowess—the *New York Times* published a 2012 Vallejo profile with the headline, "The World's Most Glamorous Revolutionary."

Vallejo eventually made her peace with the attention. "You have to recognize that beauty can be a hook," she told a reporter. "It can be a compliment, they come to listen to me because of my appearance, but then I explain the ideas."

By the time she made it to the National Congress of Chile, Vallejo was generally regarded as a key leader in Chilean politics. She parlayed that power into support of labor rights and has never given up her focus on education. She continues to fight to ensure free secondary education to Chilean teens, many of whom have no access to affordable schools.

Her presence has reverberated in the Chilean student movement. In 2018 feminist students shut down nearly every university in Chile, demanding better solutions for sexual harassment on campus and educational offerings that prioritized the academic contributions of women. Vallejo offered her full support to the protesters. "This is a feminist movement and in my eyes, revolutionary," she told the press.

The following year, after a price hike on subway tickets, many Chilean people decided they had had enough of the government's disregard for the working class. Starting in October 2019, some of the largest protests the country had ever seen erupted, with citizens calling for the resignation of Piñera and a replacement of Chile's Pinochet-era national constitution. Vallejo avidly supports the movement, using her platform to publicize the military police's abuse of demonstrators and denouncing the government's misdeeds against the Chilean working class.

## AWESOME ACHIEVEMENTS

- Vallejo's leadership strength also helped change the face of the FECH presidency. In the first eight years after her term, four women held the position.
- Omaha punk rock band Desaparecidos recorded a 2013 ode to Vallejo's fiery political passion, "Te Amo Camila Vallejo."

## QUOTABLES

"We realized the problem was bigger, the problem was structural."

"We don't want violence, our fight is not versus the police or to destroy commercial shops . . . our fight is to recover the right to education, on that we have been emphatic and clear."

"Today I am a feminist for the same reasons that I am a communist, because I believe (in) and want equality and emancipation for all."

"The youth has taken control . . . and revived and dignified politics."

# ELIZABETH WARREN

née Elizabeth Ann Herring (born 1949)

"I don't want happy face conclusions.
I want the truth."

Years in political office: 2013-present

Position: US senator from Massachusetts, 2013-present

Party affiliation: Democrat, 1996-present; Republican, before 1996

Hometown: Oklahoma City, Oklahoma

Top causes: childcare, home mortgage issues, bankruptcy issues, and parks and environment

# LIFE STORY

Oklahoma Dust Bowl survivors Pauline and Donald Jones Herring had three boys before their first girl, Elizabeth, was born. The future US senator's dad was a salesman, but when Elizabeth was a teenager, he had a heart attack, and with the sudden onset of medical bills and pay cuts, the family had to hustle to adjust financially. They lost their car, and Warren's mom took a minimum-wage job at Sears, on which they managed to scrape by. Given her personal history, perhaps it was no surprise that young Elizabeth would eventually become one of the United States' leading experts on the financial disasters that low- and middle-class families often face.

But her rise to office was still a long way off. Warren grew up in a time when, in her words, "she could become a nurse or she could become a teacher." After high school, Elizabeth earned a debate scholarship at George Washington University and, indeed, went off to be a teacher. She got married at nineteen, and at twenty-two had her first child—and eventual coauthor—Amelia.

Raising her first kid temporarily slowed down Warren's career, but two years later, she got into Rutgers University and started classes on Amelia's second birthday. It turned out, Warren loved law and respected its study as "an advanced degree in thinking." She became a well-known law professor, teaching at many universities throughout the country.

At this point in her life, Warren was a pretty conservative thinker. That shifted when she dove deeper into her chosen specialty, bankruptcy law. She took part in a massive research project in the early '80s for which she toured the country, talking to individuals who had filed for bankruptcy. She now admits that she went into the research looking to expose people who were gaming the system and costing taxpayers money. But she was surprised to discover that most of the people she spoke with were middle-class families who had hit rough times—they had gone through a death or a job loss and were often victims of predatory mortgage and credit card companies that profit off customers' debt.

Warren began to realize that she'd have to step outside the ivory tower of academia to tackle these problems, but she was hesitant to become a politician. Until, that is, she was appointed to the National Bankruptcy Review Commission, a federal organization that investigated bankruptcies until it shut down in 1997. She went on to become a top financial adviser for the federal government, and President Barack Obama named her special adviser for an important new agency to protect US residents from predatory behavior by banks.

With her indisputable expertise, Warren proved essential in setting up the Consumer Financial Protection Bureau, a federal agency that makes sure financial companies treat people fairly, but she was denied a leadership position. Some said that Obama thought the banking industry would block her appointment because she was such a known adversary of the financial industry. Warren got so frustrated that she decided to run for the Senate, her first foray into electoral politics. At sixty-three years old, she won, besting an incumbent Republican to take over the Massachusetts US Senate seat—a position once held by President John F. Kennedy.

# WHAT'S ON HER AGENDA

Warren was immediately appointed to the Senate Banking Committee and established herself as a formidable opponent to CEOs who valued their financial bottom line over the lives of US families. She did not hesitate to speak out against the decisions of more powerful politicians—even Obama and Hillary Clinton (page 22) had to deal with her public critiques when they sided with the banking industry on key issues.

Warren's profile has skyrocketed during her relatively brief political career, and she is considered one of the country's most progressive senators. Convinced that her understanding of the average American's financial realities belongs in the White House, she announced she would run for president in 2020. At first, in a move that some said would severely limit her campaign's finances, she vowed not to accept money or assistance from PACs or Super PACs, but in February 2020 she reversed that decision. After the early 2020 primaries, she decided to end her campaign.

For all of her accomplishments, Warren is no stranger to controversy. She claimed to be of Cherokee and Dakota ancestry—which more than a few people found dubious. In response, she doubled down, publishing DNA test results of her faint (1/64th to 1/1,024th) Native American heritage. Actual Native leaders were offended, explaining to Warren that DNA tests have little to do with tribal affiliation. She offered a formal apology to the Cherokee Nation in 2019 before announcing her campaign for the White House, though many Native spokespeople still consider her out of touch with their concerns.

Warren inspired one of the best-known feminist rallying cries of the decade in 2017 when Trump nominated Jeff Sessions to be attorney general. While she read a rather scathing 1986 letter by civil rights activist Coretta Scott King protesting Sessions, Senate majority leader Mitch McConnell rebuked her. "She had appeared to violate the rule," McConnell said. "She was warned. She was given an explanation. Nevertheless, she persisted." McConnell could hardly have expected that scores of women would find strength in that last sentence, adopting it as a motto for perseverance in the face of challenge.

## AWESOME ACHIEVEMENTS

- Warren is Massachusetts's first woman senator.
- She has published eleven books, including two she coauthored with her daughter, Amelia Warren Tyagi, on issues facing the US middle class.
- During her career as a law professor, Warren taught at the Universities of Texas, Houston, Michigan, and Pennsylvania, in addition to Harvard University.
- *Time* magazine named her one of the hundred most influential people in the world—thrice.

## QUOTABLES

"The constant tension in a democracy is that those with money will try to capture the government to turn it to their own purposes."

"The word's out: I'm a woman, and I'm going to have trouble backing off on that."

"Credit cards are like snakes: Handle 'em long enough, and one will bite you."

"My first choice is a strong consumer agency. My second choice is no agency at all and plenty of blood and teeth left on the floor."

"Millions of women have taken up 'Nevertheless, She Persisted' as their rallying cry because they know that together, we can make change. We know because we are doing it."

# MAXINE WATERS
née Maxine Moore Carr (born 1938)

## "Reclaiming my time."

Years in political office: 1976–present

Position: US representative from California, 1991–present;
California Assembly member, 1976–1990

Party affiliation: Democrat

Hometown: Kinloch, Missouri

Top causes: women's health, HIV/AIDS funding, fighting predatory lending
practices, and community development

# LIFE STORY

Maxine Moore Carr was born August 15, 1938, to Velma Lee Carr and Remus Moore
in Kinloch, an all-Black town outside of Saint Louis, Missouri. Her dad left the family
when Maxine was two, and Velma Carr became a single mother, raising Maxine as
the fifth of thirteen children. Young Maxine quickly noticed social injustices. Her first
job was busing tables at a restaurant in downtown Saint Louis that did not serve Black
people. She married her first husband, Edward Waters, right out of high school, and
they had two kids, Karen and Edward Jr., before moving to Los Angeles in 1961.

After divorcing her husband, Waters put herself through college, graduating with
a bachelor's degree in sociology from Los Angeles State College. She became deeply
involved with Watts, the LA neighborhood that had been made desperate by poorly
funded services, segregationist policies on buying houses, and the Los Angeles Police
Department's racially biased policing. The police force was led by Chief William
Parker, who was infamous for calling Black people "monkeys." Black people reported
facing police harassment for even being in the "wrong" neighborhood after dark. The
neighborhood exploded with what came to be known as the 1965 Watts Rebellion.

The rebellion arose when white police officers pulled over two Black brothers,
Marquette and Ronald Frye, who were driving their mother's car. A crowd gathered as
Marquette failed a sobriety test, and he panicked, resisting arrest. The police put the
men and their stepmother—who had arrived on the scene and moved to protect them
from the police—into cop cars. The incensed neighbors, all too familiar with LAPD's
racially motivated policing, launched a spontaneous protest that would intensify into
a six-day conflict pitting the Black community against riot police. Thirty-four people
died, over one thousand were injured, and $40 million in property damage occurred.

It was in the aftermath of the Watts Rebellion that Waters first entered into
community service as an assistant teacher for Head Start, a national program that

works with low-income families to make sure that their young children have access to the classes, nutrition, and support they need. Waters helped organize Head Start parents to lobby their local politicians to demand more federal funds for the program. The work led her to consider politics as a job, eventually becoming chief deputy to a Los Angeles city councilperson.

In 1976 she won her first election to the California Assembly, where she would represent South Central Los Angeles and its surrounding suburbs for fourteen years. She attributes the win to her team's offbeat election tactics, which included mailing out seed packets for people's gardens with her campaign literature! Waters made a name for herself as a fierce advocate for communities of color, passing legislation that limited the police's ability to conduct strip searches, bolstered tenants' rights, and barred the government from supporting businesses with links to South Africa (which was being run as an apartheid system that stratified society based on race).

She also became a major force in the growing women's movement of the 1970s. Waters joined with powerful activists such as Bella Abzug, Gloria Steinem, and Patsy Mink at the National Women's Conference. Steinem invited Waters to serve on the board of the Ms. Foundation, a nonprofit related to Steinem's seminal feminist publication, Ms. The foundation was an early funder of domestic abuse shelters and created Take Our Daughters to Work Day in 1993.

Waters lives in the Vermont Knolls neighborhood of Los Angeles with her second husband, Sidney Williams, a former linebacker for the NFL and US ambassador to the Bahamas under the Clinton administration. Auntie Maxine, as she is fondly known by many of her constituents and fans, says her favorite rapper is Tupac Shakur.

# WHAT'S ON HER AGENDA

In 1990 Waters won her first election to the US House, and she continues to serve there, still immensely popular in her district. In 2018 she won her fifteenth congressional election with the support of 77 percent of her district's voters. The legislator has become one of the Democratic Party's most notorious leaders because of her uncompromising progressive values and blunt language. In 2011 Waters delighted followers and irked conservatives when she said the far-right Tea Party group could go "straight to hell." In 2018, when it came to light that the US government had been separating immigrant children from their parents when they were detained after crossing the US-Mexico border, Waters took Trump, the forty-fifth US president, and his "America first" administration policies to task. "Today I say impeach 45," she proclaimed.

Waters became one of Trump's most outspoken adversaries. She declined to attend his inauguration or his first State of the Union address in protest of his policies. Sometimes she refused to even be in the same room with him. Sharp-tongued Auntie

Maxine often vocalizes the thoughts of Trump's critics. She made headlines when she deployed the now-notorious one-liner "reclaiming my time" in response to one of the president's officials, who didn't respond to her questions about the administration's ties with the Russian government. The phrase is actually straight out of the House's procedural rule book, but Waters's stone-faced delivery immortalized the words.

Her political career has had its share of scandals. The *LA Times* published a 2004 article accusing her of using politics to fill the pockets of her family members, and in 2008 she set up meetings with the US Treasury Department and representatives of a bank at which her husband was a stockholder and former director. A House Ethics Committee investigation determined that no wrongdoing had occurred, and Waters was eventually cleared of all charges in the bank debacle.

In 2019 she was appointed to lead the House Financial Services Committee, which has immense influence over the country's economy. Waters has announced her determination to tighten Washington's oversight of the big business owners of Wall Street and use her position to investigate alleged corruption in the Trump administration.

## AWESOME ACHIEVEMENTS

- Waters was an advocate for hip-hop artists in the 1990s, calling them "poets" when many politicians wanted to censor their lyrics about life in underprivileged neighborhoods.
- She's the first Black person and woman to head the House Financial Services Committee, which oversees Wall Street, the Federal Reserve, the World Bank, and the US Treasury.
- She was a staunch voice against the Iraq War from its beginning and in 2005 created the Out of Iraq Caucus.
- In 2018 *Time* magazine honored Waters as one of the world's one hundred most influential people.

## QUOTABLES

"We have to keep to doing what we're doing in order to make this country right. That's what I intend to do, and as the young people say, 'I ain't scared.'"

"We should have hope because we've earned it. We've worked for it! It's ours."

"My spirit tells me I cannot be silent."

"I will work with those on the opposite side of the aisle who want to work on issues that we are alluding to. But, of course, if they don't, I have the gavel."

"I don't honor this president. I don't respect this president. And I'm not joyful in the presence of this president."

*Maxine Waters*

# GRETCHEN WHITMER
## (born 1971)

### "Schools are supposed to be the thing that levels the playing field."

**Years in political office:** 2001–2016; 2019–present

**Position:** governor of Michigan, 2019–present; Ingham County prosecutor, 2016; minority leader of Michigan Senate, 2011–2015; member of Michigan Senate, 2006–2015; member of Michigan House of Representatives, 2001–2006

**Party affiliation:** Democrat

**Hometown:** Lansing, Michigan

**Top causes:** road maintenance, reproductive rights, and pandemic response

# LIFE STORY

Gretchen Whitmer was born to a pair of Michigan political insiders. Her Democratic mom was an assistant state attorney general, and her Republican dad was the CEO of a major health insurance company. Politics weren't of much interest for their oldest daughter until Whitmer's junior year at Michigan State University, when her father encouraged her to get an internship at the Michigan State Capitol.

While she worked with Democratic state representative Curtis Hertel that semester, something clicked in Whitmer's head about the importance of electoral politics. From then on, her life would be driven by the endless networking and policy work of the political world. She ran for president of her sorority, Kappa Alpha Theta; studied from a mountain of law books; and worked at a series of unpaid gigs with local political campaigns before graduating from law school and practicing as an attorney.

At the age of twenty-nine, she ran for Michigan's House of Representatives. Hertel's son Curtis Jr. was thinking about running in that first election, but Whitmer managed to convince him—within the first five minutes of their conversation, according to him—that she was the better candidate for the job. With the help of her family's network, Whitmer was also preternaturally skilled in raising campaign funds. She drummed up triple the amount of the leading candidate, helping to make their competitive primary the most expensive race for the chamber in state history. Her fundraising paid off: she won by 281 votes.

Whitmer served as a state representative for five years, building a reputation as a rising power player. Somehow she found time to give birth to her first child and coordinate health care for her mother, who was diagnosed with and eventually died from brain cancer. In 2006 Whitmer was elected to the state senate. She briefly explored running for state attorney general before opting instead to become senate minority leader in 2011. Republicans outnumbered Democrats two to one that year, so Whitmer had little hope for pushing through legislative changes. She focused on providing inspired, if oftentimes symbolic, resistance through compelling speeches. An impassioned 2013 defense of unions in the face of a proposed anti-labor bill became one of her most memorable speaking events.

Whitmer's constituents will not soon forget her words when the senate debated legislation that would require people to buy separate insurance to cover abortions, even if the pregnancy had resulted from incest or rape. In front of the overwhelmingly male senate, Whitmer told her story of being raped twenty years earlier. She said thoughts of her two daughters going through a similar experience kept her up at night. "I can't imagine [them] going through what I went through, then having to consider what to do about an unwanted pregnancy from an attacker," she said. "It's something I've hidden for a long time. But I think you need to see the face of the women you are impacting by this vote today." Despite her speech, the bill passed. Whitmer says what buoyed her through was the unexpected support people sent her from across the country.

After serving the maximum number of terms in the Michigan Senate, Whitmer spent a few years practicing law and married a Republican dentist, an echo of the bipartisan union of her parents. But she was far from done with public office. She declared herself a candidate twenty months before the 2018 Michigan gubernatorial race, running on the straightforward infrastructure improvement platform of "Fix the Damn Roads," and outmaneuvered two progressive opponents in the Democratic primary. She won the general election with 53 percent of the vote, 10 percent ahead of the Republican candidate.

# WHAT'S ON HER AGENDA

Being a Democratic governor in a state where Republicans control the legislature was hardly easier than being a Democratic legislator under the same circumstances. Early in Whitmer's time in the governor's office, she highlighted her ability to work across the aisle, passing a controversial set of changes to the state's car insurance system that Republican leaders had pushed for. She also passed legislation that forwarded her increasingly progressive agenda, including a law that prevented seventeen-year-olds from being tried as adults in criminal courts.

By the beginning of 2020, she was intent on delivering on her gubernatorial campaign's promise of improving the state's roads. Having failed to get an infrastructure plan that would have depended on a hefty gas tax passed by legislators, Whitmer announced that she would issue a $3.5 billion construction bond, a power allotted to Michigan governors even without approval from other branches of the government. She was going to get creative to make sure that an opposition-led Michigan Senate and House of Representatives didn't prevent her from making the big changes she'd promised during the election.

All other matters sank to secondary importance when the global COVID-19 crisis came to Michigan in March 2020. As in many other states, COVID-19 disproportionately impacted Black communities in Michigan, which were often in dense cities and comprised many essential workers. Whitmer swung into action, shuttering schools and businesses to flatten the curve of infection before the state had seen its first death from the virus. By mid-April, Michigan had the country's third-highest number of fatalities. As the state's death toll rose, Whitmer became an outspoken critic of the federal response to the pandemic, saying that she was unable to get the supplies her state needed from national stockpiles. President Trump responded by calling her "Gretchen 'Half' Whitmer," or "halfwit," when he referred to her by name. In another press conference, Whitmer became merely "the woman from Michigan" in the president's mounting criticism of Democrat governors who had been critical of his administration's response to the pandemic.

Headlines about her friction with Trump powered a wave of national admiration for Whitmer's COVID-19 response. Then Democratic presidential hopeful Joe Biden admitted he was considering Whitmer as a potential running mate. Trump had narrowly won Michigan during his first presidential election in 2016, and Biden potentially partnering with the state's popular governor would have been a good strategy for flipping the state blue in 2020.

## AWESOME ACHIEVEMENTS

- Whitmer was the second woman to be governor of the Great Lakes State.
- When she became the minority leader of the Michigan Senate, she was the first woman to hold such a leadership position in the chamber.
- As Michiganians saw a rise in lung-related injuries associated with tobacco and marijuana vaporizers in the fall of 2019, Whitmer became the country's first governor to issue a ban against flavored tobacco products.

## QUOTABLES

"If we're successful (in combating the coronavirus), people will never fully appreciate how many lives we saved."

"I was always in the minority. I was the leader of the resistance. The whole damn time."

"A woman's health care, her whole future, her ability to decide if and when she starts a family is not an election. It is a fundamental to her life. It is life sustaining and it's something that government should not be getting in the middle of."

Gretchen Whitmer

# SAHLE-WORK ZEWDE

**(born 1950)**

"I am a product of people who fought for equality and political freedom in this country, and I will work hard to serve them."

Years in political office: 1989-present

Position: president of Ethiopia, 2018-present; under-secretary-general of the United Nations to the African Union, 2018; director-general of the United Nations Nairobi office, 2011-2018; ambassador to France, 2002-2006; ambassador to Djibouti, 1993-2002; ambassador to Senegal, 1989-1993

Party affiliation: independent

Hometown: Addis Ababa, Ethiopia

Top causes: women's empowerment, peace and security, and international relations

# LIFE STORY

Sahle-Work Zewde is the oldest of four daughters born to parents who believed in the power of women's education, despite widespread patriarchal views in Ethiopia at the time. Her family sent her to France to study science at the University of Montpellier, and she lived there for nine years. When Sahle-Work returned to Ethiopia, the second most populous nation in Africa, she began to work for the government in the ministries of education and foreign affairs.

Sahle-Work became Ethiopia's second-ever woman ambassador when she was appointed as Ethiopia's liaison to Senegal in 1989. She worked in embassies for seventeen years, mainly with Ethiopia's neighboring nation Djibouti and, later on, in France. She was so successful in those roles that she became Ethiopia's representative to the UN's Educational, Scientific and Cultural Organization (UNESCO) and then to the Economic Commission for Africa (ECA). In 2018 Portuguese UN secretary-general António Guterres appointed her to the United Nations' third most powerful office, under-secretary-general and special representative to the African Union.

Through the positions she held, Sahle-Work became an important voice internationally for Ethiopia, which was constantly plagued with threats to its national stability.

Sahle-Work Zewde

The country and its neighbor Eritrea had had an antagonistic relationship since a controversial World War II-era UN decision to form a federation between the two very different nations. In 1998 Ethiopia deported seventy-five thousand of its ethnic Eritrean residents, which was declared a human rights disaster. By the twenty-first century, Ethiopia was home to over ninety ethnic groups that often had violent conflicts with one another under the country's long-standing authoritarian rule, which blatantly repressed political opposition.

# WHAT'S ON HER AGENDA

Times would change in 2018, when Abiy Ahmed was appointed prime minister of Ethiopia. He pledged to work toward democracy and open the door to political debate. He officially ended the state of war with Eritrea, invited its Eritrean exiles back into the country, and worked to reform the government. These dramatic changes were widely seen as positive steps toward improving civil rights in the country. But liberating political prisoners, allowing opposition parties, and taking steps to repartition land between ethnic groups unleashed new political frictions that led to a failed coup attempt and rash of political assassinations in 2019.

One of Ahmed's goals was to ensure that the Ethiopian government had a higher level of gender equality. The tactic drew a clear line between his and past administrations that did not prioritize women's leadership. Inclusion is not just a political tactic. Studies show that women's voices are a key element in maintaining governmental stability. The International Peace Institute once studied 182 peace agreements signed between 1989 and 2011. When women were included in the treaties, the probability that peace would prevail for fifteen years or longer increased by 35 percent! Shortly after he was elected, Ahmed presented a cabinet composed of equal parts men and women.

To cap off the dramatic changes, Ahmed announced the appointment of Sahle-Work as the country's new president for a six-year term. Though she is Ethiopia's first woman president, Sahle-Work is not the country's first woman leader. Zewditu, the first woman in Africa to rule an internationally recognized country, reigned as Ethiopia's empress from 1916 to 1930.

In Ethiopia the prime minister and not the president is the country's top executive. The 1995 Ethiopian Constitution says that Sahle-Work's duties as president include hiring ambassadors (at which she should be very capable, considering her background), granting pardons, welcoming foreign dignitaries, authorizing foreign treaties alongside the lower chamber of parliament, and opening parliamentary sessions. But though Sahle-Work's other professional responsibilities can be largely ceremonial, she is an important symbol for the country's future. As the prime minister's chief of staff, Fitsum Arega, said upon her appointment, "In a patriarchal society such as ours, the appointment of a female head of state not only sets the standard for the future but also normalizes women as decision-makers in public life."

Sahle-Work has her work cut out for her in maintaining equilibrium among all Ethiopia's various factions. In her first presidential address to parliament, she focused on women's empowerment and its role in maintaining national stability. "I urge you all to uphold our peace in the name of a mother, who is the first to suffer from the absence of peace," she told her fellow Ethiopians.

## AWESOME ACHIEVEMENTS

- Sahle-Work speaks three languages: French, English, and Amharic, Ethiopia's official language.
- Her appointment as president made her the only female head of state currently serving in Africa.
- In 2018 Forbes named her to its list of the World's 100 Most Powerful Women.

## QUOTABLES

"Service is my passion, especially serving a country and serving a cause. I have been a civil servant all my life and public service has been the core of my life."

"If the current change in Ethiopia is headed equally by both men and women, it can sustain its momentum and realize a prosperous Ethiopia free of religious, ethnic and gender discrimination."

"In mission trips and delegates meetings, I take others with me and give them the opportunity to interact with others, answer questions and allow them to experience diplomacy both by observing as well as acting. I allow them to fail and rise. Delegation is my way of enabling people."

"If you thought I spoke a lot about women already, know that I am just getting started."

# SOURCE NOTES

**Stacey Abrams**

10   K. K. Ottesen, "Stacey Abrams: Being a Black Woman in Politics Isn't 'Some Fatal Diagnosis,'" *Washington Post*, May 14, 2019, https://www.washingtonpost.com/lifestyle/magazine/stacey-abrams-being-a-black-woman -in-politics-isnt-some-fatal-diagnosis/2019/05/10/f8027e16-5fc6-11e9-9412-daf3d2e67c6d_story.html.

12   Jim Galloway, "Stacey Abrams: 'I Will Not Concede Because the Erosion of Our Democracy Is Not Right,'" *Atlanta Journal-Constitution*, November 16, 2018, https://www.ajc.com/blog/politics/stacey-abrams-will-not -concede-because-the-erosion-our-democracy-not-right/JQqttbuF09NYkMQbIYx9BM/.

13   "Stacey Abrams on 2020: You Don't Run for Second Place," CNN, accessed June 15, 2019, https://www.cnn .com/videos/politics/2019/03/27/stacey-abrams-2020-zeleny-dnt-vpx.cnn.

13   Astead W. Herndon, "Stacey Abrams Says She's Open to Being Vice President for Any Democratic Nominee," *New York Times*, August 14, 2019, https://www.nytimes.com/2019/08/14/us/politics/stacey-abrams-vice -president.html.

13   Ottesen, "Stacey Abrams."

13   Stacey Abrams, "Full Speech: Stacey Abrams Ends Candidacy for Georgia Governor," YouTube video, 12:01, posted by NBC News, November 16, 2018, 4:43, https://www.youtube.com/watch?v=G1YXTP7u8Ds/.

13   Abrams, 3:34.

13   Lucia Graces, "Meet the Democrat Who Wants to Be America's First Black Female Governor," *Guardian* (US edition), May 3, 2017, https://www.theguardian.com/us-news/2017/may/03/stacey-abrams-governor -georgia-democrat/.


**Jacinda Ardern**

14   Jacinda Ardern, "Jacinda Ardern: 'It Takes Strength to Be an Empathetic Leader,'" BBC video, 2:02, November 14, 2018, 0:01, https://www.bbc.com/news/av/world-asia-46207254/jacinda-ardern-it-takes-strength-to-be-an -empathetic-leader/.

15   Derek Flynn, "Jacinda Ardern a 'Pretty Little Thing,' Would 'Look Good' as PM—Graham Lowe," Stuff, August 26, 2015, https://www.stuff.co.nz/national/politics/71471800/.

16   Jacinda Ardern (@jacindaardern), "@Hilary Barry and for this, I thank you Hilary. I hope your shoes were pointy," Twitter, August 25, 2015, 1:37 p.m., https://twitter.com/jacindaardern/status/636276238844235776/.

16   Jacinda Ardern, "Jacinda Ardern's Speech at Christchurch Memorial—Full Transcript," *Guardian* (London), March 28, 2019, 4:31, https://www.theguardian.com/world/2019/mar/29/jacinda-arderns-speech-at -christchurch-memorial-full-transcript/.

17   Amelia Lester, "The Roots of Jacinda Ardern's Extraordinary Leadership after Christchurch," *New Yorker*, March 23, 2019, https://www.newyorker.com/culture/culture-desk/what-jacinda-arderns-leadership-means-to -new-zealand-and-to-the-world/.

17   Eleanor Ainge Roy, "Ardern's First Year: New Zealand Grapples with Hangover from Jacindamania," *Guardian* (London), October 21, 2018, https://www.theguardian.com/world/2018/oct/21/jacinda-ardern-first-year-new -zealand-grapples-with-jacindamania-hangover/.

17   Lester, "Roots of Jacinda Ardern's Leadership."

17   Toby Manhire, "Jacinda Ardern: 'Very Little of What I Have Done Has Been Deliberate. It's Intuitive,'" *Guardian* (London), April 6, 2019, https://www.theguardian.com/world/2019/apr/06/jacinda-ardern-intuitive -courage-new-zealand/.

17   Eleanor Ainge Roy, "Jacinda Ardern: New Zealand Prime Minister Announces First Pregnancy," posted by Guardian News, 1:47, January 18, 2018, 1:10, https://www.youtube.com/watch?v=-q7Do7aOViE/.


**Elaine Chao**

18   Elaine Chao, "Interview with Elaine L. Chao (part 1)," YouTube video, 12:25, posted by National Committee of Asian American Republicans, November 30, 2016, 0:43, https://www.youtube.com/watch?v=tL6rtQ3KfoU/.

19   Chao, 3:13.

19   Chao, 4:14.

19   K. K. Ottesen, "Elaine Chao Explains Why She Doesn't See Herself as a Washington Insider," *Washington Post*, January 29, 2019, https://www.washingtonpost.com/lifestyle/magazine/elaine-chao-explains-why-she-doesnt -see-herself-as-a-washington-insider/2019/01/25/0cf6892e-0edd-11e9-831f-3aa2c2be4cbd_story.html.

19   Elaine Chao, interviewed by Dana Bash, "Elaine Chao: From Immigrant Roots to a President's C . . .," YouTube video, 6:29, posted by CNN, June 5, 2017, 3:03, https://www.youtube.com/watch?v=xnetM2NZBu8/.

19   Chao, 3:37

19   Chao, 5:11.

20   Michael Forsythe et al., "A 'Bridge' to China, and Her Family's Business, in the Trump Cabinet," *New York Times*, June 2, 2019, https://www.nytimes.com/2019/06/02/us/politics/elaine-chao-china.html.

20   Forsythe et al.

20   Chao, "Interview with Elaine L. Chao," 6:21.

21   Forsythe et al., "A 'Bridge' to China."

21   Chao, "Interview with Elaine L. Chao," 0:01.

21   Chao, 0:25.

21   Chao, 6:10.

## Hillary Clinton

22   Hillary Rodham Clinton, "Excerpt from Remarks to the UN 4th World Conference on Women Plenary Session, delivered September 5, 1995, Beijing, China," in *Reproduction and Society: Interdisciplinary Readings*, ed. Carole Joffe and Jennifer Reich (New York: Routledge, Taylor & Francis, 2015).

23   "Vast Right Wing Conspiracy," Hillary Rodham Clinton, interview by Matt Lauer, aired January 1998, YouTube video, 0:20, posted by Who2TV, January 27, 2010, 0:11, https://www.youtube.com/watch?v=EwtkorQKGFE/.

24   Evan Halper, "Clinton: Trump Is Blaming the System Again by Refusing to Say He'll Accept Election Results," *Los Angeles Times*, October 20, 2016, https://www.latimes.com/nation/politics/trailguide/la-na -trailguide-third-presidential-trump-calls-clinton-such-a-nasty-1476931080-htmlstory.html.

24   Alex Ward, "Trump Rally Crowd Chants 'Lock Her Up' as Trump Ignores Manafort and Cohen," Vox, August 21, 2018, https://www.vox.com/2018/8/21/17766468/trump-rally-manafort-cohen-clinton-lock-her-up-west-virginia/.

25   "Hillary Clinton: 'Women Rights Are Human Rights,'" YouTube video, 1:40, posted by MSNBC, February 19, 2016, 0:18, https://www.youtube.com/watch?v=MXU5wGX3yUs/.

25   "Clinton Resigns as US Secretary of State," Al Jazeera, February 1, 2013, https://www.aljazeera.com/news /americas/2013/02/201321201935419574.html.

25   Eleanor Clift, "Hillary Then and Now," *Newsweek*, July 19, 1992, https://www.newsweek.com/hillary-then -and-now-200208.

25   Katie Reilly, "Read Hillary Clinton's Historic Victory Speech as Presumptive Democratic Nominee," *Time*, June 8, 2016, http://time.com/4361099/hillary-clinton-nominee-speech-transcript/.

## Tatiana Clouthier

26   Karla Zabludovsky, "Meet the Woman Running the Show for Mexico's Likely Next President," BuzzFeed, April 24, 2018, https://www.buzzfeednews.com/article/karlazabludovsky/tatiana-clouthier-amlo-mexico-election/.

28   K. Frankel and C. Sabatini, "An Interview with Tatiana Clouthier, Congresswoman and Former Campaign Manager for President AMLO," audio podcast episode, in *Two Gringos with Questions*, Global Americans and the Canadian Council for the Americas, March 22, 2019, 10:04, https://open.spotify.com/episode/3SbQ0cLrE f8Jn4cvOiOh8k?si=rUE8U1zBTfCCjBk_5g-jjg/.

28   Frankel and Sabatini, 58:08.

29   Nacha Cattan, "Mexico's AMLO Will Work to Calm Markets: Campaign Chief," Bloomberg, November 9, 2018, https://www.bloomberg.com/news/articles/2018-11-09/mexico-s-amlo-will-work-to-calm-markets-campaign-chief/.

29   "5 Revelations of Tatiana Clouthier's Interview with the Magazine 'Who,'" Nacion321, December 28, 2018, https://www.nacion321.com/gobierno/5-revelaciones-de-la-entrevista-de-tatiana-clouthier-a-la-revista-quien/.

29   Zabludovsky, "Meet the Woman."

29   Frankel and Sabatini, "An Interview," 58:15.

29   Tatiana Clouthier (@tatclouthier), "Estefanía, tengo que reconocer que fue un error. Sobre los espacios de trabajo me refería a que sí, las mujeres ya tenemos participación, sin embargo, como mencionas, hace falta mucho camino por recorrer hacia la paridad. Estoy abierta a aprender de ti y de todas, mujeres unidas," Twitter, April 26, 2018, 11:54 a.m., https://twitter.com/tatclouthier/status/989578411512422405/.

**Susan Collins**

30  Susan Collins, *Our Children Are Watching: Ten Skills for Leading the Next Generation to Success* (Barrytown, NY: Station Hill, 1996), 59.

32  Matthew Kacsmaryk, "The Inequality Act: Weaponizing Same-Sex Marriage," Public Discourse, September 4, 2015, https://www.thepublicdiscourse.com/2015/09/15612/.

33  Nikki Schwab, "Women Senators Awarded for Getting Stuff Done," *U.S. News*, February 27, 2014, https://www.usnews.com/news/blogs/washington-whispers/2014/02/27/women-senators-awarded-for-getting-stuff-done/.

33  Collins, *Our Children*, 59.

33  Collins, 192.

33  "Senator Collins Completes Another Congress with a Perfect Consecutive Roll Call Vote Record," press release, Senator Susan Collins, January 3, 2019, https://www.collins.senate.gov/newsroom/senator-collins-completes-another-congress-perfect-consecutive-roll-call-vote-record/.


**Historic Heavyweights**

34  "ABZUG, Bella Savitzky," US House of Representatives: History, Art & Archives, accessed June 20, 2019, https://history.house.gov/People/Detail/8276/.

35  "Quotes from Ann Richards," *New York Times*, September 14, 2006, https://www.nytimes.com/2006/09/14/us/richards_quotes.html.

35  Ann Richards, "Inaugural Address," Legislative Reference Library of Texas, January 15, 1991, https://lrl.texas.gov/scanned/govdocs/Ann%20W%20Richards/1991/IA_Richards_1.15.91.pdf.


**Carmen Yulín Cruz Soto**

36  NBC News (@NBC News), "San Juan mayor: 'I cannot fathom the thought . . . ,'" Twitter, September 29, 2017, 2:02 p.m., https://twitter.com/NBCNews/status/913871652768878592/.

38  Amanda Holpuch, "San Juan Mayor's Harrowing Plea: 'Mr Trump, I Am Begging. We Are Dying Here,'" *Guardian* (London), September 29, 2017, https://www.theguardian.com/world/2017/sep/29/san-juan-mayor-plea-donald-trump-puerto-rico/.

39  "Carmen Yulín Cruz Stands with Protestors amidst Ricardo Rosselló Scandal," *NowThis News*, July 22, 2019, https://nowthisnews.com/videos/politics/carmen-yulin-cruz-stands-with-ricardo-rossello-protestors/.

39  Morgan Pehme and Gerson Borrero, "A Q&A with Carmen Yulín Cruz Soto," *City & State Magazine*, SOMOS Special Issue, November 5, 2014, 36, https://issuu.com/cityandstate/docs/cs_10282014_all_b379689e4cb413/.

39  Lauren Gambino, "Carmen Yulín Cruz, Six Months after Hurricane Maria: 'I Did What Had to Be Done,'" *Guardian* (London), March 21, 2018, https://www.theguardian.com/world/2018/mar/21/hurricane-maria-storm-san-juan-mayor-carmen-yulin-cruz-all-changed/.

39  Pehme and Borrero, "A Q&A with Carmen Yulín Cruz Soto."

39  Gambino, "Carmen Yulín Cruz."


**Sharice Davids**

40  Lindsay Wise, "Kansan Sharice Davids Gets Boost from National Democratic 'Red to Blue' Program," *Kansas City Star*, August 10, 2018, https://www.kansascity.com/news/politics-government/article216296940.html.

41  Isaac Stanley-Becker, "Sharice Davids, Who Sees Past Discrimination as Her Asset, Could Become the First Gay Native American in Congress," *Washington Post*, August 14, 2018, https://www.washingtonpost.com/news/morning-mix/wp/2018/08/14/sharice-davids-who-sees-past-discrimination-as-her-asset-could-become-the-first-gay-native-american-in-congress/.

42  Associated Press, "GOP Official out after 'Reservation' Quip about 'Lesbian Indian' Democrat," NBC News, October 10, 2018, https://www.nbcnews.com/feature/nbc-out/gop-official-slammed-saying-lesbian-indian-democrat-be-sent-back-n918786/.

42  Karim Zidan, "How Sharice Davids Traded in MMA for a Shot at Political History," *Guardian* (US edition), August 6, 2018, https://www.theguardian.com/sport/2018/aug/06/sharice-evans-us-congress-mixed-martial-arts/.

42  "Live from Rep. Sharice Davids' town hall at St. Andrew Christian Church in Olathe," Facebook, posted by *Shawnee Mission Post*, 59:36, March 24, 2019, https://www.facebook.com/shawneemissionpost/videos/2225135291034731/.

43  Matt Remle, "Hoka! Coffee Company: Indigenous from the Ground to the Cup," LRInspire, August 26, 2014, https://lrinspire.com/2014/08/26/hoka-coffee-company-indigenous-from-the-ground-to-the-cup-by-matt-remle/.

43  Emily Davies, "Ex-MMA Fighter Sharice Davids Could Become the First Lesbian Native American Congresswoman," *People*, August 9, 2018, https://people.com/politics/sharice-davids-first-lesbian-native-american-congresswoman/.

43  Sharice Davids, "Democrat Sharice Davids Wins Kansas' 3rd Congressional District," YouTube video, 5:15, posted by *Kansas City Star*, November 7, 2018, 3:48, https://www.youtube.com/watch?v=EpSNgoBEBMM/.

43  Wise, "Kansan Sharice Davids Gets Boost."

**Wendy Davis**

44  Amy Davidson Sorkin, "What Wendy Davis Stood For," *New Yorker*, June 26, 2013, https://www.newyorker.com/news/amy-davidson/what-wendy-davis-stood-for/.

45  Robert Draper, "Can Wendy Davis Have It All?," *New York Times Magazine*, February 12, 2014, https://www.nytimes.com/2014/02/16/magazine/wendy-davis.html.

45  Jay Root, "Spotlight on Wendy Davis, the Democrats' Big Hope," *New York Times*, August 31, 2013, https://www.nytimes.com/2013/09/01/us/spotlight-on-wendy-davis-the-democrats-big-hope.html.

46  "Wendy Davis Tells of Her Own Difficult Abortions in 'Forgetting,'" NPR, September 13, 2014, https://www.npr.org/2014/09/13/347958028/wendy-davis-tells-of-her-own-difficult-abortions-in-forgetting/.

46  Lauren Kelley, "Wendy Davis on Abortion-Rights Win and Why Women Should Fear Trump," *Rolling Stone*, June 27, 2016, https://www.rollingstone.com/politics/politics-news/wendy-davis-on-abortion-rights-win-and-why-women-should-fear-trump-87189/.

47  "Wendy Davis Tells of Her Own Difficult Abortions," NPR.

47  Kelley, "Wendy Davis on Abortion-Rights Win."

47  Pam LeBlanc, "Wendy Davis Launches Deeds Not Words to Spur Young Women to Activism," *Austin American-Statesman*, September 25, 2018, https://www.statesman.com/NEWS/20160903/Wendy-Davis-launches-Deeds-Not-Words-to-spur-young-women-to-activism/.

47  Emily Ramshaw, "A Filibuster Creates an Overnight Celebrity," *New York Times*, June 4, 2011, https://www.nytimes.com/2011/06/05/us/05ttdavis.html.

**Leila de Lima**

48  FP staff, "A Message from Philippine Sen. Leila de Lima," *Foreign Policy*, December 5, 2017, https://foreignpolicy.com/2017/12/05/a-message-from-philippine-senator-leila-de-lima/.

49  Rishi Iyengar, "The Killing Time: Inside Philippine President Rodrigo Duterte's War on Drugs," *Time*, August 25, 2016, https://time.com/4462352/rodrigo-duterte-drug-war-drugs-philippines-killing/.

50  Nash Jenkins, "The Fighter: How Leila de Lima Ended Up Leading the Opposition to Rodrigo Duterte's Drug War," *Time*, December 15, 2016, http://time.com/4603123/leila-de-lima-philippines-opposition-duterte-drug-war/.

51  Leila de Lima, "Dispatch from Crame No. 186," Facebook, October 19, 2019, https://www.facebook.com/leiladelimaofficial/posts/dispatch-from-crame-no-186101917just-a-reflection-my-consolation-is-that-im-livi/2062219160675295/.

51  "Sen. Leila M. de Lima's Statement on her arrest," Facebook, posted by Leila de Lima, 10:53, February 23, 2017, 10:43, https://www.facebook.com/leiladelimaofficial/videos/vb.1658419084388640/1938091426421403/.

51  Leila De Lima, "#EveryWoman: A call to protect human rights and uphold democratic principles," Facebook, October 5, 2016, https://www.facebook.com/notes/leila-de-lima/everywoman-a-call-to-protect-human-rights-and-uphold-democratic-principles/1858362134394333/.

51  Senate of the Philippines, "Sen. Leila de Lima's statement . . . ," Facebook, February 26, 2018, https://www.facebook.com/senateph/posts/sen-leila-de-limas-statement-on-the-presidential-spokespersons-claim-that-she-is/1796127107078229/.

**Betsy DeVos**

52  Tim Alberta, "The Education of Betsy DeVos," Politico, December 2017, https://www.politico.com/magazine/story/2017/11/01/betsy-devos-secretary-education-profile-2017-215768/.

53  Jay Nordlinger, "A Matter of Fairness," *National Review*, November 13, 2018, https://www.nationalreview.com/2018/11/betsy-devos-education-secretary-matter-of-fairness/.

53  Betsy DeVos, "Soft Money Is Good: 'Hard-Earned American Dollars That Big Brother Has Yet to Find a Way to Control,'" *Roll Call*, September 7, 1997, https://devosprize.wordpress.com/2009/08/28/soft-money-is-good-hard-earned-american-dollars-that-big-brother-has-yet-to-find-a-way-to-control/.

54    Betsy DeVos, "Guns in School Protect against Grizzly Bears," YouTube video, 0:33, posted by Business Insider, January 18, 2017, https://www.youtube.com/watch?v=e3xBGq3bvcQ/.

54    Alberta, "Education."

55    Erica L. Green, "To Understand Betsy DeVos's Educational Views, View Her Education," *New York Times*, June 10, 2017, https://www.nytimes.com/2017/06/10/us/politics/betsy-devos-private-schools-choice.html.

55    Betsy DeVos, "Prepared Remarks by Secretary DeVos at the Education Writers Association 72nd National Seminar," US Department of Education, May 6, 2019, https://www.ed.gov/news/speeches/prepared-remarks -secretary-devos-education-writers-association-72nd-national-seminar/.

55    DeVos.

## Maria Elena Durazo

56    Jennifer Medina, "Immigrant Workers Give New Direction to Los Angeles Unions," *New York Times*, May 17, 2013, https://www.nytimes.com/2013/05/18/us/los-angeles-labor-leader-puts-focus-on-immigrants.html.

57    Patt Morrison, "Maria Elena Durazo: Labor of Love," *Los Angeles Times*, September 5, 2009, https://www .latimes.com/la-oe-morrison5-2009sep05-column.html.

57    Morrison.

58    Christopher Cadelago, "Key Labor Leader Maria Elena Durazo to Run for Kevin de León's Senate Seat," *Sacramento Bee*, April 6, 2017, https://www.sacbee.com/news/politics-government/capitol-alert /article143093544.html.

59    Medina, "Immigrant Workers."

59    Bobbi Murray, "Conversations on Trump's America: The Coming Immigration Wars," Capital & Main, November 30, 2016, https://capitalandmain.com/conversations-on-trumps-america-the-coming-immigration-wars-1130/.

59    Eric A. Gordon, "Labor's Maria Elena Durazo on the Ballot for California State Senate," *People's World*, May 10, 2018, https://www.peoplesworld.org/article/labors-maria-elena-durazo-on-the-ballot-for-california-state-senate/.

## Dianne Feinstein

60    Robert Reinhold, "California Race Is Becoming Symbolic for Women," *New York Times*, June 4, 1990, https:// www.nytimes.com/1990/06/04/us/california-race-is-becoming-symbolic-for-women.html.

61    Dianne Feinstein, "Special Episode: The Last 'Year of the Woman,'" August 25, 2018, in *Daily*, produced by Annie Brown and Jessica Cheung, podcast, 27:07, https://www.nytimes.com/2018/08/25/podcasts/the-daily /women-midterm-elections.html.

62    John Woolfolk, "When Did Dianne Feinstein Start Opposing the Death Penalty?," *San Jose (CA) Mercury News*, May 23, 2018, https://www.mercurynews.com/2018/05/23/when-did-dianne-feinstein-start-opposing -the-death-penalty/.

62    "Senators Introduce Assault Weapons Ban," United States Senator for California Dianne Feinstein, press release, January 9, 2019, https://www.feinstein.senate.gov/public/index.cfm/press-releases?id=EFC76859 -879D-4038-97DD-C577212ED17B/.

63    Dana Bash, "Sen. Dianne Feinstein's Rise: How One Badass Woman Fought to Keep Going," CNN, August 9, 2017, https://edition.cnn.com/2017/06/06/politics/dianne-feinstein-badass-women-of-washington/index.html.

63    Robert Scheer, "LOS ANGELES TIMES INTERVIEW: Dianne Feinstein; A Senator in a Hurry for a State Facing a Lot of Troubles," *Los Angeles Times*, January 31, 1993, https://www.latimes.com/archives/la-xpm -1993-01-31-op-1006-story.html.

63    Feinstein, "Special Episode."

## Marielle Franco

64    Franco MarielleVerified (@mariellefranco), "Mais um homicídio de um jovem que pode estar entrando para a conta da PM . . . ," Twitter, March 13, 2018, 7:38 a.m., https://twitter.com/mariellefranco/status/973568966403731456.

66    John Lee Anderson, "Jair Bolsonaro's Southern Strategy," *New Yorker*, March 25, 2019, https://www.newyorker .com/magazine/2019/04/01/jair-bolsonaros-southern-strategy/.

66    Bill Langlois, "Brazil Condemns Violence against a Candidate, but Marielle Franco's Killers Remain Free," *Washington Post*, September 12, 2018, https://www.washingtonpost.com/news/global-opinions/wp/2018/09/12 /brazil-condemns-violence-against-a-candidate-but-marielle-francos-killers-remain-free/?utm_term=.35eb7bf2de93/.

67    "Mangueira Pays Tribute to Marielle Franco in Samba-Plot of the Upcoming Carnival," *Jornal do Brasil*, October 14, 2019, https://www.jb.com.br/rio/2018/10/947190-mangueira-faz-homenagem-a-marielle-franco -em-samba-enredo-do-proximo-carnaval.html.

67 Lia De Mattos Rocha, "The Life and Battles of Marielle Franco," openDemocracy, March 20, 2019, https://www.opendemocracy.net/en/democraciaabierta/life-and-battles-marielle-franco/.

67 Marielle Franco (@mariellefranco), "Frases do manual de sobrevivência pra mulheres no meio de monte de homem . . . ," Twitter, March 7, 2018, 12:03 p.m., https://twitter.com/mariellefranco/status/971476385238839297/.

67 Chitra Ramaswamy. "Marielle Franco Had to Resist—No Wonder She Didn't Survive," *Guardian* (US edition), March 19, 2018, https://www.theguardian.com/lifeandstyle/2018/mar/19/marielle-franco-brazilian-political-activist-black-gay-single-mother-fearless-fighter-murder/.

## "Fix What Ain't Right"

68 Tammy Baldwin, "Leaning toward Justice," *Metro Weekly*, October 17, 2007, https://www.metroweekly.com/2007/10/leaning-toward-justice/.

69 Hannah Ellis-Petersen, "'I Am Not Here to Entertain': Meet Thailand's First Transgender MP," *Guardian* (London), April 8, 2019, https://www.theguardian.com/world/2019/apr/06/i-am-not-here-to-entertain-meet-thailands-first-transgender-mp/.

69 "Transsexual Stands Proud in a Land of Conformity," *Sydney Morning Herald*, May 3, 2003, https://www.smh.com.au/world/transsexual-stands-proud-in-a-land-of-conformity-20030503-gdgp90.html.

## Kirsten Gillibrand

70 Kirsten Gillibrand (@SenGillibrand), "You cannot silence me," Twitter, December 12, 2017, 5:53 a.m., https://twitter.com/sengillibrand/status/940580340560809984?lang=en.

71 Anna Peele, "The Ignoring of Kirsten Gillibrand," *Washington Post*, July 6, 2019, https://www.washingtonpost.com/news/magazine/wp/2019/07/08/feature/why-america-is-ignoring-kirsten-gillibrand/?utm_term=.3438a536afec.

71 Kirsten Gillibrand, *Off the Sidelines: Raise Your Voice, Change the World* (New York: Ballantine Books, 2014).

71 Kirsten Gillibrand, interviewed by Rick Newman, "Meet Presidential Candidate Kirsten Gillibrand," Yahoo Finance video, 3:26, July 17, 2019, https://finance.yahoo.com/news/meet-presidential-candidate-kirsten-gillibrand-154916273.html.

71–72 Kirsten Gillibrand, interviewed by Chris Wallace, "Town Hall with Kirsten Gillibrand: Part 1," Fox News video, 3:36, June 2, 2019, https://www.foxnews.com/politics/nra-fires-back-after-gillibrand-points-to-her-2008-letter-praising-gun-rights-group/.

72 Shane Goldmacher, "As Gillibrand Pushes Left, Her Economic Agenda Tilts to Populism," *New York Times*, July 24, 2018, https://www.nytimes.com/2018/07/24/nyregion/kirsten-gillibrand-2020-economic-agenda.html.

72 MSNBC (@MSNBC), "Look up at that tower. A Shrine to greed, division and vanity," Twitter, posted on March 24, 2019, 10:57 a.m., 0:23, https://twitter.com/msnbc/status/1109876988024623104/.

72 Peele, "Kirsten Gillibrand."

73 Edward-Isaac Dovere, "This Isn't Going according to Plan for Kirsten Gillibrand," *Atlantic*, June 16, 2019, https://www.theatlantic.com/politics/archive/2019/06/kirsten-gillibrand-2020-plan/591754/.

73 Jonathan Van Meter, "Senator Kirsten Gillibrand on Trump, Feminism, and Hitting Her Stride in Washington," *Vogue*, October 12, 2017, https://www.vogue.com/article/senator-kirsten-gillibrand-trump-feminism-vogue-november-issue-2017/.

73 Lisa Lerer and Shane Goldmacher, "'This Is My Space': Kirsten Gillibrand's Unabashedly Feminist Campaign," *New York Times*, February 12, 2019, https://www.nytimes.com/2019/02/12/us/politics/kirsten-gillibrand-president-feminist.html.

## History's Firsts

74 Shirley Chisholm, "Chisholm '72: Unbought and Unbossed (2004)," YouTube video, 1:20, posted by iamnotatv, June 21, 2012, https://www.youtube.com/watch?v=bLHewo_lO08/.

74 Vanessa Williams, "'Unbought and Unbossed': Shirley Chisholm's Feminist Mantra Is Still Relevant 50 Years Later," *Washington Post*, January 26, 2018, https://www.washingtonpost.com/news/post-nation/wp/2018/01/26/unbought-and-unbossed-shirley-chisholms-feminist-mantra-is-as-relevant-today-as-it-was-50-years-ago/?utm_term=.321337ebac00/.

75 Megan Carpentier, "Tammy Duckworth Shows Her Strength in Senate Fight: 'These Legs Don't Buckle,'" *Guardian* (US edition), August 25, 2016, https://www.theguardian.com/us-news/2016/aug/25/tammy-duckworth-senate-race-illinois-profile/.

### Deb Haaland

76   Simon Romero, "New Mexico Could Elect First Native American to Congress," *New York Times*, June 6, 2018, https://www.nytimes.com/2018/06/06/us/deb-haaland-new-mexico-congress.html.

77   Debra Haaland, "Victory Speech—Nov. 6, 2018," Iowa State University, Archives of Women's Political Communication, November 6, 2018, https://awpc.cattcenter.iastate.edu/2019/02/25/victory-speech-nov-6-2018-6/.

79   "'Kill the Indian, and Save the Man': Capt. Richard H. Pratt on the Education of Native Americans," History Matters, accessed July 15, 2019, http://historymatters.gmu.edu/d/4929/.

79   Deb Haaland, "House Session," C-Span video, 9:12:54, May 9, 2019, 6:51:30, https://www.c-span.org/video /?460396-2/house-continues-special-orders/.

79   Deb Haaland, quoted in Amanda Gorman, "Native People Are Taking Center Stage. Finally," *New York Times*, November 27, 2018, https://www.nytimes.com/2018/11/27/smarter-living/the-edit-native-american-heritage -month.html.

79   "Deb Haaland for Congress—Ready," YouTube video, 0:30, posted by Deb Haaland, May 8, 2018, 0:21, https://www.youtube.com/watch?v=GL9aiZtbz-8/.

79   Ruairí Arrieta-Kenna, "'We Call Ourselves the Badasses': Meet the New Women of Congress," Politico, January 18, 2019, https://www.politico.com/interactives/2019/photos-new-women-of-congress/.

79   Tessa Stuart, "Meet Deb Haaland, Likely to Be the First Native Woman Elected to Congress," *Rolling Stone*, August 18, 2018, https://www.rollingstone.com/politics/politics-news/deb-haaland-first-native-woman-elected -congress-712408/.

### Nikki Haley

80   Maggie Haberman, Mark Landler, and Edward Wong, "Nikki Haley to Resign as Trump's Ambassador to the UN," *New York Times*, October 9, 2018, https://www.nytimes.com/2018/10/09/us/politics/nikki-haley-united -nations.html.

82   Hanna Rosin, "Good Ol' Girl," *Atlantic*, January/February 2011, https://www.theatlantic.com/magazine /archive/2011/01/good-ol-girl/308348/.

82   Jake Knotts, "SC Sen. Jake Knotts Calls Barack Obama and Nikki Haley 'Ragheads,'" YouTube video, 0:34, posted by PalmettoPublicRecord, May 15, 2012, https://www.youtube.com/watch?v=Zq5xMT3z560/.

82   Nikki Haley, "Gov. Nikki R. Haley Gives the Republican Response to the State of the Union," *New York Times* video, 9:14, January 13, 2016, https://www.nytimes.com/video/us/politics/100000004141321/gop-responds-to -state-of-the-union.html.

82   Nikki Haley, "'We Don't Trust Russia': Nikki Haley Lowers the Boom on Putin, Puts Iran on Notice," YouTube video, 2:41, posted by CBN News, July 23, 2018, 0:38, https://www.youtube.com/watch?v=Z71oVE0S_cE/.

83   "Nikki Haley: First Indian-American Woman to Be Elected Governor," *Time*, accessed February 25, 2020, https://time.com/collection/firsts/4898554/nikki-haley-firsts/.

83   Nikki Haley (@AmbNikkiHaley), "@realDonaldTrump, Bless your heart," Twitter, March 1, 2016, 11:55 a.m., https://twitter.com/AmbNikkiHaley/status/704756959019474948/.

83   Andrew Goldman, "The Comet: Gov. Nikki Haley of South Carolina," *New York Times Magazine*, March 4, 2011, https://www.nytimes.com/2011/03/06/magazine/06talk-t.html.

83   Nikki Haley, "Nikki Haley Resigns: 'I'll Never Truly Step Aside from Fighting for Our Country,'" YouTube video, 4:33, posted by "unwatch," October 9, 2018, 4:19, https://www.youtube.com/watch?v=7rQuZbtdf5I/.

83   Melissa Frick, "Nikki Haley Says Socialism Leads to 'Poverty, Oppression' at Grand Rapids Event," mlive, May 30, 2019, https://www.mlive.com/news/grand-rapids/2019/05/nikki-haley-says-socialism-leads-to -poverty-oppression-at-grand-rapids-event.html.

83   "Transcript: Nikki Haley on 'Face the Nation,' Dec. 10, 2017," CBS News, December 10, 2017, https://www .cbsnews.com/news/transcript-nikki-haley-on-face-the-nation-dec-10-2017/.

83   Goldman, "The Comet."

### Sarah Hanson-Young

84   Sarah Hanson-Young, "Sarah Hanson-Young's Marriage Equality Debate Speech," Greens, November 28, 2017, https://greens.org.au/sa/news/media-release/sarah-hanson-youngs-marriage-equality-debate-speech/.

85   Gemma Jones, "Taxing Year for Green Warrior," *Advertiser* (Adelaide, South Australia), November 12, 2011, https://www.adelaidenow.com.au/news/national/taxing-year-for-green-warrior/news-story /8fd6c5ff135abed366b528a68f8e32d7/.

85  Sarah Hanson-Young, *En Garde* (Melbourne: Melbourne University Press, 2018), accessed May 1, 2019, https://archive.bookfrom.net/sarah-hanson-young/456625-en_garde.html.

85  Dan Harris, "Senate Rules Far from Child's Play," *Sydney Morning Herald*, June 19, 2009, https://www.smh.com.au/national/senate-rules-far-from-childs-play-20090618-clzb.html.

86  Sarah Hanson-Young, "Leyonhjelm Tells Senator to 'Stop Shagging Men' during Women's Safety Debate," *Guardian* (US edition) video, 0:43, June 28, 2018, 0:17, https://www.theguardian.com/australia-news/2018/jun/28/david-leyonhjelm-sarah-hanson-young-senator-stop-shagging-men-womens-safety-debate/.

86  Caroline Overington, "Sarah Hanson-Young Denies She Said All Men Are Rapists," *Australian* (New South Wales), May 1, 2019, https://www.theaustralian.com.au/nation/sarah-hansonyoung-denies-she-said-all-men-are-rapists/news-story/c91f3e6c9557e864c6eddfb20f4c2e0f/.

86  abc730 (@abc730), "'He's brought the entire parliament into disrepute.' @sarahinthesen8 hits back at @DavidLeyonhjelm's comments about her. #abc730 #auspol @LaTrioli," Twitter, July 2, 2018, 2:46 a.m., https://twitter.com/abc730/status/1013720602446721025/.

86  Sarah Hanson-Young, "Sarah Hanson-Young: Asylum Policy Is Designed to Hurt People," posted by the *Guardian* (US edition) video, 0:46, May 3, 2016, 0:30, https://www.theguardian.com/australia-news/video/2016/may/03/sarah-hanson-young-refugee-policy-designed-break-people-video/.

86  Oliver Laughland, "Australian Government Targets Asylum Seekers with Graphic Campaign," *Guardian* (US edition), February 11, 2014, https://www.theguardian.com/world/2014/feb/11/government-launches-new-graphic-campaign-to-deter-asylum-seekers/.

87  "Sarah Hanson-Young on Sky News—Bush Fires and Climate," YouTube video, 10:59, posted by Sarah Hanson-Young, January 29, 2020, 5:00, https://www.youtube.com/watch?v=g1wK5C3CkSY/.

87  Hanson-Young, "Sarah Hanson-Young's Speech."

87  Sarah Hanson-Young, "Australia's Climate and Extinction Crises Are Crying Out for Political Solutions," *Guardian* (US edition), June 6, 2019, https://www.theguardian.com/commentisfree/2019/jun/07/australias-climate-and-extinction-crises-are-crying-out-for-political-solutions/.

87  Sarah Hanson-Young, "Our planet is in crisis . . . ," Facebook, May 7, 2019, https://www.facebook.com/169115193111983/posts/2308978892458925/.

87  Sarah Hanson-Young, "'You're Not Fit to Call Yourselves Men,' Sarah Hanson-Young Tells Senators—Video," *Guardian* (US edition) video, 2:44, November 28, 2018, 1:20, https://www.theguardian.com/global/video/2018/nov/28/youre-not-fit-to-call-yourselves-men-sarah-hanson-young-tells-senators-video/.

## Kamala Harris

88  Elizabeth Weil, "Kamala Harris Takes Her Shot," *Atlantic*, May 2019, https://www.theatlantic.com/magazine/archive/2019/05/kamala-harris-2020-campaign/586033/.

89  Jamilah King, "The Secret to Understanding Kamala Harris," *Mother Jones*, January 2018, https://www.motherjones.com/politics/2018/01/the-secret-to-understanding-kamala-harris/.

90  Kamala D. Harris, *Smart on Crime: A Career Prosecutor's Plan to Make Us Safer* (San Francisco: Chronicle Books, 2009).

91  Weil, "Kamala Harris."

91  ABC News (@ABC), "In my whole life, I've only had one client: the people," Twitter, January 27, 2019, 2:08 p.m., https://twitter.com/abc/status/1089646399204003845/.

91  Kamala Harris, "Kamala Harris Talks 2020 Presidential Run, Legalizing Marijuana, Criminal Justice Reform + More," YouTube video, 44:18, posted by *Breakfast Club Power 105.1 FM*, February 11, 2019, https://www.youtube.com/watch?v=Kh_wQUjeaTk/.

91  CNN Politics (@CNNPolitics), "2020 candidate Kamala Harris responds to President Trump . . . ," Twitter, May 2, 2019, 5:10 a.m., https://twitter.com/cnnpolitics/status/1123922793907806220/.

91  Kamala Harris (@KamalaHarris), "My advice to all young women: Surround yourself with really good friends who will celebrate your successes and know that no matter what you do, you are not alone," Twitter, January 17, 2019, 5:00 p.m., https://twitter.com/KamalaHarris/status/1086065706179932160/.

## Mazie Hirono

92  Mazie Hirono, "Sen. Hirono to Barr: 'Give Us Some Credit for Knowing What the Hell Is Going on around Here,'" WNBC-TV, May 1, 2019, https://www.nbcnewyork.com/multimedia/Sen-Hirono-to-Barr-Give-Us-Some-Credit-for-Knowing-What-the-Hell-Is-Going-on-Around-Here-509330392.html.

93   Robbie Dingeman, "Political Survivor: A Closer Look at Hawai'i's First Female Senator, Mazie Hirono," *Honolulu Magazine*, July 23, 2017, http://www.honolulumagazine.com/Honolulu-Magazine/July-2018/Political-Survivor-A-Closer-Look-at-Hawaiis-First-Female-Senator-Mazie-Hirono/.

93   Nina Totenberg, "The Quiet Rage of Mazie Hirono," NPR, June 7, 2018, https://www.npr.org/2018/06/07/617239314/the-quiet-rage-of-mazie-hirono/.

94   Dingeman, "Political Survivor."

94   Mazie Hirono, "Sen. Hirono: Where Is Your Compassion?," YouTube video, 1:53, posted by CNN, July 28, 2017, 0:21, https://www.youtube.com/watch?v=HS0iDKGvsbI/.

94   Mazie Hirono, "On Kavanaugh Debate, Senator Mazie Hirono Tells Men of Country to 'Shut Up and Step Up,'" YouTube video, 0:58, posted by NBC News, September 18, 2018, 0:27, https://www.youtube.com/watch?v=htGmvHKcCNY/.

95   Donald Trump, "Speech: Donald Trump Delivers a Speech at the 2019 CPAC Convention in Maryland—March 2, 2019," YouTube video, 2:02:33, posted by Factbase Videos, March 2, 2019, 1:12:22, https://www.youtube.com/watch?v=YBpbTm6i_cU/.

95   Philip Elliott, "Mazie Hirono Is the Only Immigrant in the Senate. She's Ready to Take on Trump," *Time*, May 17, 2018, https://time.com/5280460/mazie-hirono-senate-donald-trump/.

95   Jordain Carney, "Hirono Electrifies Left as Trump Antagonist," Hill, May 4, 2019, https://thehill.com/homenews/senate/442091-hirono-electrifies-left-as-trump-antagonist/.

95   Elliott, "Mazie Hirono."

95   Totenberg, "The Quiet Rage."

95   Dingeman, "Political Survivor."

95   Dingeman.

95   Elliott, "Mazie Hirono."

## Katrín Jakobsdóttir

96   John Nichols, "Meet Katrín Jakobsdóttir, Iceland's Left-Wing, Environmentalist, Feminist Prime Minister," *Nation*, March 8, 2018, https://www.thenation.com/article/meet-katrin-jakobsdottir-icelands-left-wing-environmentalist-feminist-prime-minister/.

98   Jon Henley, "Iceland's New Leader: 'People Don't Trust Our Politicians,'" *Guardian* (London), February 9, 2018, https://www.theguardian.com/world/2018/feb/09/icelands-new-leader-people-dont-trust-icelandic-politicians/.

98   Manuela Kasper-Claridge, "Gender Equality: 'Battle for Fundamental Human Rights,'" *DW*, November 20, 2018, https://www.dw.com/en/gender-equality-battle-for-fundamental-human-rights/a-46363378/.

99   Henley, "Iceland's New Leader."

99   Kasper-Claridge, "Gender Equality."

99   Nichols, "Meet Katrín Jakobsdóttir."

99   "Weird That I'm Only the Second Woman," *Iceland Monitor*, December 1, 2017, https://icelandmonitor.mbl.is/news/politics_and_society/2017/12/01/weird_that_i_m_only_the_second_woman/.

## Pramila Jayapal

100   Rep. Pramila Jayapal (@RepJayapal), "A message to women of color out there: stand strong. Refuse to be patronized or minimized. Let the small guys out there be intimated by you," Twitter, September 7, 2017, 5:24 p.m., https://twitter.com/RepJayapal/status/905949851862618112/.

101   Bob Young, "An Immigrant Herself, Seattle's Pramila Jayapal Leads the Push for Reform," *Pacific Northwest Magazine—Seattle Times*, August 7, 2010, https://www.seattletimes.com/pacific-nw-magazine/an-immigrant-herself-seattles-pramila-jayapal-leads-the-push-for-reform/.

103   Ella Nilsen, "Pramila Jayapal Is Congress's Activist Insider," Vox, February 20, 2019, https://www.vox.com/2019/2/20/18141001/pramila-jayapal-congressional-progressive-caucus-house-democrats/.

103   Pramila Jayapal, "Rep. Jayapal Tearfully Reveals Child Came Out as Gender Nonbinary," YouTube video, 4:20, posted by NBC News, April 2, 2019, 0:39, https://www.youtube.com/watch?v=EIYxr79E8XM/.

103   Heather Caygle and Sarah Ferris, "Meet the Woman Mentoring Omar, Tlaib and Ocasio-Cortez," Politico, March 22, 2019, https://www.politico.com/story/2019/03/22/jayapal-freshmen-dems-1231513/.

103   Pramila Jayapal, "A New Moral Imagination on Immigration," *NYR Daily*, December 3, 2018, https://www.nybooks.com/daily/2018/12/03/a-new-moral-imagination-on-immigration/.

**Andrea Jenkins**

104    Rafi Schwartz, "Talking to Andrea Jenkins, the First Out Trans Woman of Color Elected in American History," Splinter, November 13, 2017, https://splinternews.com/talking-to-andrea-jenkins-the-first-out -trans-woman-of-1820339679/.

105    Michelle Bruch, "Building an Archive of Transgender History," *Minneapolis Southwest Journal*, May 5, 2015, https://web.archive.org/web/20160618165716/http://www.southwestjournal.com/news/2015/05/building-an -archive-of-transgender-history/.

105–106    Cory Zurowski, "Andrea Jenkins Archives LGBTQ Stories for the Ages," *Minneapolis City Pages*, June 24, 2015, https://web.archive.org/web/20160529123321/http://www.citypages.com/arts/andrea-jenkins-archives-lgbtq -stories-for-the-ages-7427689/.

106    Julie Kendrick, "Zen Master," *Minnesota Good Age*, November 2, 2018, https://www.mngoodage.com/living /features/2018/11/zen-master/.

106    Mike Mullen, "Rep. Mary Franson Tweets Terrible Opinion after Andrea Jenkins' Win," *Minneapolis City Pages*, November 9, 2018, http://www.citypages.com/news/rep-mary-franson-tweets-terrible-opinion-after -andrea-jenkins-win/456454183/.

107    Marwa Eltagouri, "Meet Andrea Jenkins, the First Openly Transgender Black Woman Elected to Public Office in the U.S.," *Washington Post*, November 8, 2017, https://www.washingtonpost.com/news/the-fix/wp /2017/11/08/meet-andrea-jenkins-the-openly-transgender-black-woman-elected-to-public-office-in-the-u-s/.

107    Davis Richardson, "Andrea Jenkins on Becoming the US' First Black Transgender Elected Official," *New York Observer*, November 14, 2017, https://observer.com/2017/11/andrea-jenkins-on-becoming-the-u-s-first-black -transgender-elected-official/.

107    Bruch, "Building an Archive."

107    Kendrick, "Zen Master."

**Amy Klobuchar**

108    "Klobuchar on Immigration Order: Difference between Being Bold and Rash," This Week video (@ThisWeekABC), 0:48, Twitter, February 5, 2017, 10:00 a.m., 0:22, https://twitter.com/ThisWeekABC /status/828272131599278080/.

109    Julia Felsenthal, "Personable, Popular, Pragmatic: Is Minnesota Senator Amy Klobuchar the Democrats' Secret Weapon?," *Vogue*, January 15, 2019, https://www.vogue.com/article/amy-klobuchar-minnesota-senator-interview/.

110    "Kavanaugh Tangles with Senators over FBI, Drinking," YouTube video, 3:24, posted by AP Archive, October 2, 2018, 3:14, https://www.youtube.com/watch?v=7CdAeMzVY9E/.

110    "Senator Amy Klobuchar Presidential Campaign Announcement (C-SPAN)," YouTube video, 23:55, posted by C-SPAN, February 11, 2019, 6:30, https://www.youtube.com/watch?v=bX8rwqsdOCA/.

110    Lisa Lerer, "Amy Klobuchar's Big Idea: Bipartisan Appeal Can Beat Trump," *New York Times*, April 22, 2019, 1:57, video, 1:47, https://www.nytimes.com/2019/04/22/us/politics/amy-klobuchar-2020-president.html.

111    Patrick Condon and Torey Van Oot, "Sen. Amy Klobuchar Says She Will 'Do Better' in Treatment of Staffers," *Minneapolis Star Tribune*, March 2, 2019, http://www.startribune.com/sen-amy-klobuchar-says-she-will-do -better-in-treatment-of-staffers/506582872/.

111    Sarah Stein Kerr and Robin Lindsay, "Who Is Amy Klobuchar? 2020 Presidential Candidate," *New York Times*, February 10, 2019, 1:57, video, 1:27, https://www.nytimes.com/video/us/politics/100000006346241/amy -klobuchar-2020-presidential-candidate.html.

111    Amy Klobuchar, "Women Are Getting the Job Done," Huffington Post, last modified February 6, 2014, https://www.huffpost.com/entry/women-are-getting-the-job_b_4741106/.

111    Lerer, "Amy Klobuchar's Big Idea."

**Barbara Lee**

112    Gary Younge, "Congresswoman Barbara Lee: Once the Lone Voice against the Afghanistan War," *Guardian* (US edition), July 27, 2012, https://www.theguardian.com/world/2012/jul/27/barbara-lee-congresswoman-interview/.

113    Fergal Keane, "Barbara Lee: Public Enemy Number One?," *Independent* (London), February 4, 2003, https:// www.independent.co.uk/news/world/americas/barbara-lee-public-enemy-number-one-938.html.

113    Dayna Evans, "Congresswoman Barbara Lee Knows What It Takes to Fight Power," *New York Magazine*, August 22, 2017, https://www.thecut.com/2017/08/congresswoman-barbara-lee-interview-aumf.html.

114  "Public Law 107-40—Sept. 18, 2001," https://www.govinfo.gov/content/pkg/PLAW-107publ40/pdf/PLAW
     -107publ40.pdf.

114  Younge, "Congresswoman."

114  Austin Wright, "How Barbara Lee Became an Army of One," Politico, July 30, 2017, https://www.politico.com
     /magazine/story/2017/07/30/how-barbara-lee-became-an-army-of-one-215434/.

115  Younge, "Congresswoman."

115  Evans, "Congresswoman."

115  Rebecca Traister, "6 Minutes with Barbara Lee: Talking Iraq, Poverty, and Getting a Seat at the Table with the
     House's Lefty Conscience," *Intelligencer*, November 11, 2018, http://nymag.com/intelligencer/2018/11/barbara
     -lee-on-iraq-poverty-and-a-seat-at-the-table.html.

115  Evans, "Congresswoman."

## Mia Love

116  Mia Love, "Mia Love Takes on Trump, GOP in Concession Speech," YouTube video, 2:13, posted by
     Associated Press, November 26, 2018, 2:00, https://www.youtube.com/watch?v=KvV_f0zS4aM/.

117  "Rising GOP Star Mia Love Glides into the Spotlight at Convention," Fox News, August 28, 2012, https://
     www.foxnews.com/politics/rising-gop-star-mia-love-glides-into-the-spotlight-at-convention.

117  Winston Ross, "Mia Love Tries to Be the First Black Republican Woman in Congress," *Newsweek*, October 29,
     2014, https://www.newsweek.com/2014/11/07/utah-love-280643.html.

118  Josh Dawsey, "Trump Derides Protections for Immigrants from 'Shithole' Countries," *Washington Post*, January
     12, 2018, https://www.washingtonpost.com/politics/trump-attacks-protections-for-immigrants-from-shithole
     -countries-in-oval-office-meeting/2018/01/11/bfc0725c-f711-11e7-91af-31ac729add94_story.html.

118  David Wells, Ben Winslow, and Rebecca Green, "President Trump Says 'Mia Love Gave Me No Love and She
     Lost,' Race Not Yet Called," Fox 13 News, November 7, 2018, https://fox13now.com/2018/11/07/trump-says
     -mia-love-lost-too-bad-sorry-about-that-mia/.

118–119  Love, "Mia Love Takes on Trump," 0:49.

119  Ross, "Mia Love."

119  Ross.

119  Mia Love, "Republicans Have Failed to Bring Out Message to Minorities. It's Hurting the Nation," *Washington
     Post*, December 12, 2018, https://www.washingtonpost.com/opinions/2018/12/12/mia-love-republicans-have
     -failed-bring-our-message-minorities-its-hurting-nation/.

## Sanna Marin

120  Gabriela Baczynska and Anne Kauranen, "'We Have Work to Do': World's Youngest Leader Debuts at EU
     Summit," Reuters, December 12, 2019, https://www.reuters.com/article/us-eu-summit-finland/we-have-work
     -to-do-worlds-youngest-leader-debuts-at-eu-summit-idUSKBN1YG1U4/.

121  "Sanna Marin, the Prime Minister Raised in a Rainbow Family," *Foreigner*, October 12, 2019, https://
     www.foreigner.fi/articulo/news/this-is-sanna-marin-the-prime-minister-who-was-raised-by-two-women
     /20191210150129003716.html.

121  Bianca Britton and Stephanie Halasz, "Estonia Apologizes after Minister Calls Finland's New Leader Sanna
     Marin a 'Sales Girl,'" CNN, December 17, 2019, https://www.cnn.com/2019/12/17/europe/estonia-finland
     -sanna-marin-intl-scli/index.html.

121  Sanna Marin (@MarinSanna), "Olen tavattoman ylpeä Suomesta. Täällä köyhän perheen lapsi voi kouluttautua
     pitkälle ja yltää elämässään moneen. Kaupan kassasta voi tulla vaikka pääministeri. Ilman duunareita ei Suomi
     selviäisi. Arvostan jokaisen työntekijän, ammatinharjoittajan ja yrittäjän työtä korkealle!," Twitter, December 15,
     2019, 12:48 p.m., https://twitter.com/MarinSanna/status/1206315232181784582/.

122  Baczynska and Kauranen, "Work to Do."

123  Aleksi Teivainen, "Marin: Finnish Firms Were Able to Pay Eight Hours' Wage for Six Hours of Work," *Helsinki
     Times*, August 21, 2019, https://www.helsinkitimes.fi/finland/finland-news/domestic/16668-marin-finnish
     -firms-were-able-to-pay-eight-hours-wages-for-six-hours-of-work.html.

123  Megan Specia, "Who Is Sanna Marin, Finland's 34-Year-Old Prime Minister?," *New York Times*, December 10,
     2019, https://www.nytimes.com/2019/12/10/world/europe/finland-sanna-marin.html.

123  Tulikukka de Fresnes, "How Will Millennial Leaders Change the World? Finland Will Give Us a Clue,"
     *Guardian* (US edition), December 11, 2019, https://www.theguardian.com/commentisfree/2019/dec/11
     /millennial-leaders-world-finland-prime-minister-sanna-marin/.

123  Jon Henley, "Finland Anoints Sanna Marin, 34, as World's Youngest Serving Prime Minister," *Guardian* (US edition), December 9, 2019, https://www.theguardian.com/world/2019/dec/09/finland-anoints-sanna-martin-34-as-worlds-youngest-serving-prime-minister/.

123  Sanna Marin (@MarinSanna), "Neljässä vuodessa Suomi ei tule valmiiksi, mutta se voi tulla paremmaksi. Sen eteen me teemme töitä. Haluan rakentaa yhteiskuntaa, jossa jokaisesta lapsesta voi tulla mitä vain ja, jossa jokainen ihminen voi elää ja vanheta ihmisarvoisella tavalla," Twitter, December 9, 2019, 11:23 p.m., https://twitter.com/MarinSanna/status/1204300583282323461/.

## Martha McSally

124  ABC News (@ABC), Martha McSally, "JUST IN: In emotional moment at hearing . . . ," Twitter, posted on March 6, 2019, 12:03 p.m., 1:03, https://twitter.com/abc/status/1103385555629273088/.

125  Ann Gerhart, "McSally: No Muslim Garb at War," *Washington Post*, January 7, 2002, https://www.washingtonpost.com/politics/decision2012/mcsally-no-muslim-garb-at-war/2012/10/25/6f215608-1d38-11e2-9cd5-b55c38388962_story.html?utm_term=.ef7f3960c163.

126  Martha McSally, interviewed by Lesley Stahl, "Female Pilot Sues Over Muslim Garb," CBS News, January 17, 2002, https://www.cbsnews.com/news/female-pilot-sues-over-muslim-garb/.

126  "Prohibiting Members of Armed Forces in Saudi Arabia from Being Required or Compelled to Wear the Abaya Garment," *Congressional Record*, May 14, 2002, https://www.congress.gov/congressional-record/2002/05/14/house-section/article/H2422-1/.

126  Kristina Peterson, "Arizona Rep. Martha McSally Alleges Sexual Abuse by High-School Coach," *Washington Post*, April 23, 2018, https://www.wsj.com/articles/arizona-rep-martha-mcsally-alleges-sexual-abuse-by-high-school-coach-1524518307/.

127  Martha McSally, "Sen. McSally (R-AZ): 'I Was Preyed upon and Then Raped by a Superior Officer.' (C-SPAN)" YouTube video, 6:52, posted by C-SPAN, March 6, 2019, 3:51, https://www.youtube.com/watch?v=IHQN9KCL5HA/.

127  McSally, 5:02.

127  Martha McSally, "My Commitment: Solutions to Get People Working Again," *Inside Tucson Business*, October 19, 2012, https://www.insidetucsonbusiness.com/opinion/columnists/guest_opinion/my-commitment-solutions-to-get-people-working-again/article_7dcfdfee-1964-11e2-a253-0019bb2963f4.html

127  Ann Gerhart, "Running for Gabrielle Giffords's House Seat, Is Not Martha McSally's First Challenge." *Washington Post*, October 25, 2012, https://www.washingtonpost.com/politics/decision2012/running-for-gabrielle-giffordss-house-seat-is-not-martha-mcsallys-first-challenge/2012/10/25/d98e42ee-1de2-11e2-ba31-3083ca97c314_story.html.

127  Martha McSally, "Martha McSally: 'That's a War on Women,'" YouTube video, 1:02, posted by NRCC Communications, October 24, 2012, https://www.youtube.com/watch?v=X8CYAJ7BiIc/.

## Angela Merkel

128  "Angela Merkel: Germany's Shrewd Political Survivor," BBC, June 3, 2019, https://www.bbc.com/news/world-europe-23709337/.

129  Catherine Mayer, "Angela Merkel Savaged by Helmut Kohl, the Architect of United Germany," *Time*, October 6, 2014, https://time.com/3474479/angela-merkel-helmut-kohl-biography/.

130  Hans Kundnani, "Angela Merkel: Enigmatic Leader of a Divided Land," *Guardian* (US edition), March 12, 2016, https://www.theguardian.com/world/2016/mar/13/profile-angela-merkel/.

130  Lizzie Dearden, "Angela Merkel Calls for a Burqa Ban 'Wherever Legally Possible' in Germany," *Independent* (London), December 6, 2016, https://www.independent.co.uk/news/world/europe/germany-burqa-burka-ban-veils-angela-merkel-cdu-muslims-speech-refugee-crisis-elections-term-vote-a7458536.html.

131  Karl Vick, "Chancellor of the Free World," *Time*, 2015, https://time.com/time-person-of-the-year-2015-angela-merkel/.

131  Angela Merkel, "Angela Merkel: A Profile by Anne McElvoy—BBC Newsnight," YouTube video, 11:36, posted by BBC Newsnight, September 19, 2017, 5:27, https://www.youtube.com/watch?v=L7bg5aaWQmQ/.

131  Vick, "Chancellor."

131  Angela Merkel, "Merkel: 'If the Euro Fails, Europe Fails,'" BBC, September 7, 2011, https://www.bbc.com/news/av/business-14827834/merkel-if-the-euro-fails-europe-fails/.

131  Vick, "Chancellor."

**Lisa Murkowski**

132   Deborah Solomon, "Questions for Lisa Murkowski," *New York Times Magazine*, September 28, 2010, https://www.nytimes.com/2010/10/03/magazine/03fob-q4-t.html.

133   Lisa Murkowski, "Sen. Lisa Murkowski on Disagreeing with the President," YouTube video, 8:26, posted by *PBS NewsHour*, March 6, 2019, https://www.youtube.com/watch?v=b5KSdftJhKY/.

134   Lisa Murkowski, "Interview with Senator Lisa Murkowski," C-Span video, 26:51, July 19, 2018, 11:01 https://www.c-span.org/video/?448770-1/interview-senator-lisa-murkowski/.

135   Murkowski, 7:13.

135   Lisa Murkowski, "Lisa Murkowski—On the Impeachment Inquiry," YouTube video, 4:10, posted by State of Reform, October 7, 2019, 2:27, https://www.youtube.com/watch?v=lAon_xH_8js/.

135   Murkowski, "Interview," 18:24.


**Eleanor Holmes Norton**

136   Eleanor Holmes Norton, "Delegate Holmes Norton: DC Voting Rights Act," YouTube video, 4:09, posted by Nancy Pelosi, April 19, 2007, 1:46, https://www.youtube.com/watch?v=VV3k8nERUOQ/.

137   "Legends in the Law: Eleanor Holmes Norton," *Bar Report*, June/July 1997, https://www.dcbar.org/bar-resources/publications/washington-lawyer/articles/legend-norton.cfm.

138   Norton, "Delegate Holmes Norton," 1:49.

139   Zhiyan Zhong, "Eleanor Holmes Norton's Long, Historical and Complicated Career," *Washington Post*, June 20, 2018, https://www.washingtonpost.com/graphics/2018/local/amp-stories/eleanor-holmes-nortons-long-historical-and-complicated-career/.

139   Paul Schwartzman, "Eleanor Holmes Norton Lacks a Vote but Not a (Withering) Voice," *Washington Post*, October 22, 2012, https://www.washingtonpost.com/local/eleanor-holmes-norton-lacks-a-vote-but-not-a-withering-voice/2012/10/22/b9836b8e-188b-11e2-9855-71f2b202721b_story.html.

139   Schwartzman.


**Alexandra Ocasio-Cortez**

140   "The Courage to Change," YouTube video, 2:08, posted by Alexandria Ocasio-Cortez, May 30, 2018, 1:17, https://www.youtube.com/watch?v=rq3QXIVR0bs/.

141   Charlotte Alter, "'Change Is Closer Than We Think,' Inside Alexandria Ocasio-Cortez's Unlikely Rise," *Time*, March 21, 2019, https://time.com/longform/alexandria-ocasio-cortez-profile/.

141   Alter.

142   Alter.

142   Alexandria Ocasio-Cortez (@AOC), "The reason journos from @FoxNews to @dcexaminer can't help but obsess about my clothes, rent, or mischaracterize respectful convos as "fights" is bc as I've said, women like me aren't supposed to run for office - or win. & that's exactly why the BX and Queens sent me here," Twitter, November 16, 2018, 11:11 a.m., https://twitter.com/aoc/status/1063509811059453952/.

143   Alexandria Ocasio-Cortez, "Just like catcalling, I don't owe a response to unsolicited requests from men with bad intentions. And also like catcalling, for some reason they feel entitled to one," Twitter, August 9, 2018, 6:32 p.m., https://twitter.com/AOC/status/1027729430137827328/.

143   Alexandria Ocasio-Cortez, Twitter Profile, accessed July 7, 2019, https://twitter.com/AOC/.

143   Alter, "'Change Is Closer.'"

143   Alex Morris, "Alexandria Ocasio-Cortez Wants the Country to Think Big," *Rolling Stone*, February 27, 2019, https://www.rollingstone.com/politics/politics-features/alexandria-ocasio-cortez-congress-interview-797214/.

143   Alexandra Ocasio-Cortez, "Knock Down the House," directed by Rachel Lears, Netflix, May 1, 2019.


**Ilhan Omar**

144   Ilhan Omar, "Ilhan Omar Is Giving Her Victory Speech," YouTube video, 7:05, posted by HIDDE RAAC, November 6, 2018, 5:01, https://www.youtube.com/watch?v=EZjNV6V2aeM/.

145   Donald Trump, "Donald Trump Campaign Rally in Minneapolis, Minnesota," C-Span video, 49:30, November 6, 2018, 19:39, https://www.c-span.org/video/?418185-1/donald-trump-campaigns-minneapolis-minnesota/.

146   William Cummings, "Rep. Ilhan Omar Deletes the Controversial Tweets That Drew Charges of Anti-Semitism," *USA Today*, February 26, 2019, https://www.usatoday.com/story/news/politics/onpolitics/2019/02/26/ilhan-omar-deletes-israel-tweets-that-drew-charges-of-anti-semitism/2989404002/.

147    Ilhan Omar (@IlhanMN), "Listening and learning, but standing strong," Twitter, February 11, 2019, 11:46 a.m., https://twitter.com/IlhanMN/status/1095046561254567937/.

147    Ilhan Omar (@IlhanMN), "I am told everyday that I am anti-American if I am not pro-Israel. I find that to be problematic and I am not alone. I just happen to be willing to speak up on it and open myself to attacks," Twitter, March 3, 2019, 12:01 p.m., https://twitter.com/IlhanMN/status/1102297974154113026/.

147    Owen Daugherty, "Congress Is Now Going to Look like an Islamic Republic," Hill, December 6, 2018, https://thehill.com/homenews/media/420061-conservative-pastor-the-floor-of-congress-is-now-going-to-look-like-an-islamic/.

147    Ilhan Omar (@IlhanMN), "Well sir, the floor of Congress is going to look like America. . . . And you're gonna have to just deal," Twitter, December 6, 2018, 9:07 p.m., https://twitter.com/ilhanmn/status/1070907694339502080/.

147    Maxwell Strachan, "Ilhan Omar Won't Be Quiet," Huffington Post, May 6, 2019, https://www.huffpost.com/entry/ilhan-omar-profile_n_5ccc987ae4b0548b7359ee0f/.

147    Ilhan Omar (@IlhanMN), "My Americanness is questioned by the President and the @GOP on a daily basis, yet my colleagues remain silent. I know what it means to be American and no one will ever tell me otherwise," Twitter, March 3, 2019, 12:10 p.m., https://twitter.com/IlhanMN/status/1102300223592951808/.

147    Azmia Magane, "Congresswoman-Elect Ilhan Omar Shares Advice for Young People and How She Deals with Islamophobia," Teen Vogue, November 9, 2018, https://www.teenvogue.com/story/ilhan-omar-shares-how-she-deals-with-islamophobia/.

**Sarah Palin**

148    "The Difference between Hockey Moms & Pitbulls | Sarah Palin | 2008 Republican Nat," YouTube video, 0:43, posted by Republican National Convention, April 5, 2016, 0:29, https://www.youtube.com/watch?v=RjsGgTTIvnk/.

150    Sarah Palin, "Palin's Reasons for Stepping Down," Washington Post, July 3, 2009, http://voices.washingtonpost.com/44/2009/07/03/palins_remarks_in_stepping_dow.html.

151    Katie Couric and Brian Goldsmith, "What Sarah Palin Clearly Saw," Atlantic, October 8, 2018, https://www.theatlantic.com/ideas/archive/2018/10/what-sarah-palin-understood-about-politics/572389/.

151    Couric and Goldsmith.

151    Sarah Palin, "Address at CPAC 2012—Feb. 11, 2012," Iowa State University, February 11, 2012, https://awpc.cattcenter.iastate.edu/2017/03/21/address-at-cpac-2012-feb-11-2012/.

151    Palin.

151    Sarah Palin, "Sarah Palin at the 2014 Conservative Political Action Conference," C-Span video, 39:44, March 8, 2014, 22:56, https://www.c-span.org/video/?318148-17/sarah-palin-addresses-cpac/.

151    Palin, "Palin's Reasons."

**Noteworthy First Ladies**

152    Abigail Adams, quoted in "All Men Would Be Tyrants If They Could," Lapham's Quarterly, March 31, 1776, https://www.laphamsquarterly.org/revolutions/all-men-would-be-tyrants-if-they-could/.

152    Albert Fall, quoted in William Hazelgrove, "Madame President: The Secret Presidency of Edith Wilson" (Washington, DC: Regnery, 2016), https://books.google.com/books?id=4ob9DAAAQBAJ&pg=PT86&lpg=PT86&dq=%22petticoat+government%22+albert+fall&source=bl&ots=IGREz3VH6p&sig=ACfU3U0IGkYkyWQEmeDaAq4DITK5JCQpqg&hl=en&sa=X&ved=2ahUKEwiNrpWzy_TlAhXoITQIHS9SC4sQ6AEwA3oECAUQA#v=onepage&q=%22petticoat%20government%22%20albert%20fall&f=false/.

153    Nancy Reagan, My Turn: The Memoirs of Nancy Reagan (New York: Random House, October 19, 1989).

153    Michelle Obama, "#18, Michelle Obama," March 17, 2019, in "Conan O'Brien Needs a Friend," produced by Earwolf, podcast, 58:36, https://www.newsweek.com/michelle-obama-president-conan-obrien-2020-podcast-1367509/.

**Nancy Pelosi**

154    NYT Magazine (@NYTmag), "'No one gives you power. You have to take it from them.' Nancy Pelosi, the most powerful Democrat in Washington, is ready for battle," Twitter, November 19, 2018, 12:15 p.m., https://twitter.com/nytmag/status/1064613068729131009?lang=en.

156    Andy Kroll and National Journal, "The Staying Power of Nancy Pelosi," Atlantic, September 11, 2015, https://www.theatlantic.com/politics/archive/2015/09/the-staying-power-of-nancy-pelosi/440022/.

156 Marc Sandalow, "Pelosi Mocked as S.F.'s 'Latte Liberal,' Conservatives Say Her Rise Helps Them," *SFGate*, November 13, 2002, https://www.sfgate.com/politics/article/Pelosi-mocked-as-S-F-s-latte-liberal-2754909.php.

157 "HIV/AIDS," Congresswoman Nancy Pelosi, accessed August 1, 2019, https://pelosi.house.gov/issues/hivaids/.

157 Nancy Pelosi, "Leader Nancy Pelosi at the 2012 Democratic National Convention," YouTube video, 8:04, posted by Democratic National Convention, September 5, 2012, 2:29, https://www.youtube.com/watch?v=rx-VLUjyydM/.

157 Molly Ball, "Nancy Pelosi Doesn't Care What You Think of Her. And She Isn't Going Anywhere," *Time*, September 6, 2018, https://time.com/5388347/nancy-pelosi-democrats-feminism/.

157 Kroll and *National Journal*, "Staying Power of Nancy Pelosi."

157 Kroll and *National Journal*.


## Danica Roem

158 Danica Roem, "Roem Says Historic Virginia Election Needs to Prove 'Discrimination Is a Disqualifier,'" *Washington Post* video, 4:41, posted November 8, 2017, 2:47, https://www.washingtonpost.com/video/national /roem-says-historic-virginia-election-needs-to-prove-discrimination-is-a-disqualifier/2017/11/08/28fe30a8 -c466-11e7-9922-4151f5ca6168_video.html.

159 "About Danica," Danica Roem, accessed August 3, 2019, https://danicaroem.ngpvanhost.com/about-danica/.

160 Luke Darby, "Danica Roem Talks Serving under Trump, Thrash Metal, and How to Win Local Elections," *GQ*, January 8, 2018, https://www.gq.com/story/danica-roem-how-to-win-elections-interview/.

160 Chris L. Jenkins, "Marshall Admits No Doubts about Marriage," *Washington Post*, November 4, 2006, http:// www.washingtonpost.com/wp-dyn/content/article/2006/11/03/AR2006110301580.html.

160 Nicholas Trevino (@nitrevino) and Danica Roem (@pwcdanica), "When asked about Bob Marshall . . . ," Twitter, November 8, 2017, 11:30 a.m., https://web.archive.org/web/20190319103954/https:/twitter.com /nitrevino/status/928126868817174533/.

160 Kim Kelly, "This Trans Metalhead Stepmom Is Making a Historic Run for Office in Virginia," *Vice*, June 1, 2017, https://www.vice.com/en_us/article/ev4gep/this-trans-metalhead-stepmom-is-making-a-historic-run-for -office-in-virginia/.

160 Danica Roem, "Danica Roem Wants Queer People to Know This Is Your America Too," YouTube video, 3:51, posted by BuzzFeed News, October 13, 2018, 1:23, https://www.youtube.com/watch?v=lq1dAcrzpfo/.

161 Danica Roem, "Transgender Woman Gives Passionate Victory Speech after Virginia Election," posted by Guardian News, 1:37, November 8, 2017, https://www.youtube.com/watch?v=-DL50WhLGyk/.

161 Darby, "Danica Roem."

161 Tim Fitzsimons and Brian Latimer, "After Making History, Danica Roem Is Trying to Make a Difference," NBC News, December 27, 2018, https://www.nbcnews.com/feature/nbc-out/after-making-history-danica -roem-trying-make-difference-n952476/.

161 Kelly, "This Trans Metalhead Stepmom."


## Jeanne Shaheen

164 Emily Tamkin, "How Jeanne Shaheen Fills a Void in Trump's Foreign Policy," Politico, February 25, 2019, https://www.politico.com/magazine/story/2019/02/25/jeanne-shaheen-foreign-relations-committee-225202/.

165 Mattie Kahn, "The Lenny Interview: Senator Jeanne Shaheen," Lenny, June 3, 2016, https://www.lennyletter .com/story/the-lenny-interview-senator-jeanne-shaheen/.

166 Jeanne Shaheen, "Shaheen Vows to Fight Efforts to Overturn Roe v. Wade, Defend Reproductive Rights," YouTube video, 5:23, posted by SenatorShaheen, May 21, 2019, https://www.youtube.com/watch?v=kJnUShrKwSo/.

167 Maggie Mallon, "Democrats Hold Senate Floor to Push for Gun Control Legislation (UPDATED)," *Glamour*, June 16, 2016, https://www.glamour.com/story/democrats-hold-senate-floor-to-push-for-gun-control-legislation/.

167 Dana Bash, "How New Hampshire's First Female Senator Moved off the Sidelines," CNN, August 9, 2017, https://edition.cnn.com/2017/06/19/politics/jeanne-shaheen-badass-women-of-washington/index.html.

167 Kahn, "Lenny Interview."

167 Bash, "New Hampshire's."


## Elise Stefanik

168 Mattie Kahn, "There Are Just 13 Republican Women in Congress. One Sounds the Alarm: 'We Are at a Crisis Level,'" *Glamour*, February 20, 2019, https://www.glamour.com/story/elise-stefanik-pac-republican-women -interview/.

169   "Stefanik's Campaign Ramping Up," *Glens Falls (NY) Post-Star*, May 4, 2014, https://poststar.com/news/local/stefanik-s-campaign-ramping-up/article_d2154512-d3b7-11e3-9a69-0019bb2963f4.html.

170   Paul Kane, "House GOP Women Confront a Political Crisis—Their Party Is Mostly Men," *Washington Post*, November 17, 2018, https://www.washingtonpost.com/powerpost/house-gop-women-confront-a-political-crisis--their-party-is-mostly-men/2018/11/17/34448a4a-e9ed-11e8-b8dc-66cca409c180_story.html.

170   Mike DeBonis, "Elise Stefanik Emerges in Impeachment Hearings as Key Trump Defender—and GOP Celebrity," *Washington Post*, November 16, 2019, https://www.washingtonpost.com/powerpost/elise-stefanik-emerges-in-impeachment-hearings-as-key-trump-defender--and-gop-celebrity/2019/11/15/2d5e1afe-07f4-11ea-8ac0-0810ed197c7e_story.html.

170   Alan Fram, "GOP Woman Gets Outsized Role at Impeachment Hearing," AP, November 16, 2019, https://apnews.com/e6b64edf8a444cdf8b76c6c18c474af4/.

171   "Impeachment Hearing with Former Ukraine Ambassador Marie Yovanovitch," C-Span, November 15, 2019, 4:26:15, video, 1:38:58, https://www.c-span.org/video/?466135-1/impeachment-hearing-ukraine-ambassador-marie-yovanovitch/.

171   Kahn, "Republican Women in Congress."

171   Kayla Webley Adler, "Elise Stefanik Wants the Unthinkable: More Women in the GOP," *City & State New York*, November 17, 2019, https://www.cityandstateny.com/articles/personality/interviews-profiles/elise-stefanik-wants-the-unthinkable-more-women-in-the-gop.html.

171   Adler.

### Rashida Tlaib

172   Rashida Tlaib (@RashidaTlaib), "I will always speak truth to power. #unapologeticallyMe," Twitter, Janurary 4, 2019, 6:08 a.m., https://twitter.com/RashidaTlaib/status/1081190513691246592/.

173   Rashida Tlaib, interview by Michael Barbaro, "The Freshmen: Rashida Tlaib, Part 2," *New York Times*, May 14, 2019, https://www.nytimes.com/2019/05/14/podcasts/the-daily/rashida-tlaib-israel-palestinians.html.

173   Astead W. Herndon, "Rashida Tlaib, with Primary Win, Is Poised to Become First Muslim Woman in Congress," *New York Times*, August 8, 2018, https://www.nytimes.com/2018/08/08/us/politics/rashida-tlaib-congress-muslim.html.

174   Ian Austen, "A Black Mound of Canadian Oil Waste Is Rising over Detroit," *New York Times*, May 17, 2013, https://www.nytimes.com/2013/05/18/business/energy-environment/mountain-of-petroleum-coke-from-oil-sands-rises-in-detroit.html.

174   Rashida Tlaib, "Michigan Congresswoman on Trump: We're Going to Impeach That (expletive)," YouTube video, 2:55, posted by WXYZ-TV Detroit | Channel 7, January 4, 2019, https://www.youtube.com/watch?v=HitU_hnN2x8/.

174   Skullduggery (@SkullduggeryPod), "PT. 1 In this @SkullduggeryPod clip - @dklaidman @Isikoff ask @RepRashida about being only Dem to publicly support a one state solution . . . ," Twitter, May 12, 2019, 8:41 p.m., https://twitter.com/SkullduggeryPod/status/1127780896638144512/.

175   Herndon, "Rashida Tlaib."

175   Tlaib, interview by Barbaro.

175   Rashida Tlaib, "Rashida Tlaib Becomes the First Palestinian Muslim Women Elected to US Congress," YouTube video, 1:49, posted by Red Cache World, November 6, 2018, 1:24, https://www.youtube.com/watch?v=YfPD4u8BFBE/.

### Camila Vallejo Dowling

176   Jonathan Franklin, "Chile's Commander Camila, the Student Who Can Shut Down a City," *Guardian* (US edition), August 24, 2011, https://www.theguardian.com/world/2011/aug/24/chile-student-leader-camila-vallejo/.

177   Xamina Torres Cautivo, "Camila Vallejo: 'Feliz Había Protestado Pechugas al Aire,'" Paula, June 9, 2018, http://www.paula.cl/reportajes-y-entrevistas/camila-vallejo-feliz-habria-protestado-pechugas-al-aire/.

177   Cautivo.

177   Cautivo.

178   Francisco Goldman, "Camila Vallejo, the World's Most Glamorous Revolutionary," *New York Times*, April 5, 2012, https://www.nytimes.com/2012/04/08/magazine/camila-vallejo-the-worlds-most-glamorous-revolutionary.html.

178   Sofía Aldea, "Compañera Camila," Paula, May 16, 2011, http://www.paula.cl/reportajes-y-entrevistas/companera-camila/.

178   Goldman, "Camila Vallejo."
178   Franklin, "Chile's Commander Camila."
179   Cautivo, "Camila Vallejo."
179   Franklin, "Chile's Commander Camila."
179   Franklin.
179   Cautivo, "Camila Vallejo."
179   Franklin, "Camila Vallejo—Latin America's 23-Year-Old New Revolutionary Folk Hero," *Guardian* (US edition), October 8, 2011, https://www.theguardian.com/world/2011/oct/08/camila-vallejo-latin-america-revolutionary/.

## Elizabeth Warren

180   Charles P. Pierce, "The Watchdog: Elizabeth Warren," *boston.com*, December 20, 2009, http://archive.boston .com/bostonglobe/magazine/articles/2009/12/20/elizabeth_warren_is_the_bostonian_of_the_year/?page=2.
181   Elizabeth Warren, "Law Politics, and the Coming Collapse of the Middle Class with Elizabeth Warren— Conversations with History," UCTV video, 59:10, May 21, 2007, https://www.uctv.tv/shows/Law-Politics-and -the-Coming-Collapse-of-the-Middle-Class-with-Elizabeth-Warren-Conversations-with-History-12490/.
181   Warren.
183   Mitch McConnell, "#ShePersisted—McConnell's Explains Vote to Silence Elizabeth Warren 'Nevertheless She Persisted,'" YouTube video, 5:47, posted by the *Oregonian*, February 8, 2017, 0:09, https://www.youtube.com /watch?v=m2YY9_NfW8w/.
183   Emily Bazelon, "Elizabeth Warren Is Completely Serious," *New York Times Magazine*, June 17, 2019, https:// www.nytimes.com/2019/06/17/magazine/elizabeth-warren-president.html.
183   Samuel P. Jacobs, "Elizabeth Warren: 'I Created Occupy Wall Street,'" Daily Beast, July 13, 2017, https://www .thedailybeast.com/elizabeth-warren-i-created-occupy-wall-street/.
183   Ryan Chittum, "A Good Bloomberg Profile of Elizabeth Warren," *Columbia Journalism Review*, November 19, 2009, https://archives.cjr.org/the_audit/a_good_bloomberg_profile_of_el.php.
183   Ryan Grim, "Elizabeth Warren Rips Citigroup for Weaseling Wall Street Giveaway into Government Spending Bill," HuffPost, December 12, 2014, https://www.huffpost.com/entry/elizabeth-warrencitigroup -bill_n_6318446/.
183   Katie Reilly, "Why 'Nevertheless, She Persisted' Is the Theme for This Year's Women's History Month," *Time*, March 1, 2018, http://time.com/5175901/elizabeth-warren-nevertheless-she-persisted-meaning/.

## Maxine Waters

184   Maxine Waters, "Reclaiming My Time," YouTube video, 2:00, posted by Paul McGee, August 3, 2017, 0:24, https://www.youtube.com/watch?v=i2c4jyba6To/.
185   Mandalit del Barco, "Critics Decry Naming of LAPD Building for Ex-Chief," NPR, April 24, 2009, https:// www.npr.org/templates/story/story.php?storyId=103452604.
186   Maxine Waters, "Rep. Waters: 'Tea Party Can Go Straight to Hell,'" YouTube video, 0:50, posted by CBS, August 22, 2011, 0:25, https://www.youtube.com/watch?v=NBi2y84l1cQ/.
186   Maxine Waters, "Transcripts," CNN, June 30, 2018, http://transcripts.cnn.com/TRANSCRIPTS/1806/30 /cnr.06.html.
187   Waters, "Reclaiming My Time."
187   Maxine Waters, "EXCLUSIVE: Rep. Maxine Waters Responds to Being Targeted by Bomb Threats: 'I Ain't Scared,'" Blavity video, 2:43, posted by Kandist Mallett, October 26, 2018, 2:38, https://blavity.com/video /exclusive-rep-maxine-waters-responds-to-bomb-threats-that-targeted-her-i-aint-scared/.
187   Maxine Waters, "Representative Waters on Financial Services Committee Agenda," C-SPAN video, 54:45, January 16, 2019, 48:43, https://www.c-span.org/video/?457011-1/financial-services-chair-maxine-waters -discusses-committees-agenda/.
187   Stacey Leasca, "Rep. Maxine Waters Explains Why She Skipped Trump's Speech in 5 Simple Words," Good, March 1, 2017, https://www.good.is/articles/maxine-waters-trump/.
187   R. Eric Thomas, "This Is Maxine Waters, The Millennials' Political Rock Star," *Elle*, April 17, 2017, https:// www.elle.com/culture/career-politics/news/a44584/inside-maxine-waters-political-rock-concert/.
187   Jesse J. Holland, "Rep. Maxine Waters' No-Holds-Barred Remarks Find Fans," AP, March 29, 2017, https:// apnews.com/a7f6cdcbf297416b8f788132defa79cf/.

### Gretchen Whitmer

188   MT Staff, "Why Slow and Steady Could Win Gretchen Whitmer the Race for Governor," *Detroit Metro Times*, July 18, 2018, https://www.metrotimes.com/detroit/why-slow-and-steady-could-win-gretchen-whitmer-the-race-for-governor/Content?oid=13885557.

189–190   Tim Alberta, "'The Woman in Michigan' Goes National," Politico, April 9, 2020, https://www.politico.com/news/magazine/2020/04/09/gretchen-whitmer-governor-michigan-profile-2020-coronavirus-biden-vp-177791.

190   Gretchen Whitmer, "Fix the Damn Roads," Whitmer and Gilchrist for Michigan, accessed April 27, 2020, https://www.gretchenwhitmer.com/issues/infrastructure/.

190   Donald J. Trump (@realDonaldTrump), "I love Michigan, one of the reasons we are doing such a GREAT job for them during this horrible Pandemic. Yet your Governor, Gretchen 'Half' Whitmer is way in over her head . . ." Twitter, posted at 2:29 a.m. on March 28, 2020, https://twitter.com/realdonaldtrump/status/1243726993537073152?lang=en.

191   Kyle Melinn, "Trump Messes with the Wrong 'Woman from Michigan,'" *Lansing City Pulse*, April 2, 2020, https://www.lansingcitypulse.com/stories/trump-messes-with-the-wrong-woman-from-michigan,14065.

191   Jonathan Oosting, "Inside Michigan Gov. Whitmer's Coronavirus Fight: 'We Know We Saved Lives,'" *Bridge*, April 16, 2020, https://www.bridgemi.com/michigan-government/inside-michigan-gov-whitmers-coronavirus-fight-we-know-we-saved-lives/.

191   MT Staff, "Why Slow and Steady."

191   Gretchen Whitmer, "Ep. 380—Gov. Gretchen Whitmer," *The Axe Files with David Axelrod*, podcast episode, 45:26, April 16, 2020, 32:19, https://www.cnn.com/audio/podcasts/axe-files/.

### Sahle-Work Zewde

192   Hadra Ahmed and Kimiko de Freytas-Tamura, "Ethiopia Appoints Its First Female President," *New York Times*, October 25, 2018, https://www.nytimes.com/2018/10/25/world/africa/sahlework-zewde-ethiopia-president.html.

195   Fitsum Arega (@fitsumaregaa), "In a patriarchal society such as ours, the appointment of a female head of state not only sets the standard for the future but also normalises women as decision-makers in public life. #Ethiopia (2)," Twitter, October 25, 2018, 12:53 a.m., https://twitter.com/fitsumaregaa/status/1055366603481735168/.

195   "Sahle-Work Zewde Becomes Ethiopia's First Female President," BBC News, October 25, 2018, https://www.bbc.com/news/world-africa-45976620/.

195   "Sahlework Zewde: Embodiment of Doggedness," Association of Women in Business, September 4, 2014, http://awib.org.et/newsite/sahlework-zewde-embodiment-of-doggedness/.

195   "Sahle-Work Zewde Named Ethiopia's First Female President," Al Jazeera, October 25, 2018, https://www.aljazeera.com/news/2018/10/sahle-work-zewde-named-ethiopia-woman-president-181025084046138.html.

195   "Sahlework Zewde," Association of Women in Business.

195   Ahmed and de Freytas-Tamura, "Ethiopia Appoints."

# ABOUT THE CONTRIBUTORS

**Caitlin Donohue** is a culture writer. Raised in San Francisco and Portland, Oregon, she worked as a labor union organizer before beginning her journalism career at the rabble-rousing alternative weekly newspaper *San Francisco Bay Guardian*. She is a regular contributor to *High Times* and Remezcla, and her work has been published by McSweeney's, *Fact*, Bandcamp, Advocate, them., 48 Hills, SFMoMA's *Open Space*, and other fine and relevant publications.

Her greatest hits include a pre-#MeToo exposé of a chauvinist San Francisco progressive blogger, a piece on Mexico City's LGBTQ Central American refugees, the first English language profile of Puerto Rican Latin trap artist Bad Bunny, a history of reggaeton in Veracruz, interviews with feminist thought leader Rebecca Solnit, seminal rapper Fat Joe, and Brazilian drag queen pop star Pabllo Vittar, plus a guide to having herpes for Tavi Gevinson's online teen magazine, *Rookie*. Caitlin has lived on four continents. For the past five years, Mexico City has been her home. She considers the megapolis to be the heartbeat of the Western Hemisphere, and it is the birthplace of her cat Kiara.

**Briana Arrington** is a Philadelphia-born-and-based illustrator and graphic designer. She obtained her BFA from the Maryland Institute and College of Art in 2017. Briana's work includes pieces of her identity as she is a firm believer in the fact that representation matters. She is always hoping that her work reaches someone who may look like her, see the world like her, or has gone through similar experiences.

When her hand is not attached to creating, she is either aggressively playing volleyball with a city league or having a good cry or hearty laugh to a movie marathon. Briana is also an amateur food connoisseur. Philadelphia is a diverse table of foods, and she intends to try as much as her stomach can handle in and out of her own kitchen. Briana is joyful and loves to laugh. It is the best medicine, after all.